DICKENS'S WORKING NOTES FOR *DOMBEY AND SON*

Dickens's Working Notes for *Dombey and Son*

Facsimiles and Transcriptions of the Original Manuscript with Commentary on Dickens's Working Methods

By Tony Laing

OpenBook Publishers

https://www.openbookpublishers.com

All external links were active at the time of publication unless otherwise stated and have been archived via the Internet Archive Wayback Machine at https://archive.org/web

Digital material and resources associated with this volume are available at https://www.openbookpublishers.com/product/469#resources

ISBN Paperback: 978-1-78374-223-3
ISBN Hardback: 978-1-78374-224-0
ISBN Digital (PDF): 978-1-78374-225-7
ISBN Digital ebook (epub): 978-1-78374-226-4
ISBN Digital ebook (mobi): 978-1-78374-227-1
DOI: 10.11647/OBP.0092

Cover image and design by Heidi Carlson

All paper used by Open Book Publishers is SFI (Sustainable Forestry Initiative), PEFC (Programme for the Endorsement of Forest Certification Schemes) and Forest Stewardship Council(r)(FSC(r) certified.

Printed in the United Kingdom, United States, and Australia
by Lightning Source for Open Book Publishers (Cambridge, UK)

Contents

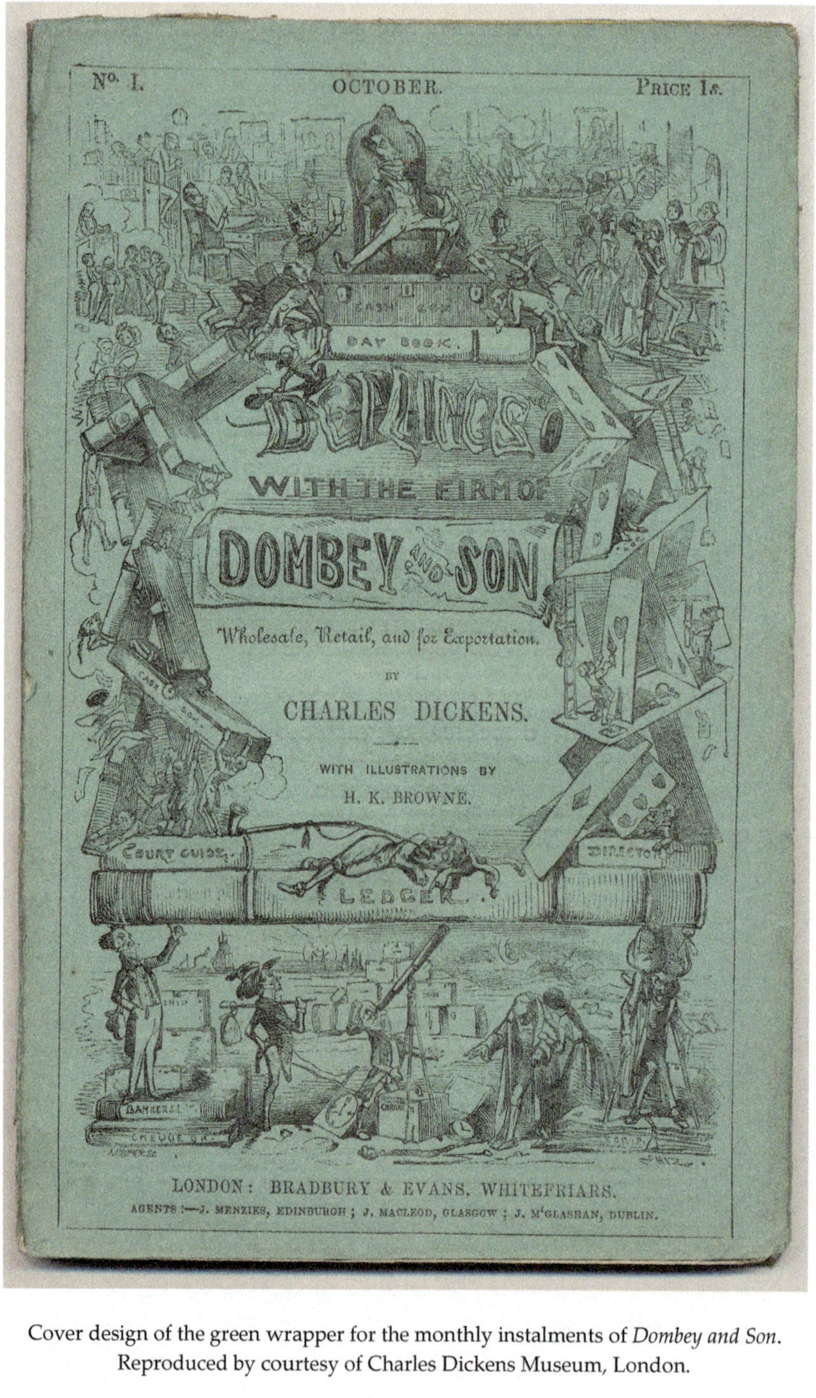

Cover design of the green wrapper for the monthly instalments of *Dombey and Son*.
Reproduced by courtesy of Charles Dickens Museum, London.

Thanks

My thanks go to David Grugeon for his good advice, to Richard Allen for his comments and close reading of an early draft, to Elizabeth James at the National Art Library within the V&A Museum, to Louisa Price at the Charles Dickens Museum, London, to East Sussex County Council public library service, and to Francesca Giovannetti and the team at Open Book Publishers for their encouragement and expertise.

Acknowledgements

The transcriptions of Dickens's working notes are made by courtesy of the Board of Trustees of the Victoria and Albert Museum, London (2011). The image of the green cover design for *Dombey and Son* is reproduced by courtesy of Charles Dickens Museum, London (2016). All facsimiles of images from the Forster Collection in the National Art Library in the V&A Museum, London are made by courtesy of the Board of Trustees of the Victoria and Albert Museum (2016). Passages from *Dombey and Son* and the image of the frontispiece from ebook 821, Project Gutenberg, http://www.gutenberg.org/ebooks/851 (released 1 February 1997) and John Forster's *Life of Charles Dickens*, 3 vols. in 2 (Boston: James R. Osgood & Co., 1875), ebook 25851, Project Gutenberg, http://www.gutenberg.org/ebooks/25851 (released 20 June 2008) are for the use of anyone anywhere at no cost and with almost no restrictions whatsoever; you may copy them, give them away or re-use them under the terms of the Project Gutenberg License online at http://www.gutenberg.org (2016).

Foreword

This critical edition of the working notes for *Dombey and Son* is for readers who wish to know more about how Charles Dickens set about writing each of the novel's twenty instalments. Most modern editions of the novel, and the various companions or guides, recognise the importance of his working notes. Many contain transcriptions of the monthly worksheets, his "Mems" as Dickens called them. This edition is an alternative to those bare transcriptions. It has twenty-three facsimiles of the original worksheets (provided by the V&A Museum), each of which is accompanied by a more detailed transcription than any published to date, and a commentary that for the first time reconstructs the order of Dickens's work on each instalment.

In 2011, developments in word processing—particularly the publication in the UK of Word 2010—made it possible to imitate, as well as transcribe the original manuscript.[1] This inexpensive software on mid-range computers can reproduce the words and the marks that go with them, imitating their position (orientation, grouping, and layout) and their appearance (size, density, colour and corrosion). Moreover, the production and distribution of an ebook is usually wider and less costly than the conventionally printed book. So now seems the right moment to publish a new, open access and reasonably priced critical edition of Dickens's working notes for *Dombey and Son*, the first novel for which he wrote systematic "Mems" to assist him in composition.[2]

Each of the nineteen units, which make up the central section of the edition, consists of a facsimile of the worksheet for a monthly instalment, its transcription, and a two-page commentary. The latter, unlike other critical approaches to the worksheets, has no overriding interpretive agenda. The commentary merely assumes that the notes are the author's distinctive response to the problems of publishing a novel that is predetermined in the length of the whole and of each instalment (sometimes formally described as fixed length, stand-alone monthly serialisation).

Although the worksheet reveals how Dickens views his fiction through the lens of the monthly instalment, he devises it in the first place to help him fulfil a growing literary ambition to give more coherence to the novel's themes and "threads", i.e. characters and actions. On the left-hand half of the monthly worksheet, he keeps his plans for the number; on the right-hand half, he records the number of the instalment, the number and title of each chapter and, in the space below each title—in this edition called the 'chapter description'—he initially makes a brief note of the chapter's content. The identification and naming of the space below each title is important, because it prepares for the later distinction between those chapter descriptions that are written before the chapter's composition and are plans, and those that are written after it and are summaries. The chapter description, like the space on the lower left-hand half of the worksheet, soon becomes useful to Dickens in ways that he probably did not anticipate when he first devised its format.

He starts writing at the end of June, well before the agreed publication date of October 1846. However, his many other activities quickly shrink the lead-time of three months to a matter of days.

https://doi.org/10.11647/OBP.0092.01

From No.4 onwards, depending on whether he managed to make a start during the first or second week of the month prior to publication, he usually has to complete his text for each instalment within ten to twenty days. The usual deadline of the 23rd or 24th, depending partly on the length of the month, was determined by the five or six days (and, if necessary, nights) for compositors to set up and run off, for printers to sew, trim, and cover, and for distribution to begin.

The demand was relentless and Dickens's commitment unwavering. He was obliged to produce over fifteen thousand words every month, for eighteen months, then in the following final month, to write at least twenty-three thousand. Yet this particular mode—in monthly, as opposed to weekly, instalments—was the one that he preferred. The pressure seems to have suited his extraordinary inventiveness, restless energy and iron will.

The commentary on the worksheet that accompanies each facsimile and transcription begins with a brief account of Dickens's circumstances during the month prior to publication. It then lists his entries with their function (and marginal number), in the order in which they were made—often not the order of their appearance in the worksheet. The commentary inserts, at the appropriate point, his other associated monthly tasks: the composition of each chapter, the compilation of his "List of Chapter Headings", and the reading of proofs. These tasks may interrupt both number planning on the left-hand side of the worksheet and chapter titling and description on the right-hand side. Analysis of the hand and layout of the worksheet, the manuscript and the List—together with the ordering in time of the various entries and tasks—gives fresh insight into his working methods, as they change with the progress of the novel.

Dickens's reputation has been sustained in the last a hundred and fifty years by successive generations of readers and, from *Pickwick Papers* onwards, by the adaptation of his fiction to the media of the day. For contemporary readers, David Timson makes a brave attempt at delivering the many voices and shapes of Dickens's prose in the Naxos audiobook of the unabridged *Dombey and Son*—and the stream continues of adaptations of his fiction for public readings, children's literature, graphic novel, theatre, film, TV and radio and their vehicles: CDs, DVDs and online/cable transmission.

However, readers whose tastes have been formed by the information revolution often have very different expectations of printed texts. *Dombey and Son*, a long-winded nineteenth century novel—one of those "large, loose, baggy monsters, with their queer elements of the accidental and the arbitrary" that Henry James maintained he disliked—may eventually be consigned to distant, seldom used, book depositories.[3] Libraries, wirelessly connected to the rapidly expanding worldwide web, multiply their PC stations and power sockets for laptops, tablets and smartphones. Like bookshops, in response to market forces, they shrink their 'classic' holdings to a few cheap editions on lower shelves.

Research for this edition has taken six years of intermittent labour. During that time, I have been sustained by Dickens's enduring qualities as a writer of fiction and by a belief that his working notes for *Dombey and Son* can be used to promote the appreciation of the novel. Reading to recapture something of the effect of periodic publication, like reading regularly shared with others, can be especially rewarding, not least because as Mark Turner says in *The Material Culture of the Victorian Novel*, Dickens '*thought* about his novels through the serial form' (Turner, p.119).[4] Any reader, by consulting each worksheet in turn, and following him in the creation of the next instalment, may alone or with others add to their understanding of the novel's themes and organisation.

Growing familiarity with the text will deepen the pleasure that comes from Dickens's astonishing linguistic creativity and his intensely visual and dramatic imagination. The reader encounters in *Dombey and Son*—more than in any other Dickens novel—an extraordinary blend of satire, comedy, pathos, sentiment and melodrama, what Paul Schlicke calls his 'complex orchestration of a variety of literary modes' (Schlicke, *Oxford Reader's Companion to Dickens* (Oxford: Oxford University Press, 1999), p.186).[5]

With two sorts of readers in mind, I have doubled most key references, citing first the text likely to be available to researchers in the field, then a less costly one (or a free online alternative) for students and the general reader. For much the same reason, this edition of Dickens's working notes for the novel—though all images are to the scale of the V&A's facsimiles and all formats are identical in content—is available in three ways:

- an online open access version with low resolution facsimiles, but with links to a 'zoomified' version of the high resolution images
- as an ebook (epub, mobi or interactive PDF) with low resolution facsimiles and links to a 'zoomified' version of the high resolution images, but low-priced and downloadable, and hyperlinked to high-resolution images that will be available on the website of Open Book Publishers, until they become accessible on the website of the V&A Museum
- an on demand print publication, as a paperback or hardback, but with high-resolution facsimiles in full colour, and each priced accordingly.

If the reader would like "a bird's eye glimpse" of the edition, there is a concluding summary in the 'Afterword', p.159.

Abbreviations, references and cross-references

General abbreviations used throughout

ch. the chapter, always followed by its number

K a text downloaded to Kindle, always followed by 'K:' and the number of its 'location'

L the Pilgrim edition of the *Letters*, edited by Graham Storey, Kathleen Tillotson and Madeline House, et al., 12 vols. (Oxford: Clarendon Press, 1982–2002), always followed by volume and page, e.g. L5:267 (vol.5, p. 267)

List Dickens's "List of Chapter Headings"

MS the manuscript of the novel *Dombey and Son*[6]

No. the monthly instalment, always followed by its number, e.g. No.5 the fifth instalment

Ws. a worksheet compiled for an instalment, always followed by the number of the instalment, e.g. Ws.15 the worksheet for the fifteenth instalment.

References

(1) For the text of *Dombey and Son*:
reference is to the text in the hardback edition in the Clarendon Dickens series, edited by Alan Horsman (Oxford: Clarendon Press, 1974) and to the same text in the paperback, also edited by Alan Horsman, in the Oxford World's Classics series (Oxford: Oxford University Press, 2008)—shown by bracketed page only, for example: (250^{270}), i.e. p.250 in hardback and p.270 superscripted in paperback.

(2) For the materials other than the text in the hardback Clarendon edition:
reference is to the Introduction, the Appendixes or the footnotes—shown, for example by: Horsman 1974, 'Introduction', p.xxxvi, or Horsman 1974, p.289 n.2.

(3) For deletions/additions to the text of *Dombey and Son*:
reference is to the footnotes of the Clarendon edition (1974) (see above) and to ebook 821, Project Gutenberg, http://www.gutenberg.org/ebooks/821 (released 01/02/1997).

(4) For Forster's *Life of Charles Dickens*:
reference is to the single volume edition edited by J. W. T. Ley, and to ebook 25851, Project Gutenberg, http://www.gutenberg.org/ebooks/25851 (released 1 February, 1997), downloaded to

https://doi.org/10.11647/OBP.0092.02

Kindle (with images), shown by page in Ley with the Kindle locations superscripted, for example: (*Life* 857[K:17253]).

(5) For Dickens's letters that are not in quoted in Forster's *Life*:
reference is to the Pilgrim edition of the *Letters*, edited by Graham Storey, Kathleen Tillotson and Madeline House, et al., 12 vols. (Oxford: Clarendon Press, 1982–2002)—shown by volume and page, for example thus: (L5:267).

The editor has had to avoid using direct online references to ebook 25851 in Project Gutenberg, because of their frequency in this ebook. Instead, he asks those readers, without access to Ley's edition, to download ebook 25851 using the free Kindle app (for PC, tablet and reader) and refer to 'location' numbers in that edition. The inconvenience of using Kindle has to be measured against the hindrances that Project Gutenberg puts in place to discourage repeated use of the same text by the same user.

Repeated calls on the same text eventually produces multiple interruptions, halting first at the Project's catalogue, then at a captcha, and finally at an instruction to stop using the text. This admirable Project seems not yet to have devised a way of distinguishing between users whom they can trust not to abuse frequent reference from those who copy texts, perhaps with robots, to re-sell them to an unsuspecting public for their own profit.

As there is no shared referencing system between any of the e-readers, the editor has had to choose an e-reader. The Kindle app for mobi is selected because its 'locations' (every 128 bytes) are reliable and frequent—and for no other reason. The improved Kindle app for PC laptop and smartphone, although in some respects it is not the easiest to manage, has all of the usual functions that enable the reader to note, copy, search and move quickly (using 'Ctrl + G') to any location.

Cross-references

(1) To a passage in this book—reference is made by page number for readers of the print version, and by 'live' bookmark or page number for readers of electronic versions, e.g. the cover design (p.viii).

(2) To the text of a repeated endnote—reference is made by 'endnote' followed by the endnote number for readers of the print version, which is 'live' for readers of electronic versions.

(3) To entries within a worksheet—reference is made *either* by the worksheet number and the relevant marginal number (subscripted) that is 'live' for readers of electronic version, e.g. 'Ws.10_5'—*or* simply by the marginal number in brackets, if the context shows the number of the worksheet that is under consideration.

(4) Marginal numbers whether standing alone or subscripted, for technical reasons, have to be part of the 'image' of each transcription. Consequently, it is not possible to make the marginal number itself a 'live' link to where the number occurs in the transcription.

(5) References to a marginal number are by the page number of its transcription (live for readers of the electronic version). For example, 'Ws.10_5' might be followed by a live page number 'p.83', which will take readers to the 'Transcription for Ws.10'. They should then scan the margins of the transcribed worksheet to find '5' and the entry to which the number refers.

Section 1. Introduction to the working notes

Dickens's "green cover" novels

The "green covers", as Dickens calls them, had their origin in the publication of his first novel *Pickwick Papers* in 1836–1837. A new venture for publishers Chapman and Hall, the monthly serial devoted to the adventures of the Pickwick Club, began as a loosely related series of episodes, which became more like a picaresque novel soon after Sam Weller joined Mr Pickwick. It turned out to be a sensational success, reaching across class divisions and transcending gender. Of the next five novels, two more were produced in a similar format *Nicholas Nickleby* (1838–1839) and *Martin Chuzzlewit* (1842–1844).

After a gap of two years, *Dombey and Son* was serialised monthly, for eighteen months, with a double instalment on the nineteenth and final month. The instalments of the novel—wrapped in the same distinctive green cover as before—appeared from October 1846, at the midpoint of author's career. Four more "green covers" followed with an increasing interval between each one. Although Dickens was always looking to publish his fiction in other ways, the format of his "green covers" remained his favourite.[7]

The number of pages in each monthly number—also referred to as 'instalment', 'issue' or 'part'—was determined by the mechanics and costs of printing. Each part consisted of two printers sheets, except for the final double number. One sheet accommodated eight leaves, which printed on both sides, resulted in sixteen pages per sheet. The fixed length therefore that Dickens worked to was thirty-two printed pages for each of the eighteen two-sheet numbers, and forty-eight printed pages for the four-sheet or double number.

Readers buying the double number might assume that it was literally a 'double number', implying sixty-four pages of text. However, only three printers sheets were given over to text. The final green wrapper had to accommodate all the other pages that buyers would need, if they wished to have their collection of twenty instalments bound together, to give the appearance of a conventional single-volume publication. Apart from the usual two illustrations, the extra pages included a frontispiece illustrative of the novel as a whole, and a title page with an engraved vignette of an evocative moment in the story, as well as twelve pages at least of letterpress. The latter consisted of a half title page, a printer's page, the full title page, dedication, preface (one or more pages), contents pages (at least four), a list of plates (two pages) and an errata sheet (usually placed at the start). With perhaps some blank leaves at the front and back, the extra pages accounted for the fourth printers sheet.

Each number was accompanied by two lengthy sections of advertisements, one before the text of the instalment and one after it. These could be extended, if demand increased as circulation rose. The whole was sewn, trimmed and enclosed in its green wrapper, which on the front gave the novel's title and the names of author and illustrator, surrounded by a cover design, which hinted at the course of the story.[8] Two loose illustrations, each of a moment in the current number, printed on stiffer paper, were slipped in between the first section of advertisements and the text.[9] The monthly part was sold for one shilling, except for the double number sold for two. The cost amounted to twenty shillings or one pound altogether.[10]

 https://doi.org/10.11647/OBP.0092.03

When the novel was published as a single volume, the publisher would first use up unsold surplus parts. Stripped of their green cover and advertisements, they formed—perhaps with a revised errata sheet—the so-called 'first issue' of the first edition. The first edition, published soon after the last instalment, on 12 April, 1848—with the page layout and pagination of the monthly issue—was sold in a cloth binding for a guinea (21/- or £1.1s).[11] During the first three decades of Dickens's career as a novelist—before the development in the 1860s of much cheaper paper, made from wood pulp as opposed to the rags used before then—the price of both the single volume and of the bound-up numbers compared favourably with the price of the conventional novel, which was generally published in three volumes, and sold for one and a half guineas (£1.11s.6d).

Apart from being cheaper to produce, serialisation had the great advantage of spreading the cost to the buyers, while enabling the printer/publisher to re-coup costs using money raised through advertising and sales during publication. Just as significant as the reduction in unit cost, the organisation and technology that underpinned book production, marketing and distribution steadily advanced over each decade from the 1830s onwards. As the market expanded along the new train lines and printing machinery improved, the scale of production grew from many thousands to tens of thousands.[12]

Dickens was well placed to benefit from the increase. By the mid-eighteen forties, he had secured contracts with his publishers that gave him a substantial share of profits. He was also becoming more ambitious as a novelist. When *Dombey and Son* was well received by the critics, and the sale of each of the early monthly numbers regularly topped 30,000, he was gratified and relieved. He felt financially secure for the first time in his life, and able to save a portion of his monthly earnings. His first investment was not in speculative railway stock, but in government consoles.[13]

The frontispiece of this book is a facsimile of the design on the green wrapper for *Dombey and Son*. The design "shadowing out [...] drift and bearing" (*Life* 437[K:8888]) implicitly conveys Dickens's determination, from beginning to end, to constrain his exuberance for the sake of coherence. Readers may like to search the design for any false trails or omissions, and compare it with his "outline of my immediate intentions" sent to John Forster (see endnote 42). Dickens feared that the cover, with "perhaps with a little too much in it" (L5:620), gave too much away.[14] (For information about abbreviations, references and cross references, see above p.7).

Brown devised the design for the wrapper some weeks before the publication of the first instalment. In modern editions, it is sometimes paired with the frontispiece, the last plate for the novel, created by Browne while Dickens was working on the double number. One of the extra items that was wrapped with the final instalment, the frontispiece p.163 can be found at end of the Afterword.

History of the working notes

Beginning with *Pickwick Papers* in 1836–1837, Dickens produced six novels in nine years. In words alone, it was an immense output. Halfway through the sixth, *Martin Chuzzlewit*, when he writes to Forster "That I feel my powers now, more than I ever did", he concludes "it is impossible to go on working the brain to that extent for ever" (L3:590–91). He plans for a lengthy break. After an unprecedented gap of two years, Dickens with some trepidation commits to another "green cover" *Dombey and Son*, to be published from October 1846, an important literary as well as an uncertain commercial undertaking for him.

Anticipating the occasion with a decisive change of surroundings—and in an attempt to save money—Dickens moves with his family and servants to Switzerland and then to Paris. For the first time he lives abroad during the composition and publication of the early numbers of a novel. The move brings problems for him, but a fortunate outcome for us.[15] We have an unusually detailed account of the period abroad in his letters home, especially in those to Forster. His letters are the basis of the biographical headnote that begins the commentary on each worksheet.

Very early in 1846, Dickens decides that his next novel should be more ambitious in theme and structure than any previous. To assist him in the task—in a development he had then for the most part quite deliberately avoided (see his letter to Gaylord Clark, p.135)—he determines from the outset to make regular systematic notes, compiling one worksheet in preparation for each instalment.[16]

To begin with, Dickens has two purposes in mind. The left-hand half of the worksheet would serve as an aid to planning the current number in the light of his later intentions. The right-hand half would record the part number and the number and the title of each chapter, with perhaps some further indication of content. As the sheets accumulate, they become a check on the relation of the part to the whole, a reminder of the story's many "threads" and a guide to his growing pile of back numbers. Once the novel is well underway, he finds that the worksheet, with a 'wafered' extension, might also assist him in planning individual chapters.[17]

Number planning (always on the left-hand side) and chapter recording (always on the right-hand side), though they vary widely in their detail and extent, are settled from the start. However, from Ws.3 to Ws.5—the end of the first quarter of the novel—Dickens experiments with different ways of using the worksheet for chapter planning. Then, after some personal and family mishaps, from Ws.9 onwards he usually plans each chapter in the 'chapter description' on the right-hand half; or on other occasions, dispenses with planning and simply keeps a record in the chapter description by summarising its contents. The decision whether to plan or to summarise changes with the progress of the novel, until in the winding-up of the double number, Dickens relies on the worksheet to plan all of the last five chapters. The distinctive indications of planning that are present in the double number help to identify the chapter plans in the previous eighteen worksheets.

It was probably "his dear and trusted friend John Forster", rather than Dickens himself, who faced with such a large collection of more than five hundred and fifty loose leaves had the notes for the novel bound together with its manuscript (see the bequest to Forster in 'The Will of Charles Dickens' in *Life* 857[K:17253]).[18] At Forster's death two years later, the volumes of manuscript with the rest of his extensive library were willed to his wife and through her to the National Art Library within what is now the V&A Museum. Perhaps Dickens entrusted them to Forster on the understanding that they would become available to future readers.[19] Such an arrangement would be consonant with the fellow-feeling he expressed for his readership and his audiences during his lifetime.[20]

The notes for *Dombey and Son* remained squirrelled away in the Museum for eight decades, until two scholars, John Butt and Sylvère Monod, apparently working independently in post-war London, used them in their postgraduate study on Dickens at Durham University and the Sorbonne published in 1948 and 1953 respectively.[21] Since then, critics of the novel have drawn on the notes, particularly if their concern was with what John Butt and Kathleen Tillotson called 'design and execution' the subtitle of the chapter on *Dombey and Son* in their pioneering study *Dickens at Work*.

With the resurgence of academic interest in Dickens, and in the light of environmental threat to the collection, the Museum remounted and rebound all of its Dickens manuscripts in the 1960s. Unfortunately, this venture was later found to have serious flaws in the choice of mounting paper used to protect each manuscript leaf, so a second project was begun in the 1990s and finished some ten years later. The manuscript of *Dombey and Son* is now freshly mounted in eight carefully crafted volumes, the first of which opens with all of his working notes for the novel.[22]

Understandably, access has been restricted to protect the originals from environmental damage. High resolution photographing of all of the Dickens's manuscripts in the Forster Collection was completed in 2015, which hopefully means that these digital images will soon become available online to the public. In the meantime, readers of this book can examine facsimiles of the original worksheets for *Dombey and Son,* supplied by the V&A Museum, along with transcriptions, intended (among other purposes) as an aid to reading Dickens's sometimes difficult hand. The images are in high or low resolution, depending on which version of the book is being used (see the end of the 'Foreword', for a description of the three versions, p.5).

Materials of the working notes

This section describes the physical materials of the working notes that are mounted with the novel's manuscript in the V&A Museum. It compares the general qualities of the paper, ink and quill of the notes with those of the manuscript of the novel.[23] The twenty-six leaves of working notes consist of:

(1) a small leaf, which gives the novel's title page as Dickens first envisages it "Some Dealings with the Firm of Dombey and Son, Wholesale, Retail and for Exportation". His underlines anticipate the use of the short title. He drops the "Some" of the longer title when he enters the heading on the top right-hand side of each worksheet. This small leaf is not transcribed.

(2) one foolscap leaf folded on its longer side (four pages) and one half-foolscap leaf (two pages), which together contain the "List of Chapter Headings".[24] Dickens began compiling the List when he finished No.5. From then on, he enters the chapter headings as they accumulate, usually number by number. The six pages are transcribed here for the first time, with commentary in 'Appendix C', where each entry is numbered in square brackets. The number(s) corresponds to the number(s) of the instalment(s) in which the chapters occur.

(3) nineteen pre-cut half-foolscap leaves, four of which have an addition. One whole leaf and three torn half-leaves are attached in different positions and by different means. Three are wafered on (see Ws.4, 5 and 19&20) and one is pasted (see Ws.6).[25] These make up the nineteen worksheets that, with four attachments, are reproduced in facsimile in 'Section 5'. [Editor's note: the abbreviation 'Ws' stands for worksheet; it is always followed by the number of part that it prepares for (see above, 'General abbreviations', p.7). The worksheet for double number is always 'Ws.19&20' and its attachment 'Ws.19&20a'].

The leaves consist of two kinds of paper: (1) a bluish paper, ribbed and watermarked from being laid on a mould of parallel wires the size of letter paper, rather small and flimsy—used for the working notes, with the exception of Ws.5a and the "List of Chapter Headings"; and (2) a paler woven paper, smoother and unwatermarked, laid on a fine wire mesh, of better quality—used for Ws.5a, the "List of Chapter Headings" and the manuscript of the novel.

The qualitative contrast between manuscript and most working notes continues in the handwriting, inks and quills. Always aware of the fixed length of each number, Dickens comes to rely on a consistently written page to estimate his progress through the number. Consequently, for page after page, the handwriting in the manuscript is often remarkably regular in size, spacing and lineation. In the worksheet, on the other hand, he varies the hand's size, style and layout, as he groups entries together to emphasise the distinctiveness of each group.

The quality and colour of the ink is also more consistent in the manuscript. In the worksheet and "List of Chapter Headings", changes in ink can add to the contrast between groups, whether it is a change to a black ink producing corrosion, or a more obvious change of colour. The latter occurs a little more frequently in the worksheet and List than in the manuscript, partly because entries in the worksheet and List are often made at different times, and partly because in the manuscript Dickens prefers, where possible, to use the same ink for each chapter. For an account of the only exception, see the last two paragraphs of 'Ink colour' pp.21–2.

As for quills, some were kept, at the start at least, specifically for writing the novel. Dickens had a set of quills without which he felt unable to begin writing the first number.[26] They were presumably of the best quality goose feather, which he may have recut or mended himself as the need arose, or perhaps discarded (or demoted) as they became worn.[27] The quills he used in the worksheets, by contrast, are more varied, occasionally with a poor flow, e.g. the erratic flow throughout Ws.6a p.66, or sometimes with a thickly cut nib, e.g. the titles and descriptions of chs.46 and 47 (later 48) and many entries in Ws.15 p.102, where he uses a thickly cut and free flowing quill that threatens to blot, having used a finer quill to write his initial number plan and the plan for ch.48 (later 47).

In this description of the materials that Dickens used, the application of the word 'manuscript' has narrowed to 'the manuscript of the novel'. As mentioned earlier, the worksheets and the other working notes are a part of the manuscript that is held in the volumes of the V&A Museum. However, a clear distinction between the manuscript of the novel and the working notes has to be made in order to understand the relation between the two. From now on 'manuscript' and its abbreviation 'MS' always refers to the manuscript of the novel, excluding the working notes.

Section 2. Transcribing the worksheets

Basic issues

This section describes the more obvious difficulties of transcribing the worksheets and discusses how the transcription deals with them. They include the problem of representing the layout of the worksheet and the size of lettering, as well as giving an accurate account of words, punctuation, common abbreviations, deletions, corrections and underlining.

Layout of the worksheet

The transcription represents the worksheet by a rectangle drawn approximately to the scale of the original, about eleven centimetres from top to bottom and seventeen and a half from side to side. It is divided by a vertical dotted line showing where Dickens folds then flattens the original to form two equal halves. The rectangle, with entries grouped and positioned as in the original, reveals the ease with which he moves or glances to and fro between what is sometimes misleadingly called 'pages', here referred to as the left- and right-hand halves (or sides) of the worksheet.[28]

Entries are regularly organised into groups, often laid out as a list, with the groups separated by small idiosyncratic diagonal slashes (see below p.22). As Dickens moves down the page, he is well practised in maintaining a notional horizontal. In the worksheets for central instalments that tend to be more crowded, he sometimes uses a consistently sloping line—perhaps with a matching slope to its margin—in order to use space more effectively (or occasionally from haste and impatience). The spacing of lines or words, at one point the spread of syllables on the line, is sometimes significant ($Ws.4_{12}$ p.51). The leaf that is stuck over the unused left-hand half of Ws.5 is a unique but indicative example of Dickens's sensitivity to layout for expressive purposes. For the facsimile and transcription of Ws.5a, see below p.60; for its commentary see p.61. [Editor's note: the abbreviation for a worksheet 'Ws.' with the number of its instalment is often followed a smaller subscripted number which refers to a numbered entry in the margin of the transcription. If the context makes it clear which worksheet is under consideration, then its marginal numbers are simply shown in brackets, as, for example, in the final paragraph of this subsection].

Although the transcription generally preserves many of the effects of layout, it struggles to deal with some inevitable difference between type and the written word. If transcription were to preserve the pleasing layout of type that the modern reader takes for granted, the horizontal positioning of each word would create many anomalies, particularly at the line end. The line of type would often end a long way short of the right-hand edge, perhaps leaving the reader to wonder why Dickens does not spread his entries towards the right. On the other hand, if the starting point of each word relative to the left-hand edge of the page were to match exactly that of the written word in the original—where Dickens expands and occasionally contracts the length of each word by the way he forms letters and makes ligatures—then the arbitrary gaps between words (or the lack of them) would seem strange.

https://doi.org/10.11647/OBP.0092.04

Always matching the line beginnings, the transcription steers a middle course between matching the position of each word either to the left-hand margin or to the end of the previous word. As the discrepancy begins to arise between the start of words in transcription and the original, it imitates the length of the gaps between words in the original, by regularising the gap to one, two, three or four spaces. This preserves the appearance of the hand's movements across the page but adjusts the difference in length between the typed and written word—unless of course there is a change in letter size of the original, which is usually represented in transcription by increasing or decreasing the size of the font.

The effect of the compromise in positioning can be best appreciated through examination of a short passage. Compare for example the final entries of Ws.5 in transcription and facsimile.[29] In transcription, the order of entry is clearly (16), (15) and (17). The first entry "Paul's death" (16) in size and spacing is fourteenpoint; the second entry (15) in size and spacing is ninepoint, but with double spaces between the words after the stop; the final entry (17) in size and spacing is tenpoint, but with double or triple spaces in the inquit "said Miss Tox" and what follows, except for the phrase "Dombey and Son's" sized and spaced in eightpoint. All of these changes follow comparable alterations in Dickens's handwriting. By so doing, it conveys an impression of the way words are grouped in the manuscript. Occasionally, the layout of both transcription and the original seems visually to correspond to the rhythm of the spoken voice that sometimes seems to accompany the silent reading of Dickens's prose at moments of heightened feeling.

Lettering

As much as layout, it is the lettering—its size and hand—that confirms the unity of each group. Every sheet shows how skilful and well-practised Dickens is with a quill, varying his lettering for example in the facsimile and transcription of Ws.3 pp.46–7 from very large for emphasis e.g. "Old child" (15), to an extreme "smallhand"—his own word to describe his smallest hand—marking small but significant details, e.g. "Mirrors – hearth-rugs" (9); see p.47. To represent contrasts in size the transcription uses a full range of font sizes from eight to sixteenpoint. The representation of other qualities of the lettering is examined below in 'Special issues', p.18.

Punctuation marks and common abbreviations

Dickens's versions of common abbreviations and punctuation marks are transliterated in the usual way, e.g. q^{y}, etc, &, N$^{o/s}$ and M^{r}; similarly the stop, comma, colon, semi-colon, question and exclamation mark. His variation of long and short dashes seems in most instances random or insignificant. They are both transcribed thus '–', except where occasionally a series of short dashes falling between items seems to imply that the items are in some way equivalent, in which case they are transcribed thus '-', for example, in the transcription of Ws.1 p.39, compare '–' in (1), (2) (3) with '-' in (7).

Deletions and corrections

The wording of the corrections of the worksheets is closest to that of Harry Stone's in his transcriptions, with the difference that more weight is given to Dickens's likely intentions with regard to initial letters.

A greater degree of freedom has also been taken in conjecturing partly obscured deletions (For Stone's approach to these issues, see *Dickens' Working Notes for His Novels*, edited by Harry Stone (University of Chicago Press, 1987), pp.xxxii–iii. Hereafter 'Stone').

Dickens makes few deletions in the working notes compared with the heavily revised manuscript of the novel. Some worksheet revisions are running corrections, i.e. immediate second thoughts that are made as he writes. Most are revisions to drafts of text for chapter titles, closing texts for chapter endings, or the "letterings" for illustrations.

In making changes to chapter titles, Dickens deletes in his usual way, either by striking through words with a horizontal line, or by covering them with loops that largely obscure what lies beneath. Because of the complexity of the revisions to some chapter titles, transcription of deletions occasionally requires three different ways to show the history of deletion (see 'Deletion in transcription', p.35). The order of the revisions to many chapter titles is revealed by changes in layout, hand, and the positioning of the broken double underlines.[30]

Title revisions are made at different stages, some as he writes, others at a later stage, perhaps when he is finishing the chapter, or occasionally when he has moved on to a subsequent chapter. Late revisions are particularly obvious when they involve a change in colour, as they do in ch.26 and ch.33. Having written the first half of ch.26 in black, he writes the second half of the chapter in blue and returns to enter the title in blue. Similarly, after writing ch.33 in black and leaving the chapter untitled, he returns to title ch.33 in bright blue, during the composition in bright blue of ch.34.

Underlining for meaning

Dickens makes consistent use of emphatic underlines. Varying in weight and number, usually single or double and always continuous, they accentuates the importance of a word or entry. The source of the import varies. Sometimes they foreground an incident or character for their future significance. Sometimes they mark an idea, image, symbol, or rhetorical device that will be repeated in later contexts. Occasionally they simply confirm a decision.

He also uses less formal but still distinctive lines, as signs or gestures to convey information of different sorts, including transposition in the facsimile of Ws.15, inclusion in Ws.16$_{15}$ p.107, his pleasure or relief at completing a task (see the many 'signing off' underlines, e.g. in the transcription of Ws.10$_{7}$ p.83 or of Ws.13$_{36}$ p.95).

In transcription, lines are drawn to show their position, length and density and, very occasionally, some other distinctive quality such as curvature, where the nib opens and closes in response to changing pressure, e.g. in the transcriptions of Ws.6$_{9}$ p.63 and Ws.10$_{7}$ p.83.

Conventional double underlining

Dickens employs two sorts of routine double underlines. He uses a continuous double underline for the title of each instalment, and broken double underlines for the heading of each chapter number and title.

The broken double underlines of chapter number headings—a part of Dickens's preliminary preparations—are usually deliberate and unhurried, varying the number of breaks he makes with the length of each heading. In contrast, the broken double underlines given to chapter titles, in the early numbers especially, are often hurriedly executed, their frequent corrosion suggesting that the underlines are drawn quickly, sometimes for more than one chapter at a time. In later chapters, in titles as well as number headings, each stroke is usually shorter, more evenly made and more closely matched to its partner, reflecting his growing confidence in the format of the worksheet.

At the start, he usually leaves provisional titles unmarked, only applying broken underlines to his final choice (most exceptions are in ch.1). From Ws.2 onwards, he makes the decision to revise titles in manuscript—underlining all versions—and to transfer only the final underlined title to the worksheet (an early exception is ch.8). The general effect of the decision on the appearance of titles in the worksheet is to make them more prominent, and in the manuscript—with the deletions, revisions, insertions and broken underlines—to make the order of entry more distinct. (For the history of the entry of chapter titles, see column (4) in 'Appendix B'; for the revisions, see 'Appendix D').

In transcription, all routine underlines, whether continuous or broken, are best made 'drawn', i.e. made by inserting a drawn object, as opposed to typographical underlining. Even so, transcription represents broken underlines very approximately. Each stroke of the pair of broken underlines is reduced to a straight line, approximate as to length, angle and position, but showing the appropriate degree of blackness and of thickness, as Word 2010 defines them.[31]

The diagrammatic simplification reveals how the second stroke of each pair often leads to the first of the next pair, how Dickens sometimes tends to put a little more pressure on the quill, as he enters the first and last pair, and how each pair tends to fall away from the horizontal towards the end of the group as a whole—all variations that are reminders of a busy writer at work (see, for example, the right-hand entries in Ws.8 p.74).

Special issues

This section examines the more problematic aspects of transcribing. It describes types of significant corrosion, changes in density that ensue from alterations in hand pressure or changes of quill, the variety of Dickens's coloured inks, and his idiosyncratic diagonal slashes—and how all are imitated or represented in transcription.

Corrosion

The black iron-gall ink that Dickens uses poses a tantalising problem. It has, in many instances, corroded through oxidisation to various shades of yellowy brown. The process of decay is dependent on a number of factors acting together: in the environment, in the constitution of the ink, and in the writer's hand. In the case of the latter, for example, alterations in speed, pressure, angle of the stroke can affect the density of the ink, which in turn may make it more liable to corrode. Such a multiplicity of interrelated causes complicates interpretation. Nevertheless, a corroded group of entries does reveal a relationship—of some sort, and from whatever reason—to its surroundings.[32]

A proportion of entries, in what is called 'non-corroding black', seem to be unaffected. Other entries, which are only corroded in part, with random changes to single words, letters or strokes, can be discounted.

What remains are those groups of entries that are discoloured, so that they appear either a consistent shade of brown throughout, or a shade of brown that becomes lighter as the entry or entries advance.

In the first case, where corrosion is unvarying, it seems reasonable to see consistent corrosion as significant because, when the corrosion ends, it signals a pause or break in Dickens's note-making. He stops and resumes in a way that results in a cessation of corrosion and change in a contrast, perhaps with a different hand, ink or quill. Consistent corrosion contributes to the perception of the relationship between groups, particularly in the more crowded right-hand entries of the worksheets of the third quarter, for example in the right-hand of Ws.11 p.87 separating the consistently corroded (11)–(15) from non-corroded (19)–(21) but drawing together (19)–(21) and (25)–(27). In Ws.15, the effect of consistent corrosion helps determine the order of entry; it increases the probable concurrence of the left-hand number plans (1) and (2) with the title and plan for ch.48 (later 47) made in entries (24)–(31). There is often a marked contrast—caused by consistent corrosion of a less dense ink and lighter hand—in late final entries made on the lower left-hand half, for example, Ws.4_6 p.51, 6_9 p.63 and 7_5 p.71.

In the second case, because corrosion is progressive, it must have an immediate cause, perhaps a delay in re-dipping, or repeated re-dipping with a rapid loss of flow, or a simply a reduction in quill pressure to conserve a drying pen. Whatever the cause however, progressive corrosion happens relatively quickly, confirming that the affected entries are delivered by the same quill on the same occasion and followed by a pause or break. For example, when Dickens explains at some length the order of composition in No.15, his quill slowly dries, thinning the ink, which later corrodes (see Ws.15_6 p.103). Similarly, towards the end of his plans for Miss Tox's visit to the Toodles family, he avoids re-dipping—in another final group of entries—and as the ink supply fails, it becomes thin and later progressively corrodes (see Ws.$12_{22\ \&\ 23}$ p.91). The title and summary of ch.18 (later 17) and ch.19 are both similarly corroded and probably entered on the same occasion. However, in both groups of entries, corrosion is consistent at the start and progressive towards the end, which suggests that Dickens lightly re-dips his pen between chapter descriptions (see Ws.6 p.63).

In transcription, the imitation of corrosion is achieved by choosing the proportion of the principal constituent colours of brown (red and green) and varying the degree of transparency. Entries that are corroded to the same degree are imitated by an unchanging shade of brown. Entries that are progressively corroded are imitated in the same way, but also lightened by varying their transparency to show the degree and extent of the corrosion. In practice, the corrosion in any one worksheet is simplified to a broadly defined set of four or five contrasts, often more pronounced than in the original—to compensate for inevitable variations in colour and tone of different monitors, computers and printers.

Density

The density of black ink varies, producing a darker or lighter line. Apart from the transient darkening that can occur when a quill is re-dipped and is perhaps temporarily overloaded, a consistently denser or lighter line can arise from the cut of the nib or the flow of the barrel or from an increase or reduction in pressure (the latter especially when writing with smaller lettering or a faster hand). One or more of the quills used in the later worksheets give a much darker line, apparently more thickly cut. Occasionally a quill, with a poor nib or an unclean barrel or sullied ink, delivers an erratic ink flow (see, for example, Ws.6a recto and verso; and cf. their transcriptions, p.67).

Nevertheless, where density is consistent, it is often deliberate, and created by a lighter or heavier hand. Of course as a skilled draughtsman, Dickens varies the pressure with which he letters at will, e.g. when forming Roman numerals, he regularly makes them darker and larger than their surroundings. Generally, he is consistent in the density of those entries that he groups together. Like positioning and size, density contributes to the reader's sense of the relation of one group to another.

Transcription of changes in density, as with corrosion, is mostly limited to two sorts of entries or groups of entries: those that are distinguished throughout by a *consistent* reduction in the density of their ink, whether by change in hand or quill, and those that show a *progressive* reduction. A consistent reduction in the density of black ink can usually be transcribed by the using of one of the five gradients of black singled out in Word 2010; progressive loss of density is always shown by thinning black to lighter shades of grey using its percentage 'gradient' facility.

The distinction between density and corrosion is often difficult to sustain, because it varies with different light. In the brief number plan of Ws.9 p.79, the entry "connect Carker and Edith" loses density at "before the wedding" (2) and again at "and get in Florence" (3) and perhaps again at "Mems" (1), presumably because Dickens lightens his hand to conserve the ink supply in the pen and avoid re-dipping. The changes in density, setting aside possible corrosion, are sufficient to confirm Dickens's hasty afterthought "and get in Florence".

Even so, the close relation of density and corrosion need not affect the transcription of changes in density, however small the changes are or unreliable their corrosion. For example, in Ws.1 p.39, most of the words of the first two left-hand entries (1) and (2) are both less dense and more evenly corroded than the next three entries (3)–(5), which are more varied but more dense and less corroded. However, the next entry (6), though tinged by corrosion is much darker that either of the two earlier groups (1)–(5) while the final entry (7) is slightly denser and more corroded than (1) and (2). The effect of this representation of density with corrosion is to confirm what is also conveyed by changes in lineation and letter size. The entries Ws.$1_{1–7}$ are made in four stages (1) and (2), (3)–(5), (6), and (7)—identified by size, layout, density and corrosion—which correspond in their sequence to the order of the narrative.

Compromises in the representation of density can be found in most worksheet transcriptions. In the part and chapter number headings for Ws.1–3, for example, Dickens uses a thin hand and enlarges the numerals. The size of these numerals can be conveyed by using a larger font. But the larger the font, the thicker and darker it appears. So to retain an impression of the relation of the number headings to their surroundings, the density of the larger type has been considerably reduced, which makes the dark lighter but still leaves it without the spidery character of the original.

To convey the effect of Dickens's darkest entries, the transcription usually adjusts the density of the entries around them. The result can be seen in Ws.15 by comparing the right-hand half of the transcription with its facsimile. In the special case of the distinctive, probably consecutive, dark entries, which Dickens makes as he begins Ws.17, the transcription uses a bold type (see Ws.$17_{4,\ 5,\ 12\ \&\ 17}$ p.111, Ws.$18_{2,\ 5\ \&\ 6}$ p.115 and 19&$20_{2\ \&\ 13}$ p.119).

Despite the difficulties posed by very thin or very dark entries, the manipulation of density remains one of the more reliable ways of conveying contrast, even in those worksheets like Ws.15 or Ws.19&20 that are crowded with detail. It has often proved more useful to adjust the representation of density (and to be sure of the outcome) than to attempt to imitate too closely the degree of accompanying corrosion that seems to vary as the light changes.

Ink colour

A number of entries are written in a bright blue, a faint watery blue or a greeny blue ink. As none of the blue inks have iron derivatives in their mixture, they are not liable to corrosion. Although the quality of all the blue inks vary, the bright blue appears to be the most satisfactory. However, Dickens was probably unable to secure a reliable supply, so he tends to reserve what bright blue he has for whole chapters in the manuscript.

Bright blue is used to write all of No.7, most of No.9 and the last chapter of No.11, while in the worksheets for those numbers there are at most only three entries made in bright blue. The only use of bright blue for part of a chapter occurs in No.9 (see below). Evidence suggests that the two less satisfactory watery blue and greeny blue inks are not chosen but forced on Dickens by his temporarily living away from his usual residence. Each of the three uses of bright blue in the "List of Chapter Headings" follows soon after its use in the manuscript, confirming as might be expected that, despite a wish to conserve bright blue, Dickens moves on from completing a chapter to updating the List. 'Appendix F' summarises the consecutiveness of entries in blue, in the worksheets and all other tasks, showing if or when, and how often, they are interrupted by entries in black. The appendix is derived from a survey of the relevant commentaries.

In transcription, the range of blues in the original is represented by a brighter blue, a less faint blue and a more greeny blue—each made more distinct in transcription than it appears in the facsimiles. Headings in the accompanying commentary are coloured to match what is being described, as in the naming of colours in the previous sentence. The representation of colour, like that of density and corrosion, is intended not to copy but to show a contrast comparable to that of the original.

The marked difference between black and blue inks in transcription and commentary makes it easy to survey all of the monthly areas of work for changes in ink colour. If we examine, first of all, just those bright blue entries that are made in the worksheets, we find that most bright blue entries are consecutive. The exceptions are one entry in Ws.7 (see the unique entry (2) p.71) and the two changes to bright blue and back in Ws.9 (see below). Next, examining the commentaries for changes to bright blue ink, not just in the worksheets, but in all areas of work, we again find that most blue entries are consecutive. For No.7, all tasks in blue—from the composition and titling in manuscript to the planning and composition of the planned extension to ch.22—are consecutive (excepting Ws.7_2), as are the entries in faint watery blue in No.12 and in greeny blue in Nos.19&20 and 19&20a. In No.11, bright blue ink is used only once, for the composition of ch.34.

The use of blue ink in the production of No.9 is unusual, probably occurring because of changes to Dickens's work routine, arising from his poor health during the first three weeks of May 1847. His temporary debilitating condition and some of its effects are described in the biographical headnote for Ws.9. The letters imply that he did not begin—"had not the heart to go at my number" (L5:69)—until very late in the month, after his arrival in Brighton to convalesce on 17 May. He probably takes a supply of black ink with him when he leaves town, just as he did when he returns to Devonshire Terrace from Broadstairs during the creation of No.12, and when he lodges again in Brighton (at a different address) in order to produce the double number.

Soon after arriving in Brighton however, he probably finds a supply of bright blue ink, and in the middle of writing ch.26 changes from black to the recently obtained bright blue—the only mid-chapter change of ink colour in the entire manuscript. In No.9, from then on, he reserves the bright blue ink, which he seems to prefer for composition, only reverting to a black quill and ink at the end of the ch.26 to plan briefly the remaining chs.27 and 28. The evidence for planning is strong (see commentary on 'Plan for ch.27', p.81) so the chapter descriptions cannot be written after the composition of chs.27 and 28. Still recovering from illness, he perhaps needed an early break from the physical effort of writing ch.26, notwithstanding the advantages of using bright blue—the ink gives a sharper line, with a flow that is more even and responsive, and dries more quickly. Only in the unusual conditions prevailing during the production of No.9 does Dickens alternate between inks, changing from black to blue and back on two occasions (see 'Appendix F', p.192).

Diagonal slashes

Dickens's idiosyncratic slashes are short, slightly curved, diagonal lines, made in a controlled and consistent way, in order to separate them from what follows. Generally pulled from right to left, they are different in feel from underlines, which are pulled the other way as the hand and arm moves towards the right. The slash, comparable perhaps to a shorthand stroke, is usually made after a group, rather than before (shown for example by the colour change at Ws.$12_{6\,\&\,8}$ p.91).

Dickens uses slashes in all worksheets, on the left- or right-hand side, except in the unique Ws.7. Their omission there, in the six left-hand entries, is unusual; he is relying apparently on colour and layout to make the groups distinct. Arguably, the omission of slashes at this early stage, confirms how deliberate they later become.

Slashes regularly separate entries or groups of entries, giving them weight and position in a sequence. They are always significant, used regularly in number planning, and in chapter plans used at the start, intermittently from Ws.4 and consistently from Ws.10 onwards.[33] The slash is usually made at the start of a line or sometimes, when space is at a premium, mid-line or even towards the end of a line (see the last four slashes of ch.48 (later 47) in Ws.$15_{28\text{–}31}$ p.103). They are generally distinguishable from Dickens's horizontal underlines, although similarity can sometimes leads to misreading, e.g. the slash before "Preparation for Cousin Feenix" (Ws.10_{17} p.83) or ambiguity, e.g. the slash below "Good" (Ws.11_{25} p.87). In the case of the slash at the start of entry (12) on the left-hand side of Ws.19&20, where he has no room to shape the slash in the usual way, Dickens takes care to separate it slightly from the continuous single line that follows (see Ws.19&20_{12} p.119). We can assume from the special attention he gives to distinguishing the slash from its surroundings that it is sign of some significance.

The transcription of the idiosyncratic slash shows its position and imitates very approximately its length, slope and density, but not its curved contour.

Accidental marks

There are occasional marks throughout the worksheets that are moving reminders of a writer at work. For example, at the start of Ws.3 p.46, they seem to show Dickens tapping beneath "Mems" on the top left-hand half as he reflects on the early narrative, perhaps before he devised the worksheet format. There are also various 'transfer' errors, for example when, having almost finished a worksheet, he puts extra pressure on the second 'd' of 'odd' leaving two small transferred marks beneath (Ws.10_7 p.83), or having finished updating the List for No.15, he appears to repeat the last double underline beneath

"Florence" (see bottom of p.178). Such errors occur when Dickens transfers ink unintentionally. Some surface, acting like blotting paper, has taken up ink from his letters or lines and left marks elsewhere that faintly resemble them.[34] One writing accident—a smudge—occurs with special significance in ch.17 (see 'Title and summary of ch.17 (later 18)' in the commentary on Ws.6, p.65).

Comparison with other transcriptions

The general aim is to improve on the transcriptions currently available. Stone summed up the situation thus : '[transcriptions] have been sadly deficient, some containing hundreds of errors, and all suffering from an inability to deal satisfactorily with the problems of format and with the idiosyncrasies of Dickens' annotation' (Stone, p.xxxi).[35]

The release of photographic facsimiles of the extant working notes for all the novels with their accompanying transcriptions in Stone's edition was a notable advance in the history and treatment of the notes. However, Stone's generously sized and beautifully produced book has limitations—apart from its cost—due to the technology that was available at the time. The facsimiles, photographed and printed in black and white, distort the appearance of the original in a number of ways. They render changes in colour, whether due to corrosion or to the various blue inks, as a change of tone, i.e. as alterations in the gradation of black to grey. Readers of the facsimiles (and of the transcriptions) are therefore unable to discriminate consistently between the effect of density, corrosion and colour, distinctions that, crucial to the close analysis of Dickens's hand, make a significant contribution to the transcriptions and commentaries of this edition. Nevertheless, although developments in communication and in printing have bettered his facsimiles, Stone's introductions to the preparation and composition of the working notes for each of Dickens's novels are still among the most readable and well informed.

Stone tries to deal with the absence of colour by including a coloured frontispiece of the worksheet for No.12 in *Dombey and Son* and describing in detail all the coloured ink changes, as he sees them, in his introduction to each novel. In the section on *Dombey and Son*, however, the prose account is a poor substitute for the visual effect (Stone, pp.51–52). Arguments based on ink change—for example about the relation of Ws.7, Ws.9 or Ws.12 to the composition of their respective instalments—are very difficult to disentangle without a visual display. Moreover, although he recognises that the discoloration of Dickens's black ink is caused by oxidation (and consequently related to density), he later apparently underestimates the affect that oxidation has, when he writes "In his middle works [*Dombey and Son* to *Little Dorrit*], Dickens employed both brown and blue ink" (Stone, p.xvii). Albeit often difficult to interpret and display, most worksheets for *Dombey and Son* are affected in some way by oxidation of the varying iron gall constituent in black ink.

Stone rather unfairly berates earlier transcribers for their omissions, while in his own, by reducing all of Dickens's letters to one unvarying font size throughout, he diminishes very obvious marked differences between groups of entries in the original. In his defence, he appeals to his facsimiles, a recourse not available to those earlier transcribers, who were in any case unable to show them, because of copyright law.[36]

His edition has other lesser flaws. It is not quite true to describe the paper of all the working notes as 'blue-grey laid paper'. As he notes later, the paper for Ws.5a is taken from Dickens's store of smoother 'woven' paper that he also used for the manuscript, a sign of the importance he assigned to that attachment (Stone, p.67). Dickens also used the better quality paper for the "List of Chapter Headings". The latter goes unmentioned by Stone, perhaps because he mistakenly considered it a preparation for the contents page and as such not a part of the working notes. Yet Dickens obviously viewed the List as a necessary part of his monthly tasks, usually compiling it as he approached the end of the instalment in hand (see 'Appendix C' for a transcription of the List, its purpose and what it tells us of Dickens's working methods).

With regard to transcriptions in general, Stone claims that facsimiles of the originals 'convey nuances, emphases, spacings, afterthoughts, and immediacies which no transcription can capture'. He feels that the 'expressive and meaningful [...] variations in size, boldness, underlining, check marks, and so on [are] untranscribable' (Stone, p.xxxi). A sense of the untranscribable qualities of the original is probably shared by many readers. It arises from the skill of the writer and the nature of his medium. Finding a steel nib "scratchy" and always preferring a quill, Dickens enjoys its speed, flexibility and expressiveness. With control over size, direction, length and density of stroke, he creates a great variety of contrasts, as you would expect from someone with his life experience and shorthand skills.[37]

The more widely available transcriptions of the working notes have some of the commonly found shortcomings touched on by Stone. Published first in 'Appendix B' of the authoritative Clarendon edition of the novel in 1974, then reproduced in the Oxford World's Classics series from 1982 onwards, Horsman's transcription is derived directly from the original manuscript. Given the limitations of the conventional printed page, it is very accurate as to words and punctuation. However, it provides a poor and occasionally misleading imitation of layout and of grouping. It standardises all letters to a single font size, the orientation of all entries to the horizontal, omits colour, corrosion and all unconventional marks other than underlines. His claim to 'follow the order [...] of the original' (835^{929}) must refer to physical appearance of entries; there are no indications of their order in time. [Editor's note: (1) the first figure following the bracket refers to page number in the hardback Clarendon text of the novel, edited by Alan Horsman (Oxford: Clarendon Press, 1974); (2) the second superscripted figure refers to the same text reissued as an Oxford World's Classics paperback, edited by Alan Horsman (Oxford: Oxford University Press, 2008) as in 'References', p.7].

Verbal accuracy alone misrepresents Dickens's notation. For him making notes is an ongoing and changing process, with regular movements between left and right halves of the sheet, between notes and manuscript, with many hesitations, additions, insertions, corrections, and alterations of pace. Perhaps because of the problems of printing an effective transcription, the publishers of Penguin English Library—the chief rival in the UK to the Oxford World's Classics series—seems to hesitate over the value of publishing them at all. Their edition of *Dombey and Son* (2002) omits the 'Number Plans' whereas the parallel edition of *Little Dorrit* (2003) includes them.

The present transcription differs from previous attempts in a number of ways. As already mentioned, it avoids a misleadingly spaced separation of the number plan side from the chapter side, found for example throughout Paul Herring's article, where one follows the other, to the confusion of this reader.[38] Drawing each worksheet with approximately the same dimensions as the original is a visual reminder of close relation the two adjacent halves to each other. Furthermore, by grouping and positioning entries in a similar way to the original and by imitating the size, density, colour and corrosion of the hand, the transcription shows more clearly how entries relate to each other.[39] It also represents all nonverbal marks, including those important idiosyncratic diagonal slashes that separate and unify entries or groups of entries, which are often either omitted in transcription or if retained, done in a way that fails to distinguish them clearly from other lines. A few of the random marks that Dickens makes on the page as he pauses for thought are also included—not just for the information they carry but because they are moving reminders of the author at work.

Finally, unlike the two principal editions of Horsman and Stone, this critical edition links transcription to a descriptive commentary. All entry groups in each transcription are numbered, enabling the two-page commentary to assemble an annotated order of entry, reconstructed here for the first time from all the evidence in each facsimile and elsewhere, and incorporating Dickens's other monthly tasks that regularly interrupt the worksheet entries. The commentary lists the following in the order that Dickens appears to have made them: the six sorts of entries made in the worksheet—as described in 'Grouping and function on the left-hand half', p.28)—the composition of each chapter, the compilation of the "List of Chapter Headings" and the principal changes made to the various proofs.

'Appendix C' transcribes the "List of Chapter Headings", 'Appendix D' brings together Dickens's scattered chapter title revisions, and 'Appendix E' transcribes some of his false starts in the manuscript at chapter openings, and 'Appendix F' summarizes the use of blue inks—all shown here in detail for the first time.

Section 3. Procedures in the worksheets

Formatting the worksheet

From January 1846 onwards, Dickens experiences the usual restless preparation for a new book "wandering about (in London) at night in the strangest places", during which time according to Forster "the characters were growing in his mind" (*Life* 388[K:7934]). Nevertheless, believing he "could write better in retirement", he determines to go abroad to Italy or Switzerland, settling with his family in Lausanne in the summer of 1846. Soon after their arrival, his box of writing materials is delivered and on 28 June he "BEGAN DOMBEY!" (*Life* 400[K:8159]). [Editor's note: the abbreviation following '*Life*' refers to John Forster's *Life of Charles Dickens*, ed. J. W. Ley (London: Cecil Palmer, 1926) and to the same title, 3 vols. in 2 (Boston: James R. Osgood & Co., 1875) as ebook 25851, Project Gutenberg, http://www.gutenberg.org/ebooks/25851 (released 20 June 2008), downloaded to the Kindle app and here with the location superscripted. For more information, see the explanation in 'References', p.7].

With his materials to hand, his talismans—"certain quaint little bronze figures"—on the desk before him, and the inkwell cleansed and replenished the previous night, we can imagine Dickens preparing his first worksheet (L4:573n). He has already made a few notes, but on this occasion he takes a leaf of the poorer quality paper from one of his two pre-cut half-foolscap paper supplies and, having folded it in half parallel to its shorter side, he lays it flat, with the longer side facing him.

By folding the worksheet in the way he does, Dickens prepares to distinguish number business from chapter business, a distinction that reflects his growing ambition for his chosen method of publication. Intending to create a novel more coherent in theme and structure, he plans each number so that it relates well to what has gone before and what is to come. On the right-hand 'chapter' side, he gives the longer title of the novel with the number of the instalment and chapter number headings for the routine three chapters then, turning the worksheet over, adds another on the back. On the left-hand 'number' side, he notes what might go into the current number, in view of both his larger and his immediate intentions for the novel (see endnote 42).

After Dickens has planned the shape and substance of the number, he usually writes the opening chapter (the only exception No.15) and titles it in the manuscript. He transfer the title to the worksheet and, when the chapter is completed, he adds, if it seems necessary, a brief reminder of its contents. Then he does the same for the middle and the last chapter, alert to the special relation of the closing chapter to the predefined end of the number. Throughout the creation of each instalment, Dickens moves from one task to the next, going between the left and right-hand side of the worksheet, the manuscript, the proofs, and—from Ws.6 onwards—the "List of Chapter Headings". Keeping in mind the progress of the story as well as his "immediate intentions", he is also of course determined to make each instalment attractive in itself and likely to get and keep the interest of the reader (see endnote 42).

https://doi.org/10.11647/OBP.0092.05

Entries on the left-hand half

As soon as Dickens starts to use the worksheet, the format he has devised changes into something more elaborate. The number plan for the first instalment initially leaves blank the lower part of the left-hand half. Later, how he uses that space will vary in function more than any other part of the worksheet. On this occasion, during the composition of chapters two and three, he reverses the leaf and uses the space to trial three possible titles, perhaps for chapter headings or as lettering for the illustrations. Entry Ws.1$_{8}$ p.39 where the leaf is reversed for the first and only time, and Ws.1$_{22\ \&\ 23}$ p.37 on the right-hand side—unique entries on the under (verso) side of the worksheet—are both instances of a method of entry that is subsequently always avoided. Dickens on reflection probably decides that reversing or turning the leaf over might hamper his use of the worksheet, making it more awkward to scan or check entries.

Heading the left-hand half

In about half of the worksheets, Dickens gives the left-hand side the heading "Mems", a term that he uses elsewhere for the worksheets themselves. The heading is a reminder of what needs to be remembered as he writes each number. Although there are often some differences between worksheets headed "Mems" and those without the heading, the distinction is not made consistently.

He titles the left-hand side of Ws.3 "General mems", a heading that was probably given it before it became the worksheet "for Ws.3". Some of its misplaced entries may also have been made at that early pre-format stage evident in 'Discarded entries' in Ws.2 p.44 and 'Plan for the number' in Ws.3 p.48. He doubts the usefulness of the heading, only reviving it for the worksheet of the double number.

The number plan

Because Dickens begins entries on each left-hand side with his plans for the number as a whole, the left-hand side is usually referred to as 'the number plan', a convenient label but often only applicable to entries in the upper part of the left-hand half.

Every number has a plan, but plans vary considerably in scope and structure, partly depending on their place in the development of the novel, and to a lesser extent, on Dickens's circumstances at the time. A few number plans fill the whole page; one has only a single entry. Some are entered as whole and on the same occasion; others, as the layout and hand of the original shows, are accumulated in two or three stages.

Grouping and function on the left-hand half

Dickens regularly separates one group of left-hand entries from another by his diagonal slash. Even in the first half of the novel, where notation practices are more variable, the practice is unusually consistent. He groups without using slashes—by positioning and qualities of hand alone—in only three worksheets in the first half of the novel (Ws.3, 7 and 9), and in only one worksheet in the second half of the novel (Ws.18). In all other worksheets, entries on the left-hand half are sorted into groups by Dickens using his characteristic slash.

We can also deduce from the worksheets as a whole that each left-hand group will have a particular function. Firstly and usually in the upper part of the left-hand half, there may be:

- a preliminary—an occasional heading "Mems" (in Ws.6, 7, 9, 12, 13, 15) or "General mems" (in Ws.3 and Ws.19&20
- a plan (or 'initial plan') for the number—comprising materials for the number, occasionally haphazard, but more often roughly sorted into chapter order, particularly as to the opening and middle chapters
- an additional number plan—entries made later, some adding to the plan for the number as a whole and some concerning individual chapters
- a further number plan—entries made later than and distinct from the additional number plans, sometimes also concerning individual chapters.

Secondly, in the lower part of the left-hand half, there may be:

- a memo—a note of special significance, to be remembered for its potential use in subsequent numbers, usually entered after the composition of a chapter
- a comment—a retrospective explanation, written after completing the number, concerning his plans and their execution.

Finally, throughout the left-hand half, there may be:

- outcome(s)—replies to earlier left-hand entries if they take the form of questions or for some other reason require confirmation.

The occurrence of the single number 'plan'—as opposed to the 'initial/additional/further plans'—varies. In the first half of the novel, for very different reasons, most worksheets have just a single 'plan'. By contrast, in the third quarter of the novel, the reverse is the case; most number plans are entered in two or three different stages, largely because of the entanglement of Dickens's interrelated narrative "threads". Then in the last quarter, as the outcomes become more predictable, the number plans shrink to just three entries or less, as Dickens orders the events that wind up his two main plots.

Two unique entries on the left-hand half

Two left-hand entries fall outside of the above categories. The first is the special chapter-cum-number plan (Ws.5a) that Dickens uses to help him weave the sick Paul's viewpoint into the narrative of chs.14 and 16, which he regarded as an innovation in his fictional method. The second is the long entry giving the "social history" of Edith and her mother, which, though it prefaces Ws.7, also provides background to ch.27 (see 'Plan for ch.27' p.81). It marks a shift of direction in the plotting of the novel, which

Dickens probably had in mind from its inception (see top right in the cover design of the green wrapper, for his earliest intentions, evident in the wedding ceremony at the altar and its witnesses p.viii).

Chapter planning on the left-hand half

The point at which an idea for the number becomes an item within a chapter is usually implicit. Compare the lower left-hand entries of Ws.3 with those of Ws.4a. The lower left-hand entries of Ws.3 are four scattered groups, the first of which (8) is not yet associated with any chapter, but held back for the next number, while the other three (9)–(11) may be embedded in an imagined narrative, but not yet assigned to a particular chapter (see Ws.3 p.49). On the other hand, the lower left-hand entries of the leaf attached to the bottom of Ws.4 comprise eight items all linked to the second half of ch.12, with the last one (8)—partly re-formed from two of the previous seven—used to close the chapter (see Ws.4a p.54). Hindsight tells us the destination of all these entries, but their position on the left-hand side suggests that, for a time at least, they floated free in Dickens's imagination.

In contrast to Ws.4a, the crucial note of "Dombey musing at table...." in Ws.10 is from its inception imaginatively associated with the middle ch.30 (see Ws.10 p.83). It might appear to be placed on the left-hand half simply because there is no space for it in the adjacent right-hand plan. However, hand and quill suggests otherwise (see the commentary 'Plan for the number' in Ws.10 p.84). By placing the note of the reverie amid his general ideas for the number, Dickens singles it out as particularly significant; it evokes Dombey's buried fear of the tie to his daughter and his profound guilt.

The larger issue of the relation that number plans on the left-hand half have to chapter plans on the right-hand will be examined later, when the chapter plans have been described more fully (see third paragraph onward of 'Third quarter', p.152–53).

Entries on the right-hand half

Preliminaries: part heading and chapter numbers

The longer title of the novel and the number of the current instalment are preliminary headings, spread across the top of the right-hand half—together called 'the Part heading'—and followed by the chapter number headings for three chapters, spread evenly down the page. Once this starting routine is established, the chapter number headings tend to slip to the right as the arm moves downwards, confirming that they are entered altogether. The chapter number headings usually mark out three regions on the page, each region consisting of a number, a title and a 'chapter description' (see below).

Changes to chapter number heading(s)

Sometimes Dickens has to update chapter number heading(s) to have an accurate record of changes made after his preliminary entries (see commentaries to Ws.7, 10, 14 and 15).

Titling the chapters

Dickens takes great care over the choice and wording of chapter titles. He treats them, to begin with, as the most important part of the record on the right-hand side. The stage at which a title is entered in the worksheet changes along with alterations in choosing, revising and entering the title in the manuscript. All revisions to chapter titles, with their wording, sequence and location are given in 'Appendix D'.

The chapter description

In the context of the right-hand entries, the term 'chapter description' here refers to all entries made between the chapter title (or title gap) and the next chapter number (or the bottom of the page). It is used as the general term for those entries so as not to anticipate their purpose, whether plan or summary. Dickens discovers how best to use the space during the progress of the novel. At first, he merely adds a summary note to most chapters (Ws.1–3), which becomes a fuller summary in the opening and middle chapters of Ws.4. Then, for the short closing chapter (ch.13), he uses the space to plan the chapter, anchoring the structure of an imagined narrative by identifying the order of its main concerns. This planning method is extended in the more detailed planning that accompanies the narrative innovations of No.5.

Subsequently in Nos.6–8, partly from adverse circumstances and ill health, and partly from problems intrinsic to the story, his attention to the chapter description lapses, just as his number planning, though increasingly detailed, becomes more tentative.

In No.9, once Dickens establishes Florence within the gathering 'marriage storm', the confident invention of the earlier numbers returns, and with it the frequent use of the chapter description space for planning purposes in Ws.9–15.[40] Then in Ws.16–18, many chapter descriptions are retrospective outlines, i.e. summaries recalling the "principal landmarks of the story" (L11:161) and lacking the positive indications of planning that are found in previous numbers. [Editor's note: the numbers following 'L[etters]' refers to volume and page in the Pilgrim edition of *Dickens's Letters*, ed. Graham Storey, Kathleen Tillotson and Madeline House, et al., 12 vols. (Oxford: Clarendon Press, 1982–2002). For more on the letters, see 'References', p.7].

When entries in the description space become more detailed, Dickens begins to use his idiosyncratic diagonal slash to form them into groups. In contrast to the left-hand half, the slash is used only occasionally in isolated chapters before Ws.9. However, from then on, it is used to structure most descriptions, except for those in the shorter closing chapters, where a single paragraph is usually organised by dashes and commas.

Entries in the double number

In Ws.19&20, Dickens preserves as much as he can of the format of a single number, before adapting and extending his plans into Ws.19&20a. He continues the formal distinction between the left and right-hand half. As in single-number worksheets, preliminaries on the right-hand half in the double number cover the part heading and number headings for the first three chapters. He has already entered (2), and now adds a descriptive heading (1) and crucial number plan entries (3) and (4), filling the lower left-hand space with a unique roll call of named characters (5)–(12) (see the transcription of Ws.19&20 p.119).

The compression of the later left-hand entries (10)–(12) suggests that the additional leaf is probably not attached to Ws.19&20 at the start, but delayed until he has completed ch.59, at which point he wafers a slip to the bottom of Ws.19&20 and attaches the additional leaf Ws.19&20a to it. Then, writing with the same greeny blue ink and quill that he has just used to compose ch.59, he makes all the greeny blue entries (15, 20, 28–31, 36, 40 & 41) that are scattered through the transcription of Ws.19&20 p.119 and Ws.19&20a p.123.

One reason that Dickens has to give such sustained close attention to the double number is that the usual adjustment of number to chapter planning is complicated by his intention—implicit in the lower left-hand entries (5)–(12)—to bring a degree of closure to the stories of most named characters. A few (5), (10) and (12) are coupled with other characters because the intrigues, in which they are involved, have still to be resolved. Some are named because they require a final mention having been prominent in earlier episodes; others simply because they have played some lesser part. The list of course is not exhaustive, and probably is not intended to be so.

One group of named characters probably goes unmentioned because they are extensions of the setting in which they appear, e.g. Mrs Blockett the nurse, Mr Baps the dancing master at the Blimbers, Sownds the Beadle and Mrs Miff at the church, and Old Glubb at the seaside. Others, not mentioned in the left-hand list, are nevertheless drawn into the closing narrative, including Mrs Wickam, Berinthia, Perch and Mrs Perch, Towlinson and Anne, Briggs and "old Tozer". In the various proofs, he revives Mr Toodles, the Skettles, then for one last time Miss Tox, and finally, at the very last moment, Diogenes, who is hurriedly inserted, on Dickens's instruction, by Forster (see 'Proofs' p.125).

For further discussion of the double number worksheet, see the last part of 'Section 6', 'Planning the double number' (p.156), which describes its order of entry as well as setting out the various kinds of evidence for chapter planning found there.

Section 4. Introduction to the worksheets

Introduction to the facsimiles

Since Dickens made his worksheets wider than they are long, all facsimiles are displayed in landscape rather than portrait mode, with the exception of the unique entry on 'Worksheet for No.1 (verso)' and its transcription.[41] Consequently, apart from introductory notes on the worksheets and Ws.1 verso, all of the next section of facsimiles, transcriptions and commentary are printed or displayed in landscape mode.

Facsimile and transcription appear on opposite pages to enable the reader to compare the two without turning the page. Readers of the electronic version, depending on the e-reader's system and software, may be able to view any part of any page with any other by opening a second identical file—offsetting, to some extent, the disadvantages of a continuous prose account.

All of the V&A's images of the worksheets are high resolution (300 dpi), coloured and slightly reduced digital photographs of the original manuscript, made under controlled lighting conditions. Each version of this book contains copies of the V&A images, but the resolution of the copies varies with the different versions. For a description of the various versions of the book, see the end of the 'Foreword', p.5.

A few V&A images—four worksheets in all—are much more reduced. The original manuscript of each of the four worksheet has an additional leaf attached to it. When worksheet and attachment were photographed, they were shot within a frame of the same size and shape as a single worksheet, so that they were reduced by about twenty-five to fifty per cent (depending on the size of the attachment). This blurs the detail of those four images making them more difficult to read without magnification and, in the case of one worksheet, without reorientation. Magnification results in a proportionate reduction in resolution.

The editor's solution to the problems of the V&A's images of worksheets with attachments is to treat each of them in a slightly different way, in order to make them as readable as possible on the displayed and printed page, while keeping their proportion. The details of the adjustments are as follows:

- The facsimile of Ws.4 is shown with a part of its additional leaf (Ws.4a) visible beneath it, so that the reader can see where the attachment is positioned. The transcription and commentary of Ws.4 follows. After them, comes the facsimile of Ws.4a, with its transcription and commentary.
- The facsimile of Ws.5 is shown without the leaf (Ws.5a) that is wafered over its left-hand half. In its place—in the rectangle, where the leaf will later be positioned—is the introduction to Ws.5a. The transcription and commentary of Ws.5 follows with, on the next two pages, the facsimile of Ws.5a and its transcription and commentary.
- The facsimile of Ws.6 (recto) is shown with a part of its additional leaf Ws.6a (recto) showing beneath it, so that the reader can see where the attachment is positioned. The transcription and commentary of Ws.6 (recto) follows.

https://doi.org/10.11647/OBP.0092.06

- As Ws.6 (verso) is blank, except for its attachment Ws.6a (verso), the facsimile of Ws.6 (verso) is not shown. Instead, the facsimiles of both Ws.6a (recto) and (verso), re-oriented and to scale, are re-entered on a single page, followed by their transcriptions and commentaries.
- The facsimile of Ws.19&20 is shown with a part of its additional leaf (Ws.19&20a) showing beneath it, so that the reader can see how the attachment is made using a slip of paper between the two leaves. The transcription and commentary of Ws.19&20 follows. After them, comes the facsimile of Ws.19&20a, with its transcription and commentary (including further commentary on some entries made in Ws.19&20).

For more information on the additional leaves, see: the 'Materials of the working notes' in 'Section 1' (p.12); the introduction to Ws.4a (p.51); the introduction to Ws.5a (p.57); the introduction to Ws.6a at the start of its commentary (p.68); and the introduction to Ws.19&20a (p.123).

Numbering the entries in the transcriptions

Groups are numbered continuously from the left-hand margin to the right-hand margin, in the order of their appearance on the page. Numbering observes the group divisions that Dickens provides by his slashes, and, where these are lacking, uses the evidence of hand, ink and layout to distinguish one group from another. During the commentary, each numbered group is at some point assigned to a subheading according to its function (defined below in 'Dickens's order of work'). Most of these numbered groups on the left-hand half will eventually find a place in the published text. In which case, for the sake of conciseness in the commentary, the group is followed by an arrow '→' with a chapter number, indicating the chapter in which the content of the group first appears in the manuscript.

On the right-hand margin, each numbered group is displayed as follows:

- the part heading is numbered in red
- the chapter number headings are numbered in red and underlined
- the chapter titles are numbered in black and underlined
- the chapter description is numbered in black.

The distinctive slash is at first is confined to the occasional single chapter description: in Ws.$4_{10–12}$ for ch.11, in Ws.$6_{23–25}$ for ch.19, and in Ws.$9_{7–10}$ for ch.26. From then on, the slash is consistently used throughout, except for a few shorter chapter descriptions. Where Dickens relies solely on dashes and stops to organise entries, as sometimes happens in shorter final chapters, they are usually numbered as a single entry. Ws.7 is unique having no slashes in either left- or right-hand pages; its groups are identified by colour, positioning and hand.

Reference by number in this way may make for slow reading. However, without it, comment would be sometimes ambiguous or laboured and often repetitive. A continuous and consistent numbering system, across left- and right-hand sides, has proved essential in order to give a full but readable account of both Dickens's routines and the opportune to-ing and fro-ing typical of his working method.

Deletion in transcription

- deletion is shown by a horizontal midline, e.g. '~~Also Mis~~' (Ws.1$_{16}$ p.39)
- subsequent short deletions are by arrows, e.g. '<and character>'
- subsequent long deletions are shown by a dotted underline, e.g. 'is ~~beheld~~(?) ∧$^{seen(?)}$ in the bosom of his family' (Ws.1$_{18}$ p.39).
- conjectures of partly obscured deletions are followed by a query in brackets (see above)
- wholly obscured deletions are shown by a line of 'x's corresponding (roughly) to their length.

Dickens's order of work as shown in the commentaries

The commentary begins by providing a short biographical headnote of Dickens's life during the creation of the instalment, using the letters written at the time. From then on, it lists the order of his work, whether on the left-hand '**LH**' of the worksheet, on the right-hand '**RH**' of the worksheet, on the manuscript '**MS**', in the '**List**' of Chapter Headings , or on the '**Proofs**'.

For **LH** entries, the order of entry is determined by the grouping of the entries, their appearance on the page, their content and its relation to the final text. Each group has a function identified by a heading: whether it is a 'preliminary', a 'plan' for the number (or an 'initial/additional/further plan'), an 'outcome(s)', a 'memo' or a 'comment'. For more on the headings, see above 'Grouping and function on the left-hand half', p.28.

For **RH** entries, the commentary lays out Dickens's work using the functions that correspond to his divisions, whether 'preliminaries' (part heading and chapter number headings), 'chapter title/titling', 'changes to chapter number', or 'chapter description'.

For **MS** followed by a chapter number, the commentary gives a brief account of the chapter and its titling, to show how both relate to the worksheet.

For **List** followed by its identifying number (given in 'Appendix C'), the commentary describes the entries that Dickens adds to his "List of Chapter Headings". Changes in entry help to establish the relation between his entries in the List and his work on the instalment(s).

For **Proofs**, the commentary notes significant deletions or additions, particularly those made in reaction to the fixed length of the instalment. Other details are included to clarify the relation between the worksheets and the published text, where there are discrepancies between the two.

Abbreviations and other conventions in the commentaries

- 'LH' means the left-hand half of a worksheet
- 'List' refers to Dickens's "List of Chapter Headings", generally followed by entry number(s) in square brackets (given in 'Appendix C')
- 'MS' means the manuscript of the novel
- 'RH' means the right-hand half of a worksheet
- a bracketed number, either on its own or preceded by a worksheet number and subscripted, refers to a marginal number in a worksheet, i.e. either 'Ws.7 ... entry (2)' or 'Ws.7_2'
- comments in red signal comments of special importance, the significance of which often goes beyond the worksheet in hand
- headings in blue signal that the associated entry or text is written in blue in the original
- the symbol '→', preceded by a marginal number and followed by a chapter number, shows the chapter to which the marginal number relates, e.g. '(5)→ch.34' means 'entry (5), which relates to ch.34'
- a letter with a strike through, immediately followed by another letter, shows that the first has been overwritten by the second, e.g. '~~d~~D' (Ws.$5a_4$ p.60).

Section 5. The worksheets

Worksheet for No.1 (verso)

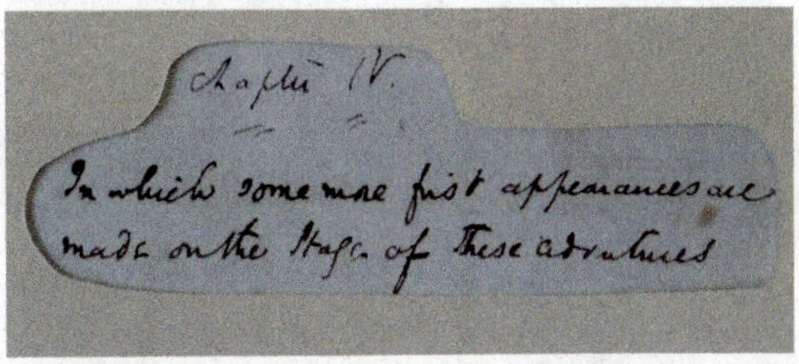
Chapter IV.
In which some more first appearances are
made on the Stage of these Adventures

Image No.2012FE1485 verso: Forster Collection, National Art Library, Victoria and Albert Museum (2015). © Victoria and Albert Museum, London.

Transcription of Ws.1 (verso)

Chapter IV. (22)

In which some more first appearances are (23)
made on the Stage of these Adventures

https://doi.org/10.11647/OBP.0092.07

Worksheet for No.1 (recto)

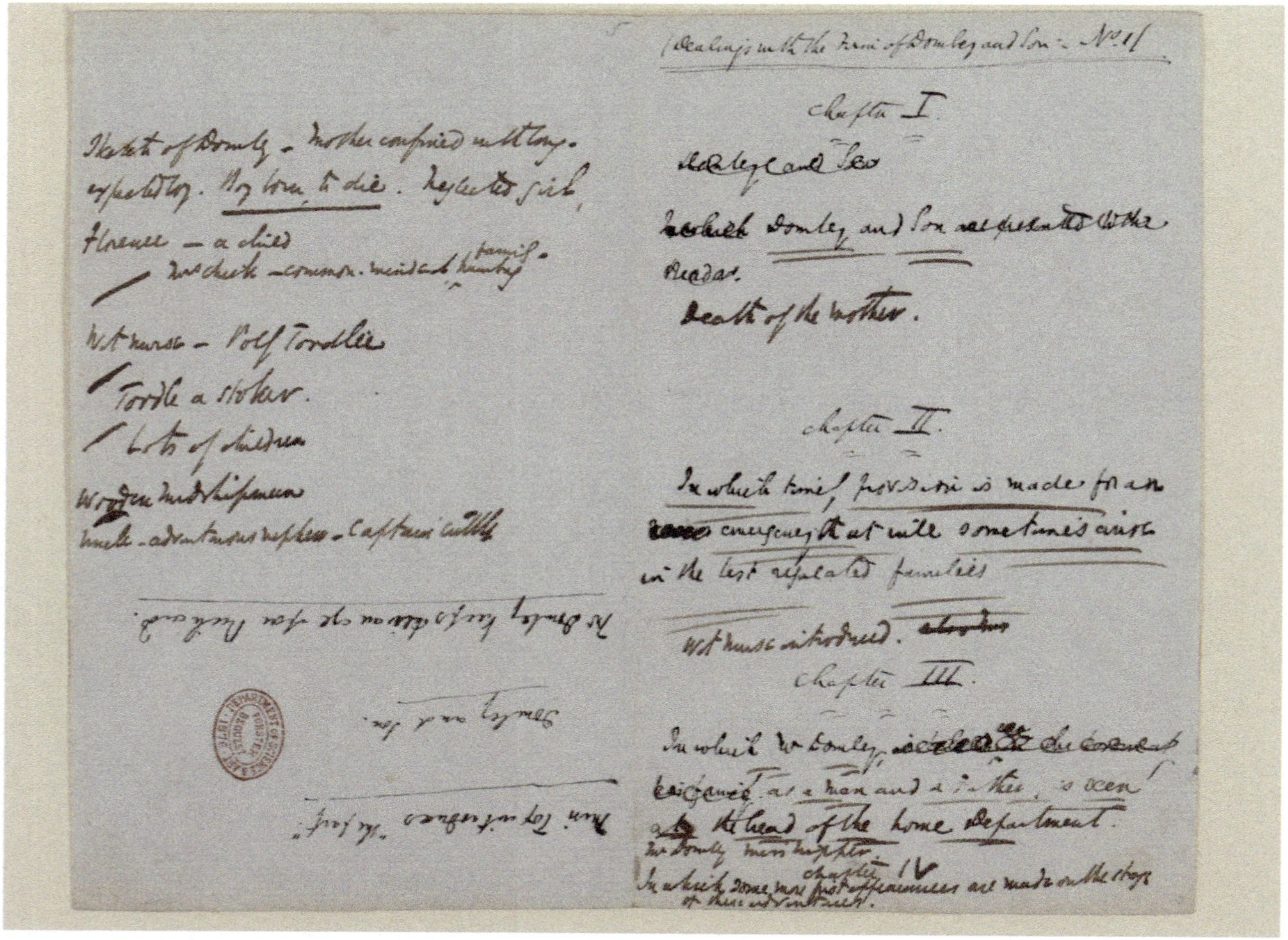

Image No.2012FE1485 recto: Forster Collection, National Art Library, Victoria and Albert Museum (2015). © Victoria and Albert Museum, London.

Transcription of Ws.1 (recto)

(1) Sketch of Dombey – mother confined with long - expected boy . Boy born, to die . Neglected girl ,

Florence – a child

(2) M[rs] Chick –common-mind and ^family - humbug

(3) Wet nurse – Polly Toodlie [sic]

(4) Toodle a stoker .

(5) Lots of children

(6) Wooden Midshipman

(7) Uncle - adventurous nephew - Captain Cuttle

(8) M[r] Dombey keeps ~~his~~ an eye upon Richards .

Dombey and Son.

Miss Tox introduces "the party".

(Dealings with the Firm of Dombey and Son – N[o]. I) (9)

Chapter I . (10)

~~Dombey and Son~~ (11)

~~In which~~ Dombey and Son ~~are presented to the Reader~~ .

Death of the mother . (12)

Chapter II . (13)

In which timely provision is made for a[n] (14) ~~Famil~~ emergency that will sometimes arise in the best regulated families

Wet nurse introduced . (15) ~~also Mis[s Tox]~~ (16)

Chapter III . (17)

In which M[r] Dombey, is ~~beheld~~[?] ^seen[?] in the bosom of his family . as a Man and a Father, is seen at the head of the home Department . (18)

M[r] Dombey Miss Nipper . (19)

Chapter IV (20)

In which some more first appearances are made on the stage of these adventures . (21)

Commentary and order of entry Ws.1 (recto and verso)

Dickens and family settle in Lausanne in June 1846. The day after the arrival of his box of writing materials on 27 June, he "BEGAN DOMBEY! I performed this feat yesterday—only wrote the first slip—but there it is, and it is a plunge straight over head and ears into the story" (*Life* 400[K:8159]). Just four weeks later, he sent the first four chapters to Forster, and with it a lengthy detailed summary of the novel's themes and structure, what he calls "the outline of my immediate intentions".[42] Nine weeks later, on 30 September, No.1 for October 1846 is published.

LH

Initial plan for the number: **(1) & (2)→ch.1; (3), (4) & (5)→ch.2**

These are identifiable by similarity of hand, ink and alignment. They are divided by idiosyncratic slashes, with one entry "Mrs Chick… humbug" (2) probably inserted soon after the others. The density and corrosion of entries is reasonably consistent in (1) and (2), though less so in (3)–(5). The corrosion of the two groupings is shown in two shades of brown. "Toodlie" is either an early version of Polly's surname or a temporary trial alternative; either way it is rejected, perhaps for its inappropriate associations. In the last three initial entries, where Dickens is assembling materials for ch.2, entries (3)–(5) slip to the right as his hand and arm move downward. The first entry of a number plan often has wider scope than later ones. After noting the opening situation and the characters involved, Dickens indicates the direction of the narrative by "Boy born to die". He frequently uses a single continuous underline to show that an entry looks forward beyond the number, in this instance to No.4, during which he initially plans to "kill Paul".

Additional number plan: **(6) & (7)→ch.4**

Dickens uses a slightly heavier hand—and/or a more laden quill—for the sign of the Midshipman. Consequently, the lettering of (6) has retained more of its blackness, whereas the lighter hand and/or the less laden quill used for (7) has begun corroding throughout. Both are distinct from (1)–(5) in alignment, hand and to a less extent size. The two groups are divided by a slash, perhaps to further emphasise the importance of the shop and its sign. The second group comprises the three characters in the order in which they appear in the text. Together they suggest that Dickens is imagining structure as well as content for ch.4.

MS and RH

Preliminary headings: **(9), (10), (13), (17) & verso (22)**[43]

In the worksheet, Dickens gives the part heading—the longer novel title with the part number—and the number headings for four chapters, three spread evenly down the page and the number heading for ch.4 (22) entered by turning the worksheet over and writing on the under (verso) side. (The facsimile and transcription of the number heading for ch.4 is shown in portrait mode, before the facsimile of No.1 (recto). For an explanation, see endnote 41).

Composition and titling of chs.1, 2, 3 & 4: **(11), (14) (18) & (23)**[44]

In ch.1, Dickens probably titles in both worksheet and manuscript, but revises in worksheet and copies the revision to manuscript. In ch.2 on the other hand, he begins by titling in worksheet (he makes a running correction there that is not in the manuscript). Similarly, in ch.3, he again revises in worksheet and transfers the final version to the manuscript. The title of ch.4 (23) is first entered, like its number heading, on the worksheet's verso side. For more on title revisions, see 'Appendix D'. He sent Forster three letters, the first when he had written ch.1, the second when "all was finished except for eight slips", i.e. chs.2 and 3 but not ch.4, and the third when he sent the manuscript of all four chapters (*Life* 472[K:9243]). The first three chapters take up thirty-two MS pages, and the initial final chapter adds another ten pages. So even allowing for irregularity of hand and spacing at the start of composition, he would know that, in his enjoyment of a "great plunge […] into the story", he had overwritten No.1 by many printed pages. After a two-year break, perhaps needing the reassurance of composition, he quite uncharacteristically paid little attention to his instalment boundary.

RH

Summary notes for chs.1–3: **(12), (15), (16) & (19)**

For chs.1 and 2, partly because the titles are teasingly uninformative, Dickens gives their subject. For ch.3, he juxtaposes Dombey and Susan, whom he intends to be "a strong character […] throughout the book" (see the final paragraph of endnote 42). All four notes are corroded, some more than others. Entry 16 "~~also Mis~~(s Tox)" is a separate entry, using a non-corroding ink like that of (8), (14) and (18) but made with a thicker nib or heavier hand. He is perhaps considering how to put right the omission of Miss Tox in the chapter record of ch.2 (and in the number plan). The entry of her name here, and its deletion, is another sign of uncertainty, in this instance over the scope of the worksheet record. At this early stage, Dickens consistently treats the left-hand as a number plan and the right-hand half as a chapter record, apparently entering the few summary chapter notes altogether, after completing the first three chapters.

LH

Further number plan: **(8)**

These three items, perhaps initially intended as trial chapter titles, could just as well be the letterings to accompany illustrations. The first referring to ch.2 becomes the lettering for the first plate; the second becomes the title of ch.1. Dickens composes the third after finishing ch.3, but before he proposes to Forster the more ironic lettering for the second plate on 7 August "'Mr Dombey and family' meaning Polly Toodle, the baby, Mr. Dombey, and little Florence" (*Life* 473[K:9283]). Dickens, viewing both illustrations as a number requirement always places their lettering on the left-hand side. But because lettering usually arises from a particular text, it is often delayed until the relevant chapter has been written. Entry (8) is the only group made by reversing the page. Finding reversal inconvenient, he avoids repeating the practice. Thinking of how he might use the worksheets, he decides to avoid reversals and keep entries easy to scan and read at a glance.

MS

Composition of an alternative ch.4 (later ch.7)

To reduce the "over-matter" which the added ch.4 creates, Dickens writes a shorter alternative chapter on Miss Tox and the Major to take the place of the one on "Wally & Co".[45] Forster objects to the change that it "might damage his interest at starting". Dickens agrees "Strength is everything" (*Life* 474[K:9297]), implying that he felt it especially important, early on, to capture the reader's interest in both the main storylines. Balancing the longer ch.4 (and the prospect of more deletions) against the alternative, Dickens prioritises what is more important for the novel as a whole. He also begins to use a smaller hand for the manuscript, with less space between words and between lines. The reductions, applied consistently from No.4 on, make it easier for him to estimate pages of manuscript as pages of print, and thus to calculate how many pages of print remain as he composes.[46]

RH

Broken underlining of titles of chs.1–3

They are probably made altogether, perhaps in a rush. Swiftly made black lines such as these usually corrode.

Chapter number heading and title for ch.4: **(20) & (<u>21</u>)**

Once the decision is made to retain the initial ch.4, its headings—already entered on the back, carefully laid out and capitalised—are squeezed onto the front, without capitals or underlines, a hurried final entry for the sake of the record. Transferring the title to the front is another practical decision that shows Dickens is thinking of how he might use the worksheet later (cf. the comment on reversal in the column opposite).

Proofs

The decision to retain the longer fourth chapter gives Dickens "great pangs" (*Life* 474[K:9286]). About thirty deletions have to be made, all to chs.1–3, but none to ch.4, which was probably at the printers.[47]

[Editor's note: references above to Forster *Life* are (1) to Ley's edition and (2) to ebook 25851 in Project Gutenberg downloaded to Kindle (see p.7)].

Worksheet for No.2

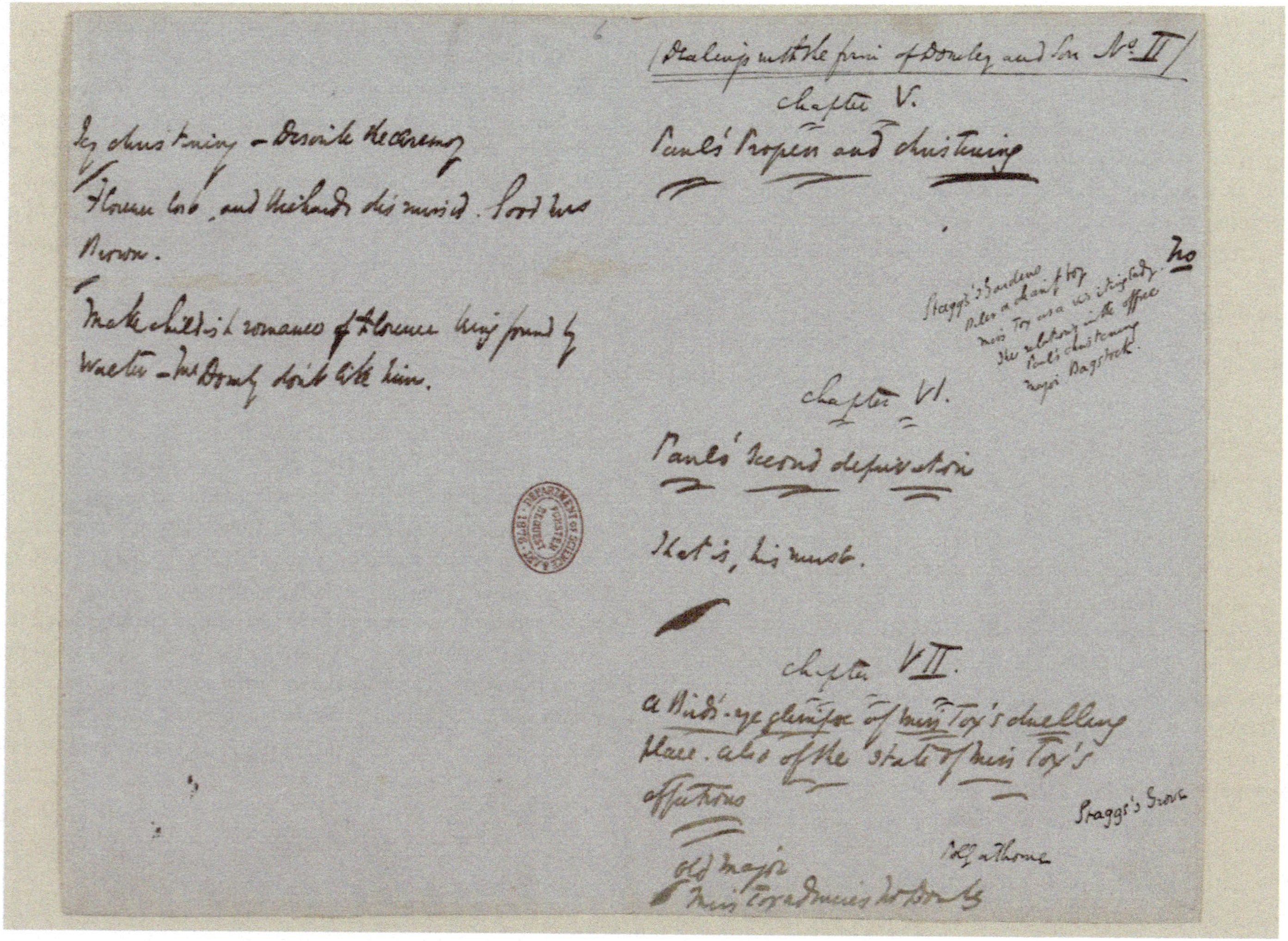

Image No.2012FE1506 (reduced): Forster Collection, National Art Library, Victoria and Albert Museum (2015). © Victoria and Albert Museum, London.

Transcription of Ws.2

(1) Icy christening – Describe the ceremony

(2) Florence lost, and Richards dismissed. Good Mrs Brown.

(3) Make childish romance of Florence being found by Walter – Mr Dombey don't like him.

(Dealings with the firm of Dombey and Son N°. II) (4)

Chapter V. (5)

Paul's Progress and christening (6)

No. (7)

Staggs's Gardens
Biler a charity boy
Miss Tox as a visiting lady.
The relations in the office
Paul's christening
Major Bagstock. (8)

Chapter VI. (9)

Paul's Second deprivation (10)

That is, his nurse. (11)

Chapter VII. (12)

A Bird's-eye glimpse of Miss Tox's dwelling place. Also of the state of Miss Tox's affections (13)

Staggs's Grove (14)

Polly at home (15)

Old Major (16)

Miss Tox admires Mr Dombey (17)

Commentary and order of entry (Ws.2)

Dickens begins No.2 on 8 August, writing with "infinite pains", and finishing in the first week of September. The rest of September and early October are given over to his Christmas book for 1846, *The Battle of Life*. "You can hardly imagine," he writes on 30 August "what infinite pains I take, or what extraordinary difficulty I find in getting on FAST. Invention, thank God, seems the easiest thing in the world; and I seem to have such a preposterous sense of the ridiculous [...] as to be constantly requiring to restrain myself from launching into extravagances in the height of my enjoyment" (*Life* 423[K:8591]). The "pains" arise, he supposes, from the long gap between *Dombey* and his previous novel, and from writing for the first time while living abroad without access to the stimulus of London.[48] Nevertheless, he is drawn into the wealthy English speaking community in Lausanne that forms "an agreeable little circle" to whom he reads the first number on ?19 September and the second on 10 October to the "most prodigious and uproariness delight of the circle" (*Life* 477[K:9366]). On 31 October, No.2 for November 1846 is published.

RH

Discarded entries (probably pre-format plans): **(7), (8), (14) & (15)**

Six items (8) on a slant, near the right-hand edge, and two others (14) and (15), directly below towards the bottom of the page, are all written in "smallhand". Most of list (8) are ideas for this number, though one is for No.4; the two misplaced below (14) and (15) are for a narrative on the Toodles' home and family. The six entries in (8) cover material that will be considerably reordered: the christening and the charitable gesture that separates Rob from his family to ch.5; "Staggs's Grove" (perhaps its earlier title) and "Polly at home" to ch.6; the "old Major" to ch.7; and the first extended account of the office to ch.13. The entry "Miss Tox as a visiting lady" may refer her as a visitor to the Dombey house (ch.1), or to her calling on Queen Charlotte's (as reported in ch.2) or more probably to the development of her visit to the Toodles (reported in ch.2 but not dramatized until much later in ch.38). These entries appear to be 'pre-format' notes, i.e. among the very first notes on the early numbers that Dickens jotted down before he had devised the worksheet format. Setting them aside is a result of two key decisions that accompany the division of the worksheet into two halves. Firstly, to always position ideas for the number as a whole on the left-hand side, and secondly to limit all entries on the right-hand side to part heading and chapter number, title and description. If the above are pre-format entries, as seems likely, the "No" of (7) applies to all eight.

RH

Preliminary headings: **(4), (5), (9) & (12)**

Reverting to the opening procedure of Ws.1, Dickens now enters the longer title with the number of the part issue, followed by three chapter number headings spread evenly down the page.

LH

Plan for the number: **1→ch.5; 2 & 3→ch.6**

These notes, written fluently on the same occasion, move smoothly though aspects of the opening and middle chapters. Each entry is twofold giving the subject and some development of it. Dickens already has their shape in mind, though not their detailed structure. In (3) he is imagining Florence speaking, rather than Walter. Compare Walter's speech to Cuttle that Dombey "does not like me" (209[223]) with Florence's cry at the prospect of saying goodnight to her father "Oh no no! He don't want me" (35[35]), where the repetitive "no no" and "don't" is used to typify the speech of a young child. Many contemporary aspiring middle class would expect Dombey, as the head of a respectable and wealthy family, to disapprove of her association with a junior clerk; Dickens deflects their disapproval somewhat by always avoiding nonstandard language when Walter speaks.

MS and RH: (6)

Composition and titling of ch.5

Dickens revises the title as he writes the chapter, and transfers the final version to the worksheet.

MS

Composition and titling of ch.6

Dickens, happy in his choice of a title that looks back to Paul's first loss in ch.1, enters it at start of composition.

RH

Titles and descriptions of chs.6 and 7: **(10), (11), (13), (16) & (17)**

Similarity of hand and progressive corrosion confirms that titles and descriptions are entered at the same time.

For the history of the revision in the manuscript of the title of ch.4 (later ch.7), see 'Appendix D', ch.7 p.182. When Dickens transfers the revised title of ch.4 to ch.7 in Ws.2, he revises it a second time. Adapting the proofs of the initial ch.4 for ch.7, he appears to copy in the title from the worksheet and, as he does so, to tighten its sentence structure. (Alternatively and perhaps less likely, he may enter the title in the worksheet from his memory of the corrected proofs of ch.4, and misremember its punctuation, in which case the second revision of the title is first made in the proofs).

Progressive corrosion begins with the title of ch.6 and continues to the end, confirming that Dickens makes these entries at the same time.

The two summary entries for ch.7 are separated by a slash (used on the right-hand side for the first time). They correspond to the two contrasting concerns of the chapter the Major's disbelief at being passed over, and Miss Tox's romantic feelings for Mr. Dombey.

Proofs

Forster corrects the proofs with Dickens's consent. He had already "put the drag on" in ch.5 so as not to offend Christian sects. He now adds a conciliatory stuffy paragraph on the sacrament of baptism; the paragraph begins "It might have been well" (60^{62}). Just before that addition, he cuts a comparison of the font to a child's toy.[49] He also deletes the two closing sentences of ch.7 that prepares for the next number to open with Paul's schooling.[50] The deletion of this plant for the opening of No.3 reflects the outcome of a choice under consideration at the time, to postpone schooling to No.4 and "kill" Paul in No.5, and "make number three a kind of halfway house between infancy and Paul being eight or nine", in contrast to the first paragraph of the outline to Forster "When the boy is about ten years old (in the fourth number), he will be taken ill, and will die" (see endnote 42). Dickens raises the possibility with Forster at the beginning of October, after writing No.2 but before starting No.3 (*Life* 477[K:9358]).

The decision to postpone opens the way for an extended portrait of Mrs Pipchin's "establishment", the first of Dickens's explorations in fiction of painful childhood memories. He writes to Forster on 4 November "I hope you will like Mrs. Pipchin's establishment. It is from the life, and I was there—I don't suppose I was eight years old; but I remember it all as well, and certainly understood it as well, as I do now. We should be devilish sharp in what we do to children" (*Life* 479[K:9396]).

Worksheet for No.3

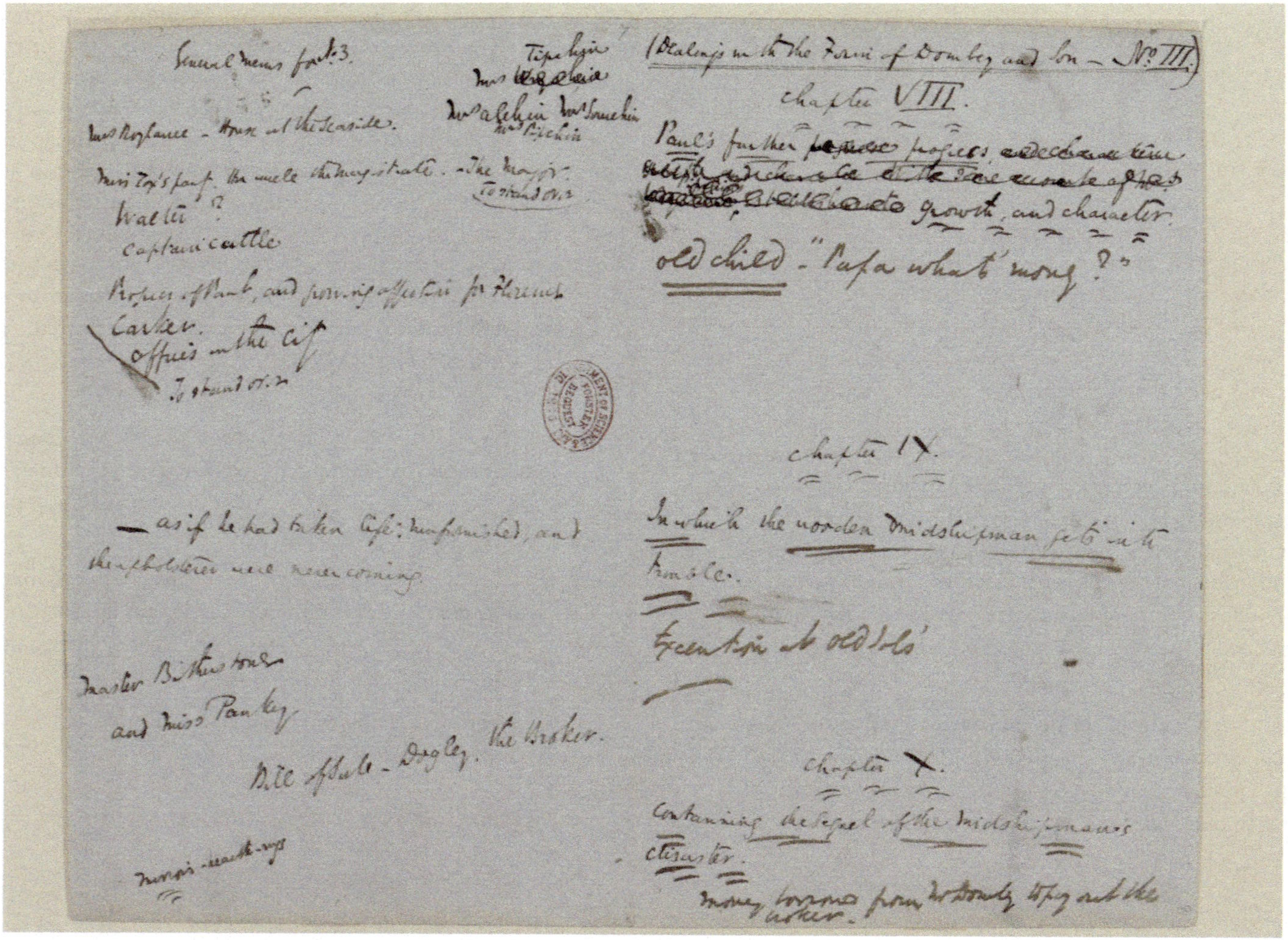

Image No.2012FE1486 (reduced): Forster Collection, National Art Library, Victoria and Albert Museum (2015). © Victoria and Albert Museum, London.

Transcription of Ws.3

(1) General Mems for N°.3.

(2) .. .. ..

(3) Mrs Roylance – House at the Seaside.

Tipchin
Mrs ~~Wrychin~~
Mrs Alchin Mrs Somechin
Mrs Pipchin

(4) Miss Tox's party, the uncle the magistrate . -The Major .
To stand over

(5) Walter ?
Captain Cuttle

(6) Progress of Paul , and growing affection for Florence

(7) Carker.
offices in the City
To stand over

(8) — as if he had taken life : unfurnished , and the upholsterers were never coming.

(9) Master Bitherstone
and Miss Pankey

(10) Bill of Sale – Dogley,[sic] the Broker.

(11) Mirrors - hearth-rugs

(Dealings with the Firm of Dombey and Son – N°:III.) (12)

Chapter VIII . (13)

Paul's further ~~progress~~ progress, <and character> growth and character . With some account of Mrs ~~Wrychin's~~ ^ Pipchin's establishment growth, and character. (14)

old child – "Papa what's money?" (15)

Chapter IX. (16)

In which the wooden Midshipman gets into trouble. (17)

Execution at old Sol's (18)

Chapter X. (19)

Containing the sequel of the Midshipman's disaster . (20)

Money borrowed from Mr Dombey to pay out the broker . (21)

Commentary and order of entry (Ws.3)

Immensely relieved by the "BRILLIANT!" sale of No.1, Dickens is anxious to sustain its success (*Life* 477[K:9363]). He writes to Forster that "A week of perfect idleness [...] has brought me round [...] I am quite glad to write the heading of the first chapter of number three to-day [26 October]. I shall be slow at first, I fear, in consequence of that change of plan [see 'Proofs' in Ws.2 p.45]. But I allow myself nearly three weeks for the number" (*Life* 478[K:9369]). On 4 November, he is half through it, on 7 November he is in the "agonies" of its last chapter, and on 9 November, as Forster says 'all was done...marvellously rapid work' (*Life* 441[K:8977]). Dickens hurries to complete the instalment early, in order to prepare for the family's move to Paris the following week. He composes fluently, inspired by the memories of childhood that were beginning to preoccupy him. The gap between completing the number and his deadline for delivering copy to the compositors (at least five days prior to issue) is narrowing. On 30 November, No.3 for December 1846 is published.

LH

Plan for the number (including some pre-format plans, cf. Ws.2):

(1); (3)→ch.8; (4); (5)→chs.9 & 10; (6)→ch.8; (7)→ch.13

Dickens's choice of word in (4) repeats the lettering for the first plate of No.1, where Miss Tox's "party" is the Toodles family, and repeats the "magistrate" detail of ch.5 (52^{54}).[51] These untypical repetitions suggest that he may have been making notes here for the opening numbers before he began work on No.1. The sheet, consisting of entries (1)–(7) excluding (2), may have begun as some "General Mems" for the first few numbers, Dickens's earliest notes (with $Ws.2_{8,\ 14\ \&\ 15}$) jotted down before he devised the worksheet format (hence the addition later "for No.3", see below).

Outcomes: **(1), (4) & (7)**

Dickens retains the heading "General Mems" because, in comparison with Ws.1 and 2, its left-hand entries go beyond the current number. The heading is not used again until Ws.19&20, when he is once again considering the story as a whole.

He inserts "for No.3" after the heading (2), adds the two "To stand over" entries, jettisons a party at Miss Tox's—perhaps attended by her uncle and part of a more extended satire of Miss Tox, apparently abandoned—and postpones both the Major (4) and James Carker in the city offices (7). He is left with early memories of Mrs Roylance (3), Walter Cuttle (5), and the development of Paul (6), particularly the boy's growing attachment to Florence.[52] The concentration on Paul, as he begins Ws.3, flows from the decision made between Nos.2 and 3, to lengthen Paul's story to five numbers (see above "that change of plan"; also the final comment in 'Proofs' in Ws.2 p.45).

RH

Preliminary headings: **(12), (13), (16) & (19)**

LH and RH

Additional number plan: **(2)**

Titling ch.8: **(<u>14</u>)**

Dickens begins by devising names for Mrs Roylance as part of the number plan, first "Alchin", then "Somechin". When he tries out the next name "Wrychin" (2), he incorporates the name into his third attempt at a chapter title in (14). Still not satisfied, he tries out "Tipchin" and then "Pipchin" in (2), which he inserts into the revised title in (14)—again moving between the left and right-hand half. This version is then copied to MS, where the revision process continues during composition ('Appendix D', ch.8 p.183).

Caught up in the memory of Mrs Roylance, Dickens feels compelled to find a name that rings true for a character "from the life". It is his detailed memory of Mrs Roylance that sways his judgment of the second illustration of Paul and Pipchin at the fireside "It is so frightfully and wildly wide of the mark" (*Life* 478[K:9383]). Despite his outrage, he is becoming aware of the difficulty that his retentive memory for visual detail posed for his illustrators.[53]

MS

Composition and titling of ch.8

When Dickens transfers the title from the worksheet, he adds what is probably an ironic reference to Mrs Pipchin's "Establishment". During the writing of the chapter, he reconsiders the emphasis, deletes the phrase, and limits the title to Paul (see reference above).

LH

Further number plan: **(8)→ch.11; (9)→ch.8; (10) & (11)→ch.9**

Dickens begins to use the lower part of the left-hand side. He notes ideas for individual chapters, here an evocative comparison (8), children's names (9), a plot detail (10), and a startlingly random but significant juxtaposition of objects (11). These are all written with a similar hand—and with (9) and (10) written on a slant—suggesting that, although his general practice is to work closely on each chapter in turn, he is at the same time imagining characters, places and other details that will find a place somewhere in later chapters.

He holds back the striking entry (8) for the end of the opening chapter of the next number (with amendments to its punctuation) in line with his decision to extend Paul's story. The entries as a whole signal an important change in the use of the worksheet. He adapts its format to include prospective details for individual chapters before they are written, in this instance using the lower left-hand.

MS

Composition and titling of chs.9 and 10

The long ch.8 has already taken up fifteen MS pages. Ch.9 fills a further ten. Consequently, ch.10 begins on MS p.26. Dickens is probably by now working to a notional 27 or 28 MS pages to thirty-two pages of print, in which case he knows, even as he writes, that cuts will be needed. The number of pages taken up by each chapter as published in each instalment is given in 'Appendix A' (see the 'Key', p.167, for how chapter length is calculated there).

RH

Titles of chs.9, 10: **(<u>17</u>) & (<u>20</u>)**

Similarity of hand suggests that Dickens transfers both titles to the worksheet at the same time.

Description of chs.8, 9 & 10: **(15), (18) & (21)**

Dickens emphasises a common theme, perhaps entering the descriptions of (21), (15) and (18) in that order (see their progressive loss of density and increasing corrosion). After adding, for some reason an extra double underline to (17)—haste rather than a blotting error—he finishes ch.9's description and the worksheet, with a flourish.

Proofs

As expected, the proofs overrun by four pages. Dickens takes out about two and a half pages, leaving the rest to Forster (*Life* 479[K:9400]). The longest of the cuts in ch.10 concerning Miss Tox's attachment to Dombey—and many early ones in ch.8 that are not so long—are restored in Project Gutenberg's edition ebook 821, chs.8 and 10).

More cuts are avoided by reducing gaps between chapters and adding a line to each printed page—both devices of last resort that were available but not invoked for No.1, perhaps because they might not be sufficient to accommodate the scale of the cuts required.

Worksheet for No.4

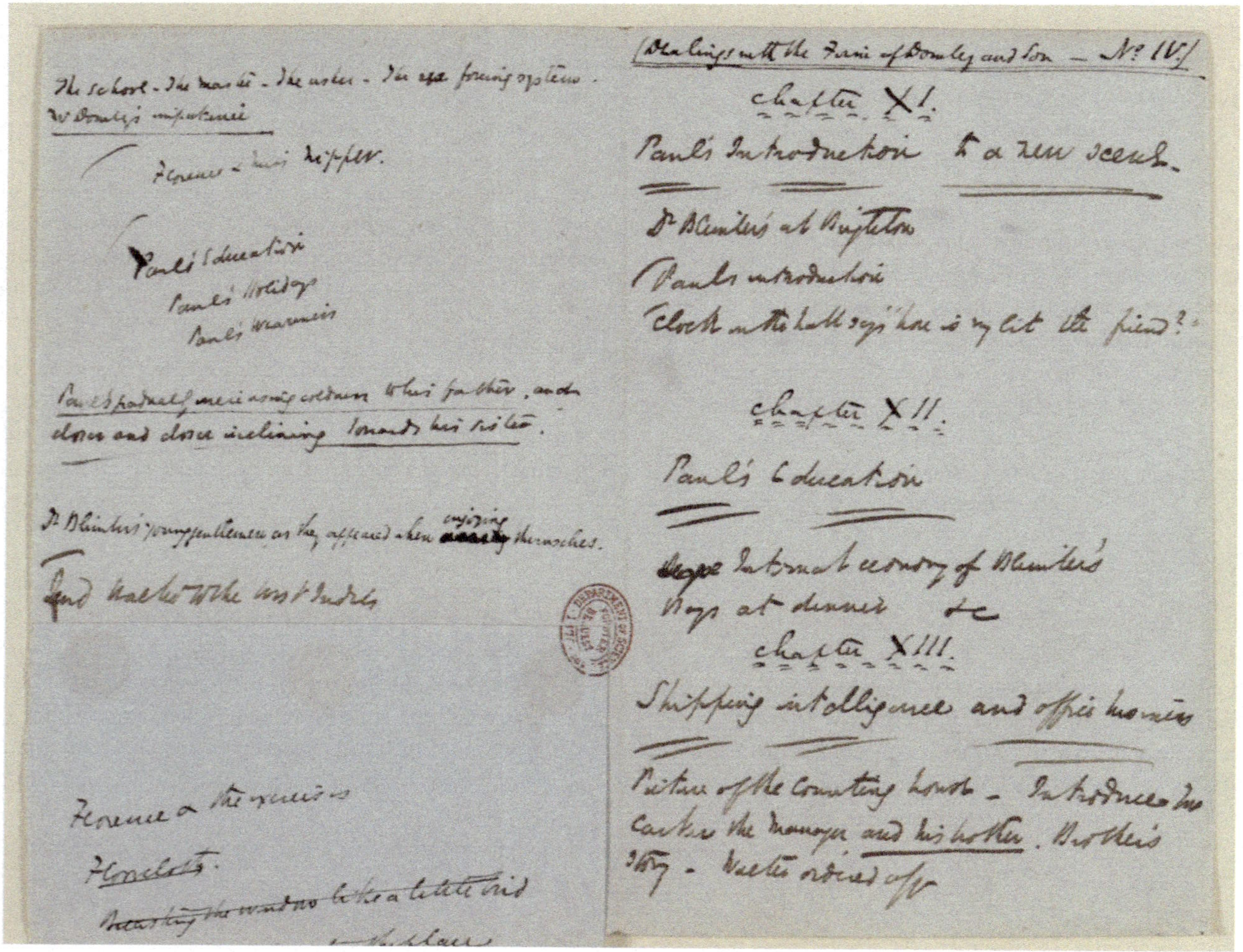
Dealings with the Firm of Dombey and Son — No. IV.

chapter XI.

Paul's Introduction to a new scene.

Dr Blimber's at Brighton

Paul's introduction

Clock in the hall says "how is my lit tle friend?"

chapter XII.

Paul's Education

Internal economy of Blimber's

Boys at dinner &c

chapter XIII.

Shipping intelligence and office business

Picture of the Counting house – Introduce Mr Carker the Manager and his brother. Brother's story – Walter ordered off

Florence – Miss Nipper.

Paul's gradually more and more weaned from his father, and closer and closer inclining towards his sister.

Dr Blimber's young gentlemen as they appeared when enjoying themselves.

Image No.2012FE1488 (reduced): Forster Collection, National Art Library, Victoria and Albert Museum (2015). © Victoria and Albert Museum, London.

Transcription of Ws.4

(1) The school - The Master - The usher - The ~~sys~~ forcing system . Mr Dombey's impatience

(2) Florence & Miss Nipper.

(3) Paul's Education
Paul's Holidays
Paul's Weariness

(4) Paul's gradually increasing coldness to his father , and closer and closer inclining towards his sister .

(5) D[r] Blimber's young gentlemen as they appeared when ~~amusing~~ enjoying themselves.

(6) Send Walter to the West Indies

[Introduction to Ws.4a
In Ws.3, Dickens used the lower left-hand side for potential chapter material. Working on No.4, he tears an additional worksheet leaf in half, to provide more space for a similar purpose. He uses it to help him compose the second half ch.12, probably as a separate sheet, before he attaches it to Ws.4. The ink smudge (not transcribed, but see facsimile) below the capital "S" of "Send" appears to be partially covered by the top edge of Ws.4a, which suggests that it is wafered into position after entry (6) and during or after his preparation for ch.13. Once used and wafered on to Ws.4, it is folded up onto itself and the worksheet.]

(Dealings with the Firm of Dombey and Son – N[o.] IV.) (7)

Chapter XI . (8)

Paul's Introduction to a new scene . (9)

D[r] Blimbers' at Brighton (10)

Pauls introduction (11)

Clock in the hall says "how is my lit tle friend ? " (12)

Chapter XII . (13)

Paul's Education (14)

~~Boys~~ Internal economy of Blimber's (15)

Boys at dinner &c (16)

Chapter XIII . (17)

Shipping intelligence and office business (18)

Picture of the Counting house – Introduce M[r] Carker the Manager and his brother . Brother's story - Walter ordered off (19)

Commentary and order of entry (Ws.4)

The Dickens entourage—himself, wife, children, servants and luggage, in two carriages and a wagon—leaves Lausanne on 16 November, arriving in Paris on the 20th. For days, he searches for a house to rent, organises the household and explores the city. "I tried to settle to my desk, and went about and about it, and dodged at it, like a bird at a lump of sugar." By 6 December, he has "written five printed pages" (*Life* 447[K:9094]). In another nine days, he completes the number, some ten days before his deadline. On the 15th he goes to London, bringing the finished manuscript with him. He stays until the 23rd, partly to read the proofs and partly to settle details of the publication of the Cheap edition, his first collected works (see *Life* 448[K:9107]). The "new preface" he had just written for *Pickwick Papers* reveals some of his artistic ambitions for *Dombey and Son*.[54] On 31 December, No.4 for January 1847 is published.

RH

Preliminary headings: **(7), (8), (13) & (17)**

Dickens returns to the procedure of Ws.1, making these entries first (cf. Ws.1–3).

LH

Initial number plan: **(1)→ch.11; (2) & (3)→ch.12 ; (4)→chs.11 & 12**

Four groups in the same hand are separated by slashes and positioning. In entry (1) Dickens notes the organisation of the school and its methods that are well matched to Dombey's ambitions for Paul. In (2), Susan now a "Miss Nipper" is a companion—and foil—to Florence. In (3) he proposes three stages to Paul's progress; the first becomes a title for ch.11 (later transferred to ch.12); the other two will be held over for No.5.

Paul's turning to Florence and away from his father (4) is underlined, like Dombey's impatience, as an ongoing and, in Paul's case, a growing feeling (cf. Ws.3_6 p.47).

MS

Composition and titling of ch.11

Dickens writes a long recapitulation, adding to the portrayal of Pipchin by her meeting with Dombey, now impatient to push ahead with Paul's formal education. He initially titles ch.11 "Paul's education" perhaps expecting to write further into the Blimber material. Then he limits the remaining pages to "introducing a new scene", arresting the action at the moment of Paul's abandonment. He can now use Ws.3_8—the image of the child sitting alone in a desolate and empty newly rented house, so expressive of loss—as a curtain to the chapter. Number openings, usually with strong links with the previous number, are often, as here, expansive and improvisatory.[55]

LH

Additional number plan: **(5)→ch.12; (6)→ch.13**

Dickens uses his smallest hand in (5) to get the lettering for the first illustration on one line, probably as he is writing ch.11. The lettering is sent to Browne (?6 Dec 1846, L.4:677) with a lengthy account of the general context (from the completed ch.11) and a brief description of the subject in ch.12 (yet to be written).

Despite the letter, Browne adds to the number of pupils (Dickens writes there are ten). He also supplies a well-developed visual contrast of his own between the formally clothed pupils and the other boys who are free to enjoy the pleasures of the seaside (cf. his final image of a young

Florence, with Paul on the seashore in his frontispiece for the finished novel p.163). Although Browne's subject of both plates for No.4 comes from the same chapter (ch.12), he maintains a strong contrast between them, by inventing the setting for his second illustration, an indoor scene at night (see "Paul's exercises").

For all other numbers, Browne finds (or is given) subjects from different chapters, presumably to heighten visually the contrast between storylines. Like other second illustrations, this one requires less detail than the first making it easier for Browne and his engravers prepare it in time.

Chapter plan: **Ws.4a→ch.12**

Ws.4a is a plan for the second half of ch.12 probably not attached to Ws.4 until entry (6) is made (see above 'Introduction to Ws.4a' p.51).

MS

Composition and titling of ch.12

Dickens uses the initial but discarded title of ch.11 for ch.12. He probably has Ws.4a alongside him to help him order the later parts of the chapter, including its ending (see below Ws.4a p.54).

RH

Titles and summaries for chs.11 & 12: **(9), (10), (11) & (12); (14), (15) & (16)**

Throughout the right-hand side, hand, quill and ink are similar. The hand is rapid, especially in the descriptions, with a great deal of elision of letterform. Both titles are similar in their generous layout, slant and hand. The descriptions of chs.11 and 12 are basic summaries, giving a setting in (10) and (15) and the central episode in (11) and (16). Among Paul's reactions in ch.11, Dickens picks out a particularly significant moment—his sensation of the great clock's machinery that begins and ends his first experience of Blimber's (12). The description of ch.12 is briefer and even hastier, the letters losing definition and increasing in their slant.

The "etc" probably refers to the rest of the repetitive daily tasks and routines, rather than the materials touched on in Ws.4a, though these also act as a record of the chapter, as well as an aid to its composition.

LH

Further number plan: **(6)→ch.13**

Dickens decides to remove Walter from the narrative until Florence is old enough for the romance plot to be resumed. After this entry, he wafers Ws.4a to the bottom of the left-hand half, overlaying the smudge in (6) (see below, top left of facsimile Ws.4a p.54).

RH

Plan for ch.13: **(19)**

Dickens allocates a generous space for the chapter title as in chs.11 and 12, but this time leaving a gap for the title to be inserted later. The description is the first plan for a whole chapter. The directive "Introduce" is a decisive indication of planning. In composition, he reworks the plan, contriving to give Dombey a prominent part in the picture of the office, in the drama that follows and in the dispatch of Walter—all understandable additions and departures when reworking a plan, but unlikely omissions in a summary.[56] Throughout the plan, he uses the same sprawling hand as before. Writing in haste, he avoids re-dipping by reducing pressure on the quill, which thins the density of the ink (see the progressive loss of density in (12) and (19)).

MS and RH: (18)

Composition and titling of ch.13

During composition, once he is satisfied with the title after much revision, Dickens transfers the final version into the gap left for it in the worksheet (see 'Appendix D', ch.13, p.183).

Facsimile of Ws.4a

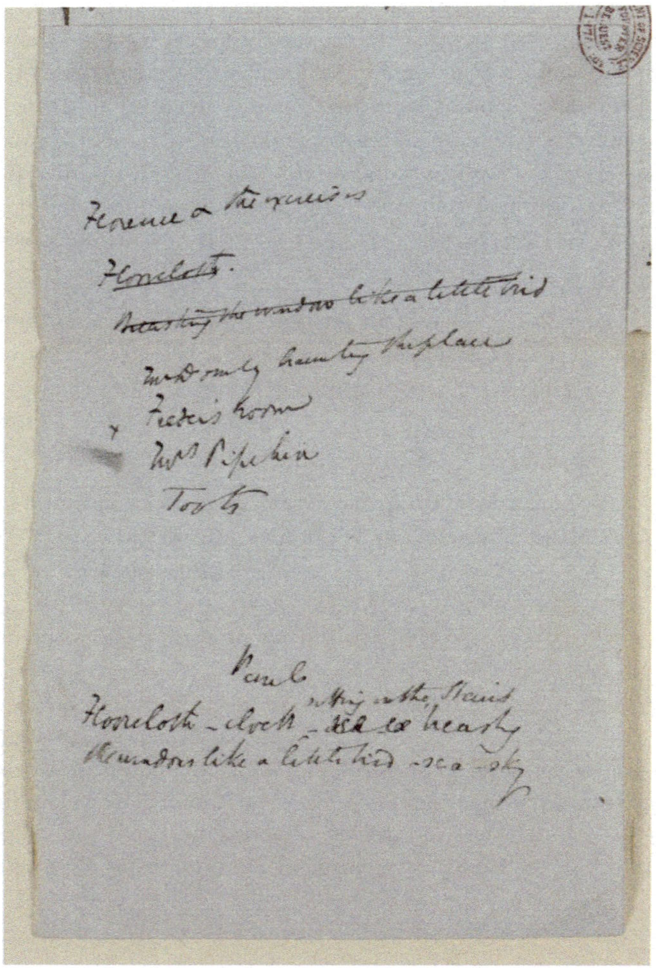

Image No.2012FE1488 (reduced): Forster Collection, National Art Library, Victoria and Albert Museum (2015).

Transcription of Ws.4a

(1) Florence & the exercises

(2) ~~Floorcloth~~ .

(3) ~~Breasting the window like a little bird~~

---

(4) M[r] Dombey haunting the place

(5) x Feeder's room

(6) M[rs] Pipchin

(7) Toots

Paul

(8) Floorcloth – clock ^[sitting on the Stairs] – <sea – s[?]> breasting the window like a little bird – sea – sky

Commentary on Ws.4a

This is the first of the four leaves that Dickens attaches to a worksheet. He wafers the leaf to the bottom left-hand of Ws.4, probably after making entry $Ws.4_6$ (see the tail end of the "S" of "Send" that is covered by Ws.4a, shown top left in the facsimile above). He spreads a list of entries down and across the page, writing in a fast hand, as though hurrying to keep abreast of thought. All are linked to ch.12, beginning "Oh Saturdays!" (162–70[177–81]).

The resonance that each entry has for him can be sensed from what it becomes in the manuscript, for example:

(1) Florence's scheme to help Paul, in which love transforms learning.

(2) Paul's withdrawal into the inner life of his imagination, seeing patterns in the floor covering.

(3) His helplessness and longing to escape is imaged as an imprisoned bird (cf. 170[181]).

(4) Dombey isolated and preoccupied is cut off by his ambition for Paul.

(5) The compensations of his own room for Feeder "the organ grinder" are prepared for in passing (159[169]), with a tiny 'x' to the left of the name, perhaps to indicate postponement—a reminder to describe the room later (see ch.14, 187[198–99]).

(6) Pipchin, still very much present in Dickens's imagination—note the slight increase in size of the name—is in charge of Florence and so occasionally at Blimber's; she interrupts Toots' conversation with Paul.

(7) Slowly, each appearance of Toots deepens Dickens's conception of him; he uses him here to draw out the portrayal of Paul (cf. 152–53[162–64], 159[169]).

(8) He creates a second list by moving (2) and (3) into a separate list of those entries that concern Paul alone. The order of the items in (8)—like those in Ws.5a—has both an emotional and a narrative logic (168–70[179–81]).

The act of making a second list gives a glimpse into Dickens's inventive intelligence. He reworks heightened moments in his imagination of the child's inner life until they join and take on a narrative order, which is then incorporated into the longer text that he has perhaps already imagined. Laying out on the page the sequence of ideas in preparation for a passage of narrative is a significant development in his use of the worksheet. In this respect, Ws.4a—laid out as narrative focalised on the ailing Paul—prepares for the notation of Ws.5a.

Worksheet for No.5

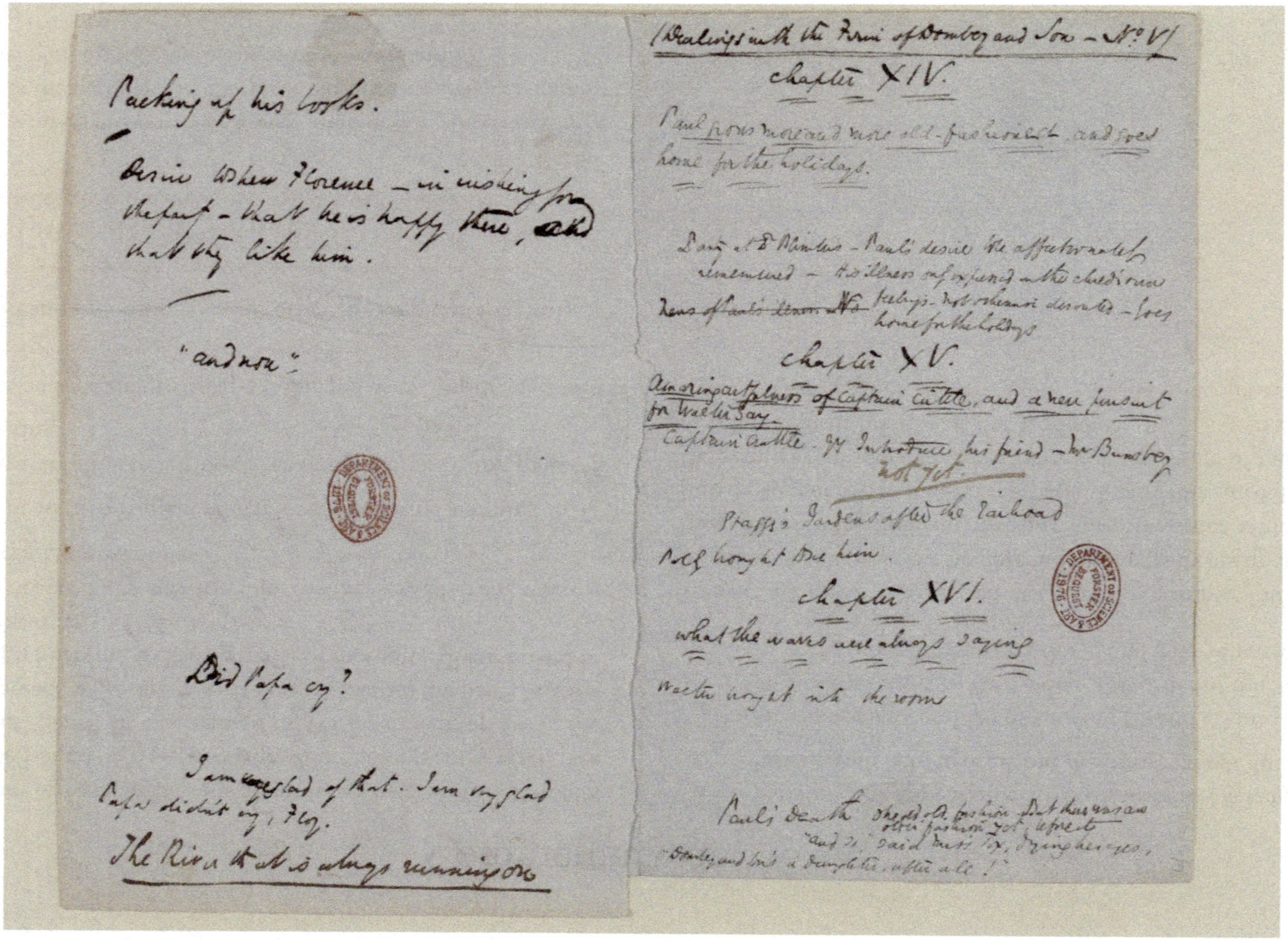
Packing up his books.

"and now"

Did Papa cry?

The River that is always running on

(Dealings with the Firm of Dombey and Son – No. V)

chapter XIV.

Paul grows more and more old-fashioned, and goes home for the holidays.

chapter XV.

chapter XVI.

What the waves were always saying

Paul's death

Image No.2012FE1496 (reduced): Forster Collection, National Art Library, Victoria and Albert Museum (2015). © Victoria and Albert Museum, London.

Transcription of Ws.5

[Introduction to Ws.5a

This rectangle represents an additional leaf, described here and later transcribed with commentary (see Ws.5a).

Pursuing the innovation of fictional method in presenting the sick child noted in Ws.54, Dickens takes special care over the next stage of his plans concerning Paul. Taking a half foolscap sheet from his supply of the better quality paper (normally reserved for the manuscript of the novel), he prepares to cover the left-hand of Ws.5 by tearing the sheet in half.

We can only conjecture as to his reasons for not using the blank left-hand page of Ws.5, but it seems he feels the occasion demands some special provision. He may be planning to have the leaf alongside him as he composes the chapter. The substance and structure of Ws.5a suggest that it was designed to help him thread the sick child's experience into the narrative of ch.14, in much the same way that he had used Ws.4a for the second half of ch.12.

A detail in the positioning of Ws.5a confirms that Dickens wafered the leaf to the left-hand of Ws.5 after using the sheet to write ch.14. The edge of Dickens's half sheet of MS is rather uneven. Its torn edge fractionally overlays the "A" of "Amazing", suggesting that he attached the leaf *after* working on ch.15. At some point, the same torn right-hand edge of Ws.5a appears to have been carefully folded under itself, to avoid obscuring the "A", and then later unfolded (a sequence of events that cannot be shown in transcription but is evident from the marks on the original). Perhaps Dickens is responsible for the folding under, then at the first mounting of the leaves, or later, it became unfolded, as it is now.]

(Dealings with the Firm of Dombey and Son – N°: V) (1)

Chapter XIV. (2)

Paul grows more and more old - fashioned , and goes home for the holidays . (3)

Party at Dr Blimber's – Paul's desire to be affectionately remembered – His illness only expressed in the child's own (4)

~~News of Paul's illness No~~ feelings- Not otherwise described – Goes home for the holidays (5)

Chapter XV. (6)

Amazingartfulness of Captain Cuttle, and a new pursuit for Walter Gay. (7)

Captain Cuttle . Qry Introduce his friend – Mr Bunsbey [sic] (8)

Not yet. (9)

Staggs's Gardens after the railroad (10)

Polly brought to see him. (11)

Chapter XVI. (12)

What the waves were always saying (13)

Walter brought into the room (14)

Paul's Death The old, old, fashion. But there was an older fashion yet, before it (15)

"And so," said Miss Tox , drying her eyes , (16)

"Dombey and Son's a daughter , after all !" (17)

Commentary and order of entry (Ws.5)

Dickens begins No.5 soon after Christmas 1846 (probably 31 December) and finishes on 15 January, once again about ten days before his deadline. Forster arrives on the 16th 'The greater part of the night of the day on which it [No.5] was written…he [Dickens] was wandering desolate and sad about the streets of Paris. I arrived there the following morning on my visit; and as I alighted…a little before eight o'clock, found him waiting for me at the gate of the post-office bureau' (*Life* 481[K:9442]). On 31 January, No.5 for February 1847 is published.

RH:

Preliminary headings: **(1), (2), (6) & (12)**

Dickens follows his established routine.

Plan for ch.14: **(4) & (5)**

He puts number planning aside and instead plans for the first of two chapters concerning Paul. He begins by entering a note of the chapter's ending, the news of Paul's illness, adds "No", and then deletes the whole entry ~~(5)~~. In its place—still leaving half of the space blank for the title—he plans the chapter from its central episode (the party) onwards. He notes Paul's displacement of feelings of loss by concern for others, and finally his intention to present illness exclusively from the sick child's viewpoint (4).

Ws.5a

Dickens breaks off from Ws.5 to prepare Ws.5a. The decision to focus on the ailing Paul is "a difficult, but a new way of doing it […] and likely to be pretty" (*Life* 404[K:8229]) something he had in mind since at least the 5th of July.[57] His use of the word "pretty" to describe the innovation is a characteristic defensive understatement. Aware of some of the difficulties, he makes special preparations in Ws.5a.

MS

Composition and titling of ch.14

Anticipating that the final chapter will be short, Dickens feels free to improvise an unusually long lead-in to the main episode the end-of-term party; it becomes ten printed pages of about seventeen (see 'Appendix A' p.165). As he writes ch.14, he weaves the substance and structure of Ws.5a into its composition. He also enlarges its title, revising it twice ('Appendix D' p.181). The leave-taking after the party is one of many extended departures that intensify pathos and the general mood of the novel (cf. the procession of farewells in chs.16, 44 and 57).

RH

Title of ch.14: **(3)**

Dickens copies the final version from manuscript into the gap left for it in the worksheet.

Plan for ch.15: **(8), (10) & (11)**

Leaving a line for the title, Dickens enters note (8), which presumably points to the first episode that ends with Cuttle seeing Walter off on a long walk. As in the other two chapters, Dickens defines an endpoint (11). The challenge then is to devise a plausible and effective narrative that links (8) to (11). He considers the introduction of Bunsby (9), leaving it as a possibility to be settled during composition. Entry (10) on the progress of the railroad explains Susan's predicament and makes more acceptable the coincidence of her meeting with Walter (in preparation for his recall). Dickens is alert throughout the novel to the different ways the development of the railway impinges on his characters.

MS and RH

Composition and titling of ch.15: **(7)**

Dickens ends with Walter being called back to the house, a plant for the opening of ch.16. He copies the title to worksheet.

RH

Outcome of (8) in ch.15: **(9)**

With a drying quill, Dickens confirms the postponement of Bunsby. The timing is conjecture; there is nothing to indicate when after writing ch.15 he made the entry (8).

Titling and plan for ch.16: **(13), (14), (15), (16) & (17)**

Dickens titles at once (13), as he sometimes does if certain of his choice. The style of broken underlining—many equal short strokes—may give it additional emphasis, though the style is used elsewhere, without that effect (see Ws.8 p.75). He notes that Walter is to be brought into the room (14), completing the action began in ch.15 (220^{236}), and adding weight to Paul's last wishes, which later are impetuously set aside by Dombey. Layout and hand suggests that he enters "Paul's Death" (16) first, then (15) and lastly (17), as the quill begins to dry.

Ws.5a

Dickens adds a final entry to Ws.5a, the river symbol (6). He can then use Ws.5a in much the same way for ch.16 as he did for ch.14.

MS

Composition and title of ch.16

Having copied in the title, Dickens incorporates Ws.5a into the composition of ch.16. The concentration on Paul's sensations and thoughts continues. Paul's feelings about his father noted in Ws.5a are echoed in what he says to him in this chapter, adding gesture to words. Throughout the chapter, the "now" gathers emphasis until a final "and now" on the last page.

Similarly, the particulars of the river are developed with every repetition. As the focus is on Paul, we hear through his ears, which conveniently keeps anonymous the speaker whose mention of Walter leads to his summons. Paul makes his last wish to his father before he describes to Florence his imagined journey on "The River that is always running on". The final narrative represents his passage into death, told in the terms that have been taught him (cf. Richards' explanation of her mother's death to Florence ($26–27^{26–27}$)).

Dickens ends with a consolatory but qualified hope "for all who see it", a plea to the reader not to estrange the spirits of children, then a "white line", then a reworked version of Miss Tox's cry (16). Her exclamation, present in his outline to Forster, is also anticipated at the end of ch.4 (see first paragraph of endnote 42).

After the experience of reading ch.16 in public, Dickens drops the exclamation from the later editions of 1859 and 1867. It was probably Forster who wrote that the sentence 'was felt a jar at the time [1848], and too light an intrusion upon a solemn catastrophe'.[58] A reading copy (1862) has "too" after "bears us to the ocean".[59]

Ws.5a

Dickens wafers Ws.5a over the left-hand half of Ws.5.

List: [1–5]

In the interval between completing the novel's first quarter and preparing for No.6, Dickens decides to keep a what he calls a "List of Chapter Headings". After preparing a few slightly larger leaves, he writes the chapter number and title for chs.1–16 in an even fine hand with consistent alignment and spacing, and without hesitation, probably copying from Ws.1–5 ('Appendix C' p.173). Once completed to the end of No.5, the list is usually compiled number-by-number. He now feels the need for a compressed record of the story's growing complexity, which perhaps reflects some uncertainty over how reliable or useful the worksheets will be in helping him oversee his larger intentions for the novel.

Proofs

There are no proofs extant, but as five long passages in manuscript do not appear in the part issue, it is likely that they were cut at proof stage. Once again, Dickens probably already suspects he has overstepped his limit; ch.16 begins on MS p.26 and ends on p.29.[60]

Facsimile of Ws.5a

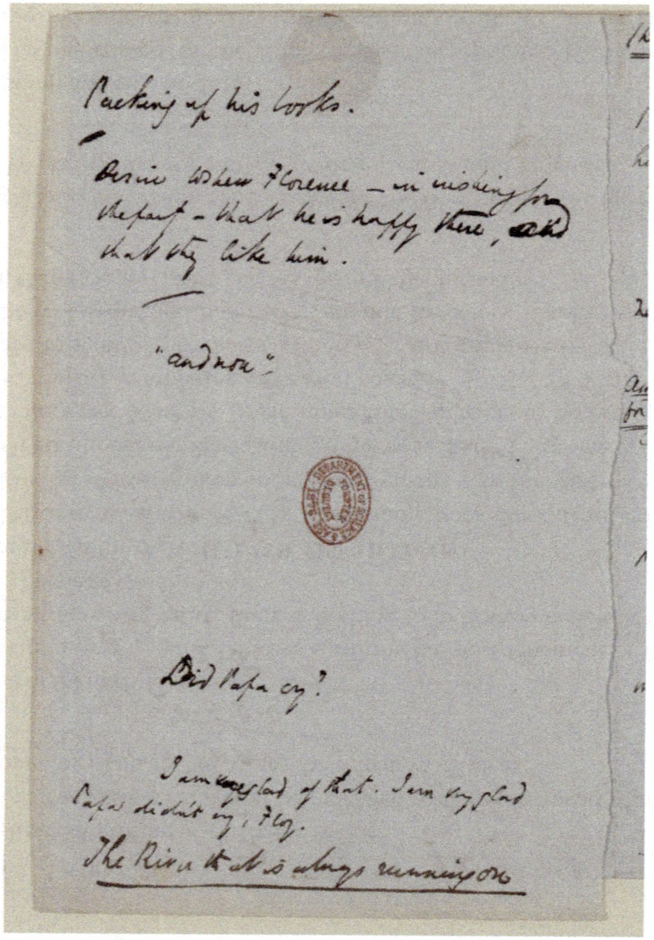

Image No.2012FE1496 (reduced and cropped): Forster Collection, National Art Library, Victoria and Albert Museum (2015). © Victoria and Albert Museum, London.

Transcription of Ws.5a

(1) Packing up his books.

/

(2) Desire to shew Florence – in wishing for the party – that he is happy there, [~~th~~]~~and~~ that they like him.

/

(3) " and now –"

(4) ~~d~~Did Papa cry ?

(5) I am ~~very~~ glad of that. I am very glad Papa didn't cry, Floy.

(6) <u>The River that is always running on</u>

Commentary on Ws.5a

Instead of a number plan for No.5, Dickens prepares an additional leaf, in which all entries are concerned with the presentation of Paul. The entries are similar in hand, quill and ink, and made on the same occasion (except for the final entry). They are spread out so that they fill the page, matching their position in an imagined narrative. He appears to wafer Ws.5a over the unused side of Ws.5, after revising the title of ch.15, and probably after the writing of ch.16 (see above 'Introduction to Ws.5a'; also 'Ws.5a' in the commentary on Ws.5 p.58).

Entry (1)

Dickens begins, in a slightly larger hand, describing an action representative of all of Paul's preparations for departure that are ways of delaying and coming to terms with loss (see $193^{205\text{–}06}$).

Entry (2)

Paul's attachment to and concern for others is noted in language appropriate to him, emphasising the present and in free indirect thought. In the text, his concern becomes more insistent as he declines; it displaces his fears, and increases the reader's empathy. At the end of the second line of (2), "th" is over-written by a large "and", which is then smudged and deleted. He removes childlike coordination to emphasise the repeated syntax and monosyllabic choice of word.

Entry (3)

The "and now" is in speech marks to suggest a special function, as if it is an authorial interjection interrupting Paul's narrative. It marks a decisive stage in Paul's illness (194^{207}). The blank space below (3) evokes the passage of time and the progress of his sickness in the intervening narrative.

Entry (4) & (5)

In the two penultimate entries, Paul questions Florence about his father's reaction to his arrival home. The irony of his repeated assertion of his protective feelings for his father provides an endpoint for ch.14 (204^{219}).

Entry (6)

Finally, in a heavier hand (that later corrodes), Dickens adds the always flowing River, underlined as a recurrent symbol. With this addition, the notes—up to this point planned for ch.14—reach into ch.16, where he also repeats the "and now" (220^{236}, 225^{241}) and further develops Paul's thoughts and gestures in his speeches to Florence about his father (222^{238}, 224^{240}).

The River, as a fact of Nature, a symbol of Time passing and a figurative allusion to death, appears at the chapter's beginning and at its end. It carries the author's closing plea "look upon us, angels of young children, with regards not quite estranged, when the swift river bears us to the ocean [too]!"[61]

Worksheet for No.6

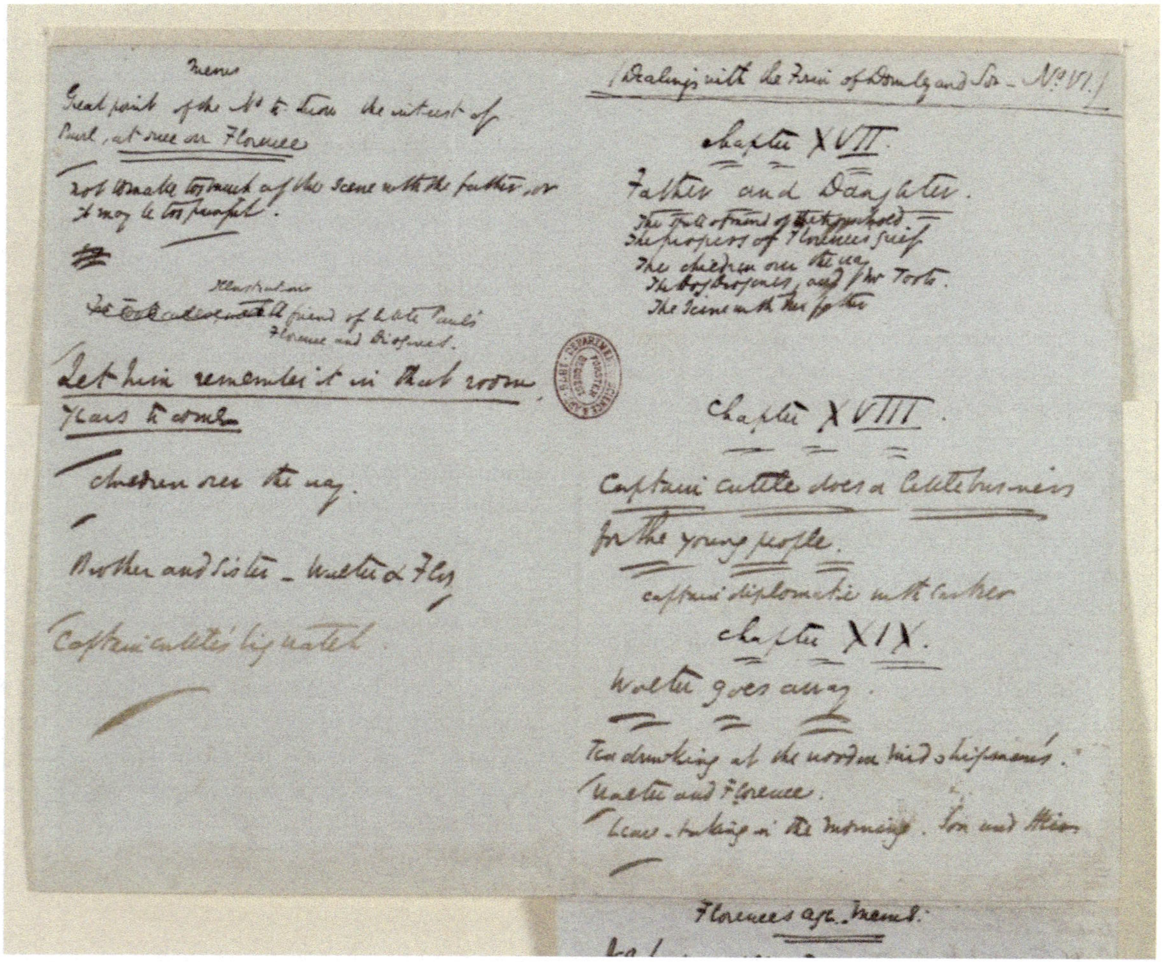

Image No.2012FE1494 recto (reduced): Forster Collection, National Art Library, Victoria and Albert Museum (2015). © Victoria and Albert Museum, London.

Transcription of Ws.6

(1) Mems

(2) Great point of the N° to throw the interest of Paul, at once on Florence

(3) Not to make too much of the scene with the father, or it may be too painful.

(4) q^y

Illustrations

(5) ~~Mr Toots calls, with D~~[?]A friend of little Paul's Florence and Diogenes.

(6) Let him remember it in that room, years to come

(7) Children over the way.

(8) Brother and sister – Walter & Floy.

(9) Captain Cuttle's big watch.

(Dealings with the Firm of Dombey and Son – N°: VI) (10)

Chapter XVII. (11)

Father and Daughter. (12)

The state of mind of the household (13)

The progress of Florence's grief (14)

The children over the way (15)

The Dog Diogenes, and Mr Toots. (16)

The Scene with her father (17)

Chapter XVIII. (18)

Captain Cuttle does a little business for the young people. (19)

Captain diplomatic with Carker (20)

Chapter XIX. (21)

Walter goes away. (22)

Tea drinking at the wooden Midshipman's. (23)

Walter and Florence. (24)

Leave - taking in the morning. Son and Heir (25)

Commentary and order of entry (Ws.6)

Forster left Dickens on 2 February with his writing-table in readiness for No.6. However, on the 4th Dickens writes he is "not under weigh [sic] yet find it very difficult indeed to fall into the new vein of the story [...] I will send the chapters as I write them, and you must not wait, of course, for me to read the end in type. To transfer to Florence, instantly, all the previous interest, is what I am aiming at" (*Life* 481–82[K:9446]). When Dickens receives the proof of ch.17 (later 18) and ch.18 (later 17), he discovers that the former is more than a page short of what he expected (*Life* 453n[K:9197 n.135]). He cannot wait for the proofs of ch.19, so rushes to London from Paris on the 18th to provide more text.[62] On 28 February, No.6 for March 1847 is published.

RH

Preliminary headings: **(10), (11), (18) & (21)**

Dickens's alignment of the number headings for three chapters slips to the right.

LH

Heading: **(1)**

He heads the left-hand half "Mems" for the first time. The heading signals that some strategic notes have to do with how the number plan relates to what is to come (see Ws.7, 9, 12, 13 and 15). By contrast, where he is concerned only with the number itself, he may omit a heading (see Ws.16–18). However, the distinction is not made consistently (cf. Ws.8, 10, 11 and 14).

Initial plan for the number: **(2), (3), (4), (6) & (7)→ch.17** (later 18)

There are signs—in the changes of hand and positioning—of an untypical hesitancy in selecting and ordering ideas (cf. Horsman 1974, 'Introduction', p.xxix). Dickens is troubled by the problem of (2), and makes no mention of Cuttle, leaving the subject of (4) temporarily undecided. He enters (6) with a heavier and larger hand, writing fluently and underlining the whole entry.

Entry (6) anticipates the importance that memory will play in the development of Dombey. However, the content of those memories—their source in crucial scenes between father and daughter—lives so vividly in Dickens's imagination that, though they are alluded to later, they are seldom planned or even recorded in the worksheets. On this occasion, already aware of the painfulness of the scene, he can only warn himself "not to make too much of it" (3).

Additional number plan: **(8)→ch.19**

Dickens enters (8) in preparation for ch.19. The young lovers-to-be make their secret relationship more acceptable, to themselves as well as others, by treating it as a close tie between brother and sister. He closes the number plan with a short slash below "Floy".

MS

Composition and titling of ch.17 (later 18)

Dickens links to ch.16 by opening with the responses to the funeral of the household, office staff, street entertainers and children opposite. Afterwards comes the moment when Dombey miswords Paul's memorial, the conversation of Chick and Tox, and the comfort they offer Florence—in all, nearly half the chapter, a long lead-in to the solitary Florence. She contemplates the rosy children and their father opposite (7), is distracted by Toots (5), comforted by Diogenes and, on the night prior to his departure, ventures to disturb her father in his study. Surprised, angered and deeply resentful, he lights her ascent on the stairs as before, aware of an earlier similar occasion, but "poisoning" the memory of it with jealous resentment. Dickens keeps the encounter brief, compressing the drama and paring down the exhortatory rhetoric. Revisions show him searching for an inclusive chapter title, but finally choosing to put the emphasis entirely on the closing scene (see 'Appendix D', ch.17, p.184).[63]

RH

Title and summary of ch.17 (later 18): **(12), (13), (14), (15), (16) & (17)**

Dickens copies in the final version of the title. Omitting the lead-in and writing at speed, he aligns the first entry with the title. He lists four phrases of similar length, structure and rhythm, his arm pulling to the right. They order four parts of the narrative focused on Florence (14–17). Then, noting the role of the household chorus, he inserts (13) almost avoiding the underlines above. Instead he smudges downwards the 'ou' of 'house', the 'nd' of 'and', and the 'a' of 'father', which confirms all five entries were made together, before the ink could dry (shown only in the facsimile; see above).

LH

Further number plan: **(5)→ch.17** (later 18)

In his smallest hand, Dickens devises two letterings for illustrations of the chapter he has just completed. Eventually, the first is rejected in favour of the second. (The second plate's subject, also involving Florence, is found later from ch.19; see 'List of plates/illustrations' (lviii[lix])).

MS

Composition and titling of ch.18 (later 17)

The title is entered at the start of composition and not revised.

List: [6]

Dickens copies in the headings for chs.17 and 18 (as numbered before their reversal at proof stage) together with a chapter number heading for ch.19 mistakenly entered as ch.9. The omission of a title confirms that these entries are made prior to the composition and titling of ch.19.

MS

Composition and titling of ch.19

Dickens leaves an empty line for a title, a 'gapping' tactic used in composition for the first time, and often employed in subsequent chapters. He had devised the ploy in Ws.4 in titling the closing ch.13 (see p.53).

Beginning the chapter on MS p.21, he has sufficient space to preface Florence's unexpected visit to the Shop with the details of Walter's recent contact with Susan. The lovers struggle to convey their feelings. When Florence gives him the purse she made for Paul "with money in it", Walter "would have left without speaking, for now he felt what parting was" (263[284]). Next morning, amidst the final farewells, he refuses Cuttle's gift of the watch. Dickens ends on MS p.27 (a half page, like MS p.13 at the end of ch.17).

RH

Title and summary for ch.18 (later 17): **(19) & (20)**

Title and summary of ch.19: **(22), (23), (24) & (25)**

LH

Memo: **(9)**

Progressive corrosion—perhaps re-dipping at (22)—and similarities of hand, suggests the order of entry is as above (19)–(25) plus (9). He memos the gift of the watch (cf. ch.10), for use in later numbers, finishing with a flourish as the quill runs dry.

Proofs

As chs.17 and 18 in their different ways both recall ch.16, Dickens can open the number with either. He transposes them, perhaps to avoid two consecutive numbers involving Cuttle and/or to enclose a "painful" scene within lighter material. He expects ch.17 (now 18) to be 15 or 16 printed pages, but finds the proofs to be only 14. Later chapters add to the shortfall. After rushing to the London office from Paris, he makes five insertions in ch.19, the last two being the most significant: Florence's conversation with Walter about her father's dislike of him, as a motive for sending him away (262–63[282–83]), and the meeting with John Carker (264–65[285–86]), a farewell that anticipates a shift of emphasis in the latter's function, from a parallel to Walter to a contrast with James.[64]

Facsimile of Ws.6a

(recto)

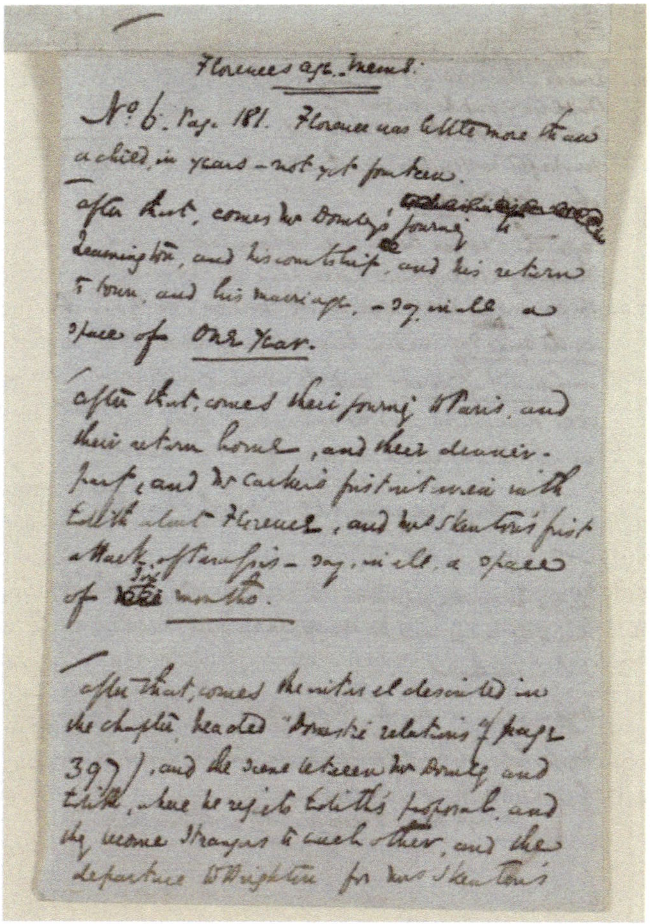

Image No.2012FE1494 recto (reduced): Forster Collection, National Art Library, Victoria and Albert Museum (2015). © Victoria and Albert Museum, London.

(verso)

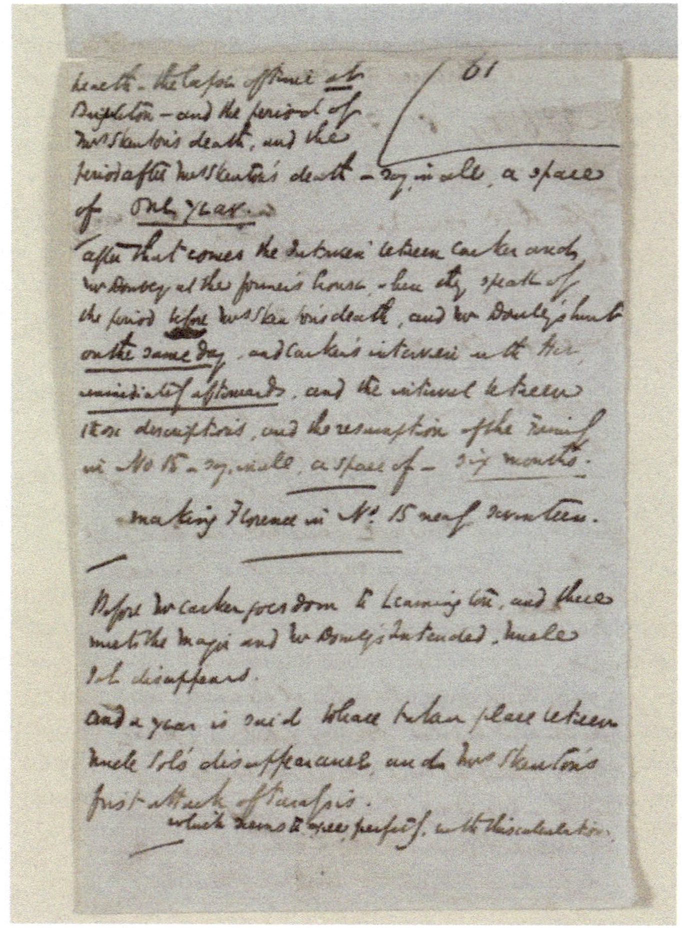

Image No.2012FE1494 verso (reduced): Forster Collection, National Art Library, Victoria and Albert Museum (2015). © Victoria and Albert Museum, London.

Transcription of Ws.6a

(recto)

Florence's age. Mems.

(1) N°. 6. Page 181. Florence was little more than a child, in years – not yet fourteen.

(2) After that, comes Mr Dombey's ^ ~~child~~(?) ~~in his own room and his tears~~[?] journey to Leamington, and his courtship, and his return to town, and his marriage, – say in all, a space of One Year.

(3) After that, comes their journey to Paris, and their return home, and their dinner-party, and Mr Carker's first interview with Edith about Florence, and Mrs Skewton's first attack of paralysis – say, in all, a space of ~~nine~~ Six months.

(4) After that, comes the interval described in the chapter headed "Domestic relations" (page 397), and the scene between Mr Dombey and Edith, where he rejects Edith's proposal, and they become Strangers to each other, and the departure to Brighton for Mrs Skewton's

(verso)

health – the lapse of time at Brighton – and the period of Mrs Skewton's death, and the period after Mrs Skewton's death – say, in all, a space of One Year.

61

(5) After that comes the Interview between Carker and Mr Dombey at the former's house - here they speak of the period before Mrs Skewton's death, and Mr Dombey's hurt on the same day, and Carker's interview with Edith, immediately afterwards, the interval between those descriptions, and the resumption of the Family in No 15 – say, in all, a space of – six months.

(6) making Florence in N°. 15 nearly seventeen.

(7) Before Mr Carker goes down to Leamington, and there meets the Major and Mr Dombey's Intended, Uncle Sol disappears.

And a year is said to have taken place between Uncle Sol's disappearance, and Mrs Skewton's first attack of Paralysis.

which seems to agree perfectly, with this calculation.

Commentary on Ws.6a (recto and verso)

Introduction

The additional leaf entitled "Florence's age. Mems" is attached to Ws.6, pasted by its top edge to the underside of Ws.6, probably because of its opening reference to that number (see the facsimile of Ws.6, p.62). However, the sheet written on both sides was always kept as a loose leaf by Dickens. Closely connected to the beginning of the narrative in No.15, it might be more appropriately attached to Ws.15. The quill and ink appear erratic in flow, perhaps due to a poor barrel and/or sullied ink. The density of the hand fluctuates irregularly throughout, the fluctuation becoming more frequent towards the end.

Aim and method

As the focus of the story changes from one group of characters to another, Dickens suspects that his management of time may lead to inconsistencies. His concern is with accuracy rather than likelihood. The purpose is to check that Florence could be almost seventeen years old at the start of No.15 (621^{686}), that he can make her seventeen *during* ch.47 (624^{689}), and that the year's gap between Sol's disappearance and Mrs Skewton's first attack is generally consistent. His method is to collate the duration of the episodes as well as the interval between them, using the relevant worksheets and parts published so far.

[Editor's note: references to the Clarendon text are by page alone, giving the page in the hardback, ed. Horsman 1974, then the page (superscripted) in the paperback, ed. Horsman 2008, superscripted (see 'References (1)', p.7)].

Entry (1)

Dickens begins with a moment in the aftermath to Paul's death, when "Florence was little more than a child in years—not yet fourteen" giving her age as in the published text, rather than the manuscript, which differs in wording.[65] He has reason to recall his starting point (1). It was a significant moment in the progress of Dombey's relationship with Florence. During preparation for the scene, he had warned himself that it "may be too painful" ($Ws.6_3$), and at proofing moved the chapter from its opening position to the middle of the number. So, familiar with the occasion, he may scan the worksheets to find "the Scene with her father" ($Ws.6_{17}$) on the evening of the funeral. From there, going to his copy of No.6—perhaps delayed for a moment until he recalls that chs.17 and 18 were later transposed—he finds the relevant quotation on "p.181" (251^{270}). Giving the printed page of the quotation as "p.181 No.6" establishes his reliance on the back number.

Entry (2)

He then calculates the gap between the departure for Leamington and the marriage. Considerations include, as a starting point, Floy's visit to Dombey's room, and afterwards his solitary tears of grief, triggered by the sight of her climbing the stairs alone (pp.182–83 of the part issue).[66] Powerful for its compression of feeling, the scene adds nothing to the prosaic calculation of time passing, so the allusion is deleted. A glance at Ws.7 for the journey, Ws.9 for the courtship and Ws.10 for the wedding would confirm "One year" as a reasonable estimate of the first interval. The events referred to in (2) are prominent in Ws.7, 9 and 10.

Entry (3)

The second interval covers the return from Paris to Mrs Skewton's first attack, to be found in No.12. The calculation depends partly on the untimed gap between the return from the three weeks in Paris and the "at home". That occasion is soon followed by Mrs Skewton's stroke, whose convalescence, Dickens hopes, can be made to concur with the first wedding anniversary. He stretches the next interval to nine months then later amends it to "Six months".

Entry (4)

Dickens refers to ch.40 by chapter title and opening "p.397" in the part issue for No.13. The chapter "describes an interval" during which Dombey confronts Edith in her bedroom (he perhaps turns on to p.399). With the rejection of Edith's proposal "they become Strangers to each other", an echo of Edith's last words "Nothing can makes us stranger to each other than we are" (p.404). From this moment, he resumes tracing the interval in the rest of the part. From the quarrel in the bedroom and the departure of Mrs Skewton, Florence, and Edith for Brighton to the time spent there and Mrs Skewton death and her "convenient" burial in Brighton (ch.41), he estimates the interval to be "**One Year**".

In contrast to entries (1) and (2), many of the details he refers to in entries (3) and (4) are not mentioned in the worksheets. Instead, when he calculates the intervals from the return from Paris to Mrs Skewton's death, he relies on two recent back numbers Nos.12 and 13.

Entry (5)

He recounts the events of the day that opens No.14, the instalment he has just completed: Dombey's exchanges with Carker at his home, the mention of the time before Mrs Skewton's death (when Carker witnessed Dombey's first rebuke to Edith see p.569[627]), the accident and Carker's interview with Edith—all on the same day. From these events to the dinner on the day preceding the second wedding anniversary, he estimates to be **"six months"**.

Entry (6)

Taking (1)-(5) together, an interval of about three years, he finds that it is possible for Florence to be **"nearly seventeen"** at the start of ch.48 (later 47).

Entry (7)

Finally he ties in the Sol/Cuttle subplot. He notes that Sol's disappearance, discovered in the last chapter of No.8 (ch.25), is prior to Carker's appearance in Leamington in the first chapter of No.9 (ch.26), and that the gap between Sol's disappearance and Mrs Skewton's first attack "is said" to be one year. There is no explicit statement defining the interval—Dickens uses "said" to mean 'said by implication'.[67]

Outcome

Dickens is now prepared, having checked the timeline in Ws.6a, to make its coherence more apparent to the reader. He is particularly concerned that the elopement should occur on the day of the second wedding anniversary, as an expression of Edith's bitter hostility to Dombey (Ws.15_2). He continues ch.47 by recapitulating Florence's experience up to the final quarrel. The new hope—to be loved by her father—is now after "nearly two years" quite gone. In its place, she clings to an idea of the father, dreaming of a man "to cherish and protect her", a change in her consciousness, which "like the change from childhood to womanhood" occurs when she is "almost seventeen" (621[686]). She grows to be seventeen a few pages later (624[689]). Visitors to the house hardly notice her. When they do, they think her pretty, but withdrawn.

Dickens buries his calculations in his description of Florence's apprehension:

> None the less so ["delicate and thoughtful in appearance"], certainly, for her life of the last six months (after the accident), Florence took her seat at the dinner-table, on the day before the second anniversary of her father's marriage to Edith (Mrs Skewton had been lying stricken with paralysis when the first came round), with an uneasiness, amounting to dread (625[690-91]).

The interpolated leaf Ws.6a shows that Dickens uses the worksheets to remind him of the content of more distant numbers and to help him retrieve detail in the pages of the part to which they refer. However, for the detail of the more recent numbers, including the number just published, as we might expect, he relies more on the parts themselves.

Worksheet for No.7

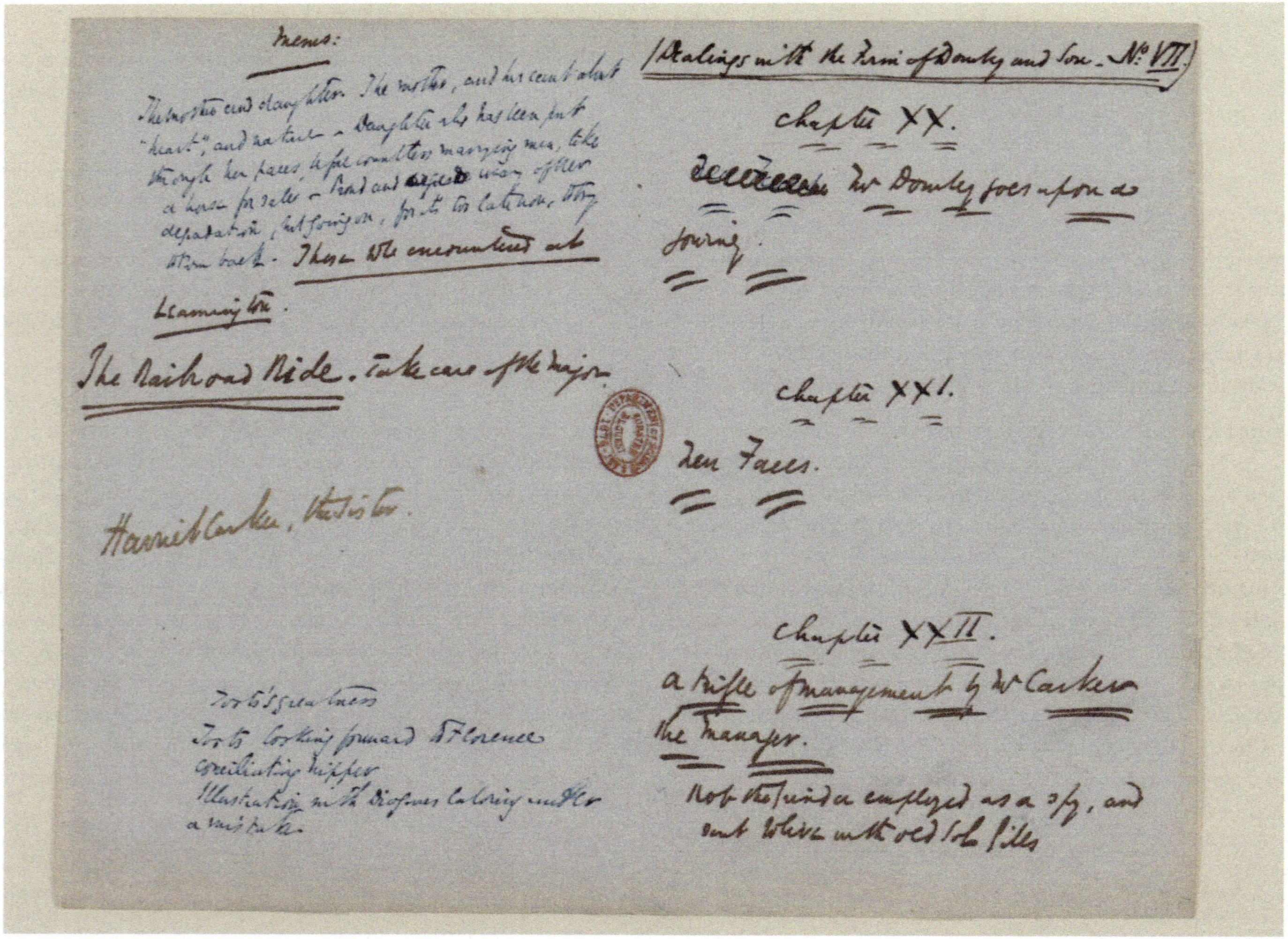

Image No.2012FE1498 (reduced): Forster Collection, National Art Library, Victoria and Albert Museum (2015). © Victoria and Albert Museum, London.

Transcription of Ws.7

(1) Mems:

(2) The mother and daughter. The mother, and her cant about "heart", and nature – Daughter who has been put through her paces, before countless marrying men, like a horse for sale – Proud and ~~disguste~~ weary of her degradation, but going on, for it's too late now, to try to turn back. These to be encountered at

(3) Leamington.

(4) The Railroad Ride. Take care of the Major.

(5) Harriet Carker, the Sister.

(6) Toots's greatness

Toots looking forward to Florence

Conciliating Nipper

Illustration with Diogenes laboring under a mistake.

(Dealings with the Firm of Dombey and Son – N$^{o:}$VII.) (7)

Chapter XX. (8)

~~New Faces~~ Mr Dombey goes upon a journey. (9) (10)

Chapter XXI. (11)

New Faces (12)

Chapter XXII. (13)

A trifle of Management by M^{r}Carker the Manager. (14)

Rob the Grinder employed as a spy, and sent to live with old Sol Gills (15)

Commentary and order of entry (Ws.7)

Once back in Paris at the end of February, Dickens is overtaken by another crisis. Charley his eldest, contracting scarlet fever at his boarding school in the Strand, is quarantined and has to be nursed. He returns to make the arrangements and get accommodation for the family. For the first time, he begins a number well into the second week of the month, probably starting on 10 March—"the moment we got housed here, I fell into a dream of work, from which I only awoke last night"—and finishing on 23 March (L5:33 and 41). On this occasion near the office, he finishes his task close to the printer's deadline. On 31 March No.7 for April 1847 is published.

LH

Preliminary: (2)

This unique entry, the backstory of Edith, is quite unlike any other in its position on the page and in the fullness of its detail. Some of that detail will re-appear in the second half of ch.20 (later ch.21), some not until ch.27. Perhaps using the opportunity to test the quality of a new ink and quill, Dickens writes in the bright blue ink that he intends to use in the number's composition. The order of entry proposed here minimises the ink changes and keeps consecutive all of the following: the other five blue entries in Ws.7, the corresponding chapters in the manuscript, and the relevant entries in the "List of Chapter Headings". Further argument for a single entry in blue (Ws.7_2), with all remaining entries consecutive, runs as follows: (1) judging from the blue inks used later elsewhere, the available blue inks are variable in quality (2) Dickens uncertain of the ink's quality may be testing it, before using blue of any sort in the manuscript for the first time (3) the bright blue seems to flow more smoothly and dry more quickly (4) having tested it, as the supply is probably uncertain, he restricts its use in the worksheet to those entries that he makes while composing chs.20 (later 20 and 21) and 22.[68]

RH

Preliminary headings: **(7), (8), (11) & (13)**

Dickens as usual makes the worksheet entries in black with some progressive loss of density.[69]

LH

Preliminary heading: **(1)**

Initial plan for the number: **(3) & (4)→ch.20**

Dickens now using black ink incorporates the mother and daughter back-story into his plan for the setting (3) and heavily stresses the importance of the railroad (4) with large lettering and double underlining, anticipating its recurrence as setting and symbol. He warns himself to attend to the key figure of the Mephistophelean Major, but perhaps not to overdo his bluster (4). The idea of a second marriage is hinted at in the cover design of the green wrapper by an altar scene involving a shadowy military figure, who becomes the "Old Major" of ch.7 (Ws.2_{16} p.43). Dickens had already made preparations for No.7; during his struggles with No.6, he wrote to Forster "I think I shall manage Dombey's second wife (introduced by the Major), and the beginning of that business in his present state of mind, very naturally and well" (endnote 62).

MS and RH

Titling and composition of ch.20 (later chs.20 and 21): **(9)**

Returning to the bright blue ink and quill, Dickens confident in his choice of title enters it in both manuscript and worksheet. On the same day that he starts the chapter, he writes a long letter to Browne about illustrating Dombey's first meeting with Edith (see below p.136).

List: [6/7]

Still in blue he corrects the numbering of ch.19, adds its title, and copies to the "List of Chapter Headings" the number heading and the initial title of ch.20 (see p.176).

MS and Proofs

Composition and titling of ch.21 (later 22)

Corrections to the Proofs of ch.20

Dickens completes the fifteen MS pages of ch.20 on about 18 March, sends it to the printers and begins ch.21 (later 22).[70] Receiving the proofs two or three days later, he is far enough into ch.21 (later 22) to know that it will become the closing chapter. On reading ch.20 in print, he divides the chapter, perhaps because it falls naturally into two parts but also because it seems too long (cf. Ws.12_8 p.91). Deleting the "New Faces", he re-titles ch.20 "Mr Dombey goes upon a journey"; then, after "with the Major arm-in-arm", he inserts the heading for a new ch.21 entitled "New Faces". He can then return to MS p.16 to change ch.21 to ch.22 by adding a Roman 'I' to "XXI".

In ch.22, Carker weaves his web, in some way touching each of the lives of John and Harriet, Sol and Walter, and Rob and Polly. After making one revision, Dickens finds an appropriately ironic title (see 'Appendix D', ch.22, p.185). With "the business of the day accomplished" Carker rides home, contemplating the daughter almost grown into a young woman (304^{330}).

LH

Additional plan to extend the close of ch.22: **(6)**

Dickens may initially have intended to end with Carker's reverie on horseback (as in chs.24 and 31). However, after following Carker through the day, he misjudges the approach to the ending. Raw from the mistake in No.6, he perhaps fears he is coming up short again. So breaking off from composition and having rehearsed in his mind's eye a Toots episode, he notes its 'salient points' on the lower left side of the worksheet, still using the blue ink and quill. He then seizes on the episode as material for a contrasting second illustration.[71]

MS

Composition of an extension to ch.22

Dickens goes back in time to get a satisfactory lead-in to the climax (see "a few digressive words are necessary" (305^{330})). From then on, he transforms the passage into a sharply comic scene. Identifying with each character in turn—even with the dog—he paces the narrative to its close as planned.[72]

RH

Titles for ch.20 & 21: **(<u>10</u>), & (<u>12</u>)**

Now using black ink, Dickens updates the worksheet entries in line with changes in proofs. Deleting the "New Faces", he retitles ch.20 "Mr Dombey goes upon a journey" and uses its initial title for ch.21, in which Dombey meets the 'new faces' for the first time.

Title and summary note for ch.22: **(<u>14</u>) & (15)**

Dickens copies in the title (14) as revised in manuscript, adding the description, a plot device (15) that establishes a link between Sol's shop and Carker.

LH

Memo: **(5)**→ch.22

In ch.22 the Carker brothers recount Harriet's story ($293–94^{317–18}$). This note of her mention is corroded, the ink probably thinning as the quill empties. It is another final entry—made after composing ch.22—serving as a reminder of the location of her backstory.

Proofs

Proofs show that, although the manuscript ends on p.26, the number is over, rather than under, written. In contrast, the manuscript of the previous number, which ended on p.27, was short by two pages of print. The discrepancy arises from differences in the amount of empty space and in the number of deletions in No.6 compared to No.7. Dickens makes three small cuts: two cuts to ch.20, one to ch.22 and increases the number of lines per page (Horsman 1974, p.270 n.1, p.278 n.4, and p.289 n.2).[73]

Worksheet for No.8

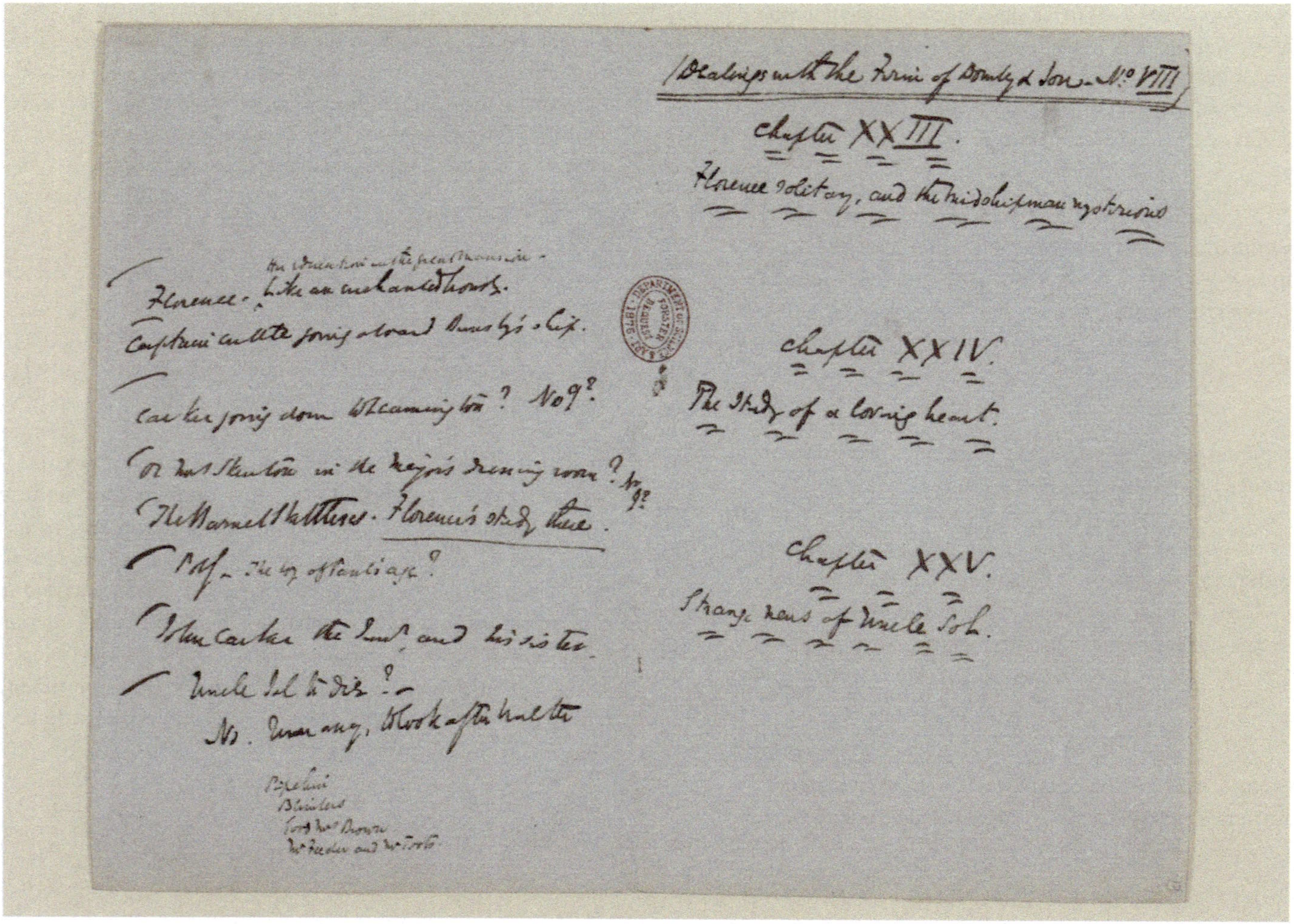
(Dealings with the Firm of Dombey & Son.—No VIII)

Chapter XXIII.

Florence solitary, and the Midshipman mysterious

Chapter XXIV.

The Study of a loving heart.

Chapter XXV.

Strange news of Uncle Sol.

Florence—like an enchanted house.

Captain Cuttle going aboard Bunsby's Ship.

Carker going down to Leamington? No 9.

Or Mrs Skewton in the Major's dressing room? No 9.

The Marwood Skettleses. Florence's study there.

Then Carker the Junior and his sister.

Uncle Sol to die?—

No. Going away, to look after Walter

Image No.2012FE1499 (reduced): Forster Collection, National Art Library, Victoria and Albert Museum (2015).

Transcription of Ws.8

(1) Florence – ^Her education in the great mansion - Like an enchanted house .

(2) Captain Cuttle going abroad Bunsby's ship.

(3) Carker going down to Leamington ? No 9 ?

(4) Or Mrs Skewton in the Major's dressing room ? N° 9?

(5) The Barnett Skettleses . Florence's study there .

(6) Polly - The boy of Paul's age ?

(7) John Carker the Junr, and his sister .

(8) Uncle Sol to die ?

(9) No . Run away , to look after Walter

(10) Pipchin
Blimbers
Good Mrs Brown .
Mr Feeder and Mr Toots .

(Dealings with the Firm of Dombey & Son – N^o: VIII) (11)

Chapter XXIII . (12)

Florence solitary , and the Midshipman mysterious (13)

Chapter XXIV . (14)

The Study of a loving heart . (15)

Chapter XXV (16)

Strange news of Uncle Sol . (17)

Commentary and order of entry (Ws.8)

Dickens writes to Forster on 10 April 1847, "I have been trying for three or four days, but really have only just begun" (L5:55). On 19 April, he was so shocked by the difficult birth of Sidney, his seventh child, that on the 20th "with half of the No [chs.24 & 25] yet to write – with my thoughts so shaken by yesterday" he was unable to "fall to work". Nevertheless, he has "infinite relish for the story I am mining at" completing the second half by 26 April, when he has "just recovered from convulsions of Dombey after which I can never write legibly" (L5:59–60). Five days later on 30 April, No.8 for May 1847 is published.

LH

Plan for the number: **(1) & (2)→ch.23; (3) & (4)→No.9, ch.26; (5)→ch.24; (6); (7)→No.11, ch.33; (8) & (9)→ch.25; (10)**

Abandoning previous routines, Dickens omits all preliminaries. He writes without much regard to layout, in a fast hand that slopes unevenly, eliding the shapes of many letters, but with many stops and starts from (5) onwards.

He collects ideas for opening with Florence: the spellbound house as (in an inserted note) the setting of *her* education (1), then the move from pathos to comedy, much as he did in Ws.6, but this time by means of Cuttle, and then Bunsby (2).

He hesitates over the order and timing of the Leamington material (3) and (4), considering a visit to the Skettles (5)—as a way of extending the portrayal of Florence's "study" of how to win her father's love, by 'studying' the children of loving fathers that she finds there.

The two queries (3) and (4) precipitate the decision to postpone the courtship to No.9, and therefore the wedding to No.10. This has the obvious advantage of ending the novel's second quarter with a climax. However, the decision to postpone leads to another problem, how to sustain a number devoted entirely to the isolated Florence.

Other notes are also set aside. The opportunity to fan Dombey's resentment of the Toodles family—aired in ch.20 (273–75[294–97])—by introducing a boy of Paul's age (6) does not arise. The John/Harriet material of (7) would lose some of its point, if it preceded the development of James Carker. Sol's death (8) might spoil the celebratory opening of his last bottle of Madeira, planned for the last chapter.

Dickens follows the suggestion of (8) with an emphatic hurried 'No' and then, after a small gap, adds that Sol should leave, unexpectedly (9), to search for Walter, and presumably return later. His departure opens the way for Cuttle to become caretaker of the Shop—an important first step in forming the small society that goes "over to the daughter" (see the last paragraph of the outline to Forster endnote 42).

Finally, using his "smallhand" for (10), Dickens lists persons for whom he has some particular intention, noted here as a reminder of their futures, but also as a part of his search for material for the current number:

"Pipchin": to become the head of Dombey's household staff (ch.40)

"Blimbers": to be visited again (ch.41), but during the composition of ch.24 to be reintroduced as guests of the Skettles

"Good Mrs Brown": to tell the fortunes of Edith and Carker, before the courtship begins (ch.27)

"Mr Feeder and Mr Toots": now both young men, to meet again (ch.41).

MS

Composition of ch.23

Dickens leaves a blank line for the title and composes the chapter. He draws out Florence's inner life through her reactions to the accelerated decay of the spellbound house and through her dreams of how to gain her father's love. Her conversation with Susan about Walter leads to their search for news, and meetings with Rob—a 'Son and Heir', whose education has trained him for service as Carker's spy—with Mrs MacStinger, Cuttle, Bunsby and Sol. Cuttle's alarm at Sol's strange behaviour prepares for the opening of the next number.

List: [7/8]

Titling of ch.23

Dickens sometimes updates his "List of Chapter Headings" as he begins writing the next number. When he updates the List on this occasion, he treats it as an opportunity to work on the title for ch.23, revising it, not in Ws or manuscript, but in the List (see 'Appendix C' [7/8] p.176). He transfers the final version to the gap left for it in the manuscript, and later to the worksheet (see below).

MS

Composition and titling of ch.24 and ch.25

The objective stated in Ws.6_2 "to throw the interest of Paul at once on Florence" still poses acute difficulties. In ch.23, Dickens relied on Florence's reactions to "living alone in the great, dreary house" and her meetings with the company at the Wooden Midshipman. But in ch.24 during her visit to the Skettles, he has to import completely new material—with the inevitable appearance of contrivance—to draw out her state of mind in the continuing search for "the road to a hard parent's heart".

Dickens is "anxious not to anticipate in this No what I design for the next [No.9], and consequently must invent and plan for it [in No.8]" (L5:55). His planning successfully delays the courtship but his invention for once appears to fail him, contriving a series of poorly motivated encounters with conveniently long passages of stilted dialogue.

Although he postpones Carker material to No.9, he still has him very much in mind (3). He ends ch.24 with Carker's offer of a message from Florence to her father (343–44[373–74] and its illustration). In the next number, he reports other earlier encounters (ch.28: 383–84[419–20]).

LH

Outcomes: (3), (4), (6)

Dickens has already given in (9) his answer to (8). He leaves implicit his answer to the other three queries. In later worksheets, where he delays replying, he records outcomes more systematically, presumably to signal clearly what might (or must) be included later.

RH

Preliminaries and chapter titles: (11), (12), **(13)**, (14), **(15)**, (16) & **(17)**

The fall towards the end of each line, especially the curve of each title down the page (not shown) and the style of underlining used throughout suggest that all entries are made at the same time, in the order of their appearance on the page. It is likely that Dickens entered these headings hurriedly, for the sake of the record, after the number was written. The absence of chapter description arises, as in Ws.7, from the pressure of circumstances. It shows that, at this stage in the development of the worksheet, when he is pressed for time and in difficulty, he reins in planning or summarizing, and relies on chapter headings as a record of the instalment—with the exception in Ws.7_{15}, which plants Rob in the shop as Carker's spy.

Worksheet for No.9

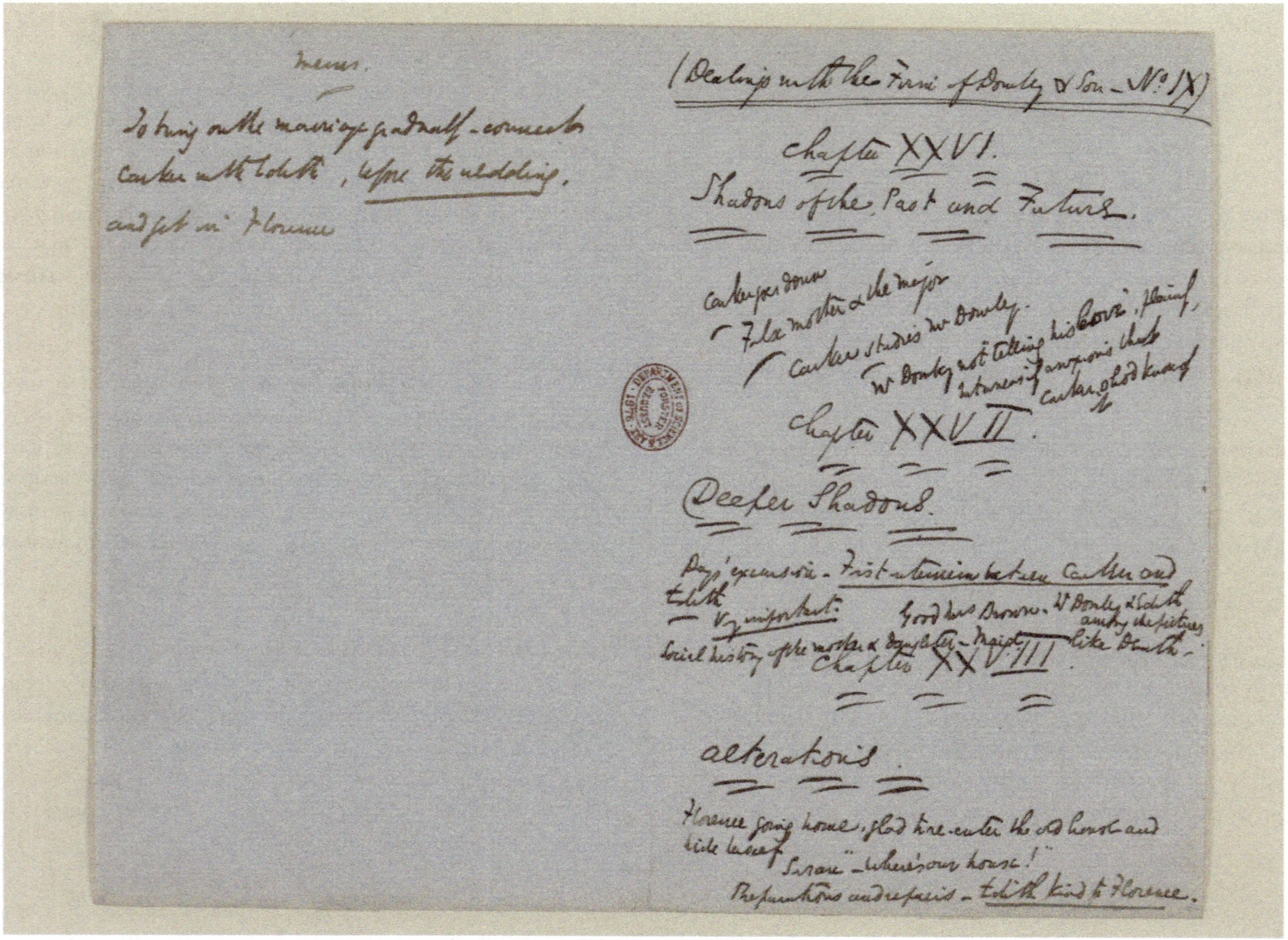

Image No.2012FE1491 (reduced): Forster Collection, National Art Library, Victoria and Albert Museum (2015). © Victoria and Albert Museum, London.

Transcription of Ws.9

(1) Mems.

(2) To bring on the marriage gradually - connect

Carker with Edith , before the wedding,

(3) and get in Florence

(Dealings with the Firm of Dombey & Son – Nº: IX.) (4)

Chapter XXVI. (5)

Shadows of the Past and Future. (6)

Carker goes down (7)

False mother & the Major (8)

Carker studies Mr Dombey. (9)

Mr Dombey not "telling his love", plainly, but uneasily anxious that Carker shod know of it (10)

Chapter XXVII. (11)

Deeper Shadows. (12)

Day's excursion - First interview between Carker and (13)

Edith Very important. Good Mrs Brown. Mr Dombey & Edith among the pictures. (14) (15) (16)

Social history of the mother & daughter – Maid like Death. (17)

Chapter XXVIII. (18)

Alterations. (19)

Florence going home, glad to re-enter the old house and hide herself (20)

Susan "– Where's our house !"

Preparations and repairs – Edith kind to Florence.

Commentary and order of entry (Ws.9)

Dickens's misfortune continues. On 3 May, he is bitten by a horse "under the impression I had gone into his stall to steal his corn" (L5:65). It affects him badly "a low dull nervousness of a most distressing kind", so much so that for two weeks he is unable to write without discomfort (L5:66). He writes only a few short letters before 16 May, making a very slow recovery from 10 May. He is still "very unwell when I left town [for Brighton 17 May], and had not the heart to go at my Number. I have gone since, however, and with such good will that the Number is very nearly gone too [23 May]" (L5:69). In Brighton "for a change" (L5:67), he produces the number in just seven or eight days, an extraordinary achievement (cf. his struggle to finish No.7, starting 10 March). After starting to write the opening ch.26 in black, he changes half way through to a bright blue ink. Presumably reserving his supply of bright blue for the manuscript (cf. his trial of the ink commented on in Ws.7, see 'LH preliminary' p.72), he changes back to black to plan both chs.27 and 28. Similar in hand, ink and quill, the plans for chs.27 and 28 seem to be prepared together. He then changes again to compose those chapters in bright blue (cf. the planning of ch.33 and 34 together in Ws.11, also followed later by a final chapter in bright blue). On 31 May, No.9 for June 1847 is published.

RH

Preliminary entries: **(4), (5), (11) & (18)**

In making these routine entries, Dickens appears to strain somewhat. He writes in a slightly larger hand, with less control than usual (see the wayward "ch" for the middle chapter, and the untypical ampersand in the novel's title—only found here and in the hurried part heading of Ws.8).

LH

Plan for the number: **(1); (2)→ch.27, (3)→ch.28**

Sure of the number's shape and content, Dickens gives himself three brief instructions. All three are concerned with events after the arrival of Carker. Progressive corrosion suggests that (2) is entered first, followed by (3) then (1). As in his preparation for the climax of the first quarter, the balance changes from number to chapter planning that is mainly concerned with the outcome of earlier plans.

RH

Plan for ch.26: **(7), (8), (9) & (10)**

Dickens leaves a gap for the title, entering four salient points in the usual black that cover the first half of the chapter: Carker has made the journey (7), the false Mrs Skewton and scheming Major conspire together (8), Carker closely watches Dombey's reactions (9), and Dombey seeks to get Carker's understanding without revealing himself (10). In composition the plan is reordered and Bagstock's part is enlarged to include his assessment of Edith and his rivalry with Carker for influence over Dombey.

MS

Composition of first half of ch.26 in black ink

Leaving the chapter untitled, Dickens begins in the middle of the introductions. He follows the order of his plan, except for the meeting of Bagstock with Mrs Skewton, held back for the long central section of the chapter, during which he breaks off to write in blue.

Composition of second half of ch.26 and its titling

While writing the second half of the chapter, he inserts the most teasingly oblique title thus far (the blue of the title confirms its late entry). The action follows Bagstock to his meeting with the "False mother" in the longest episode of the chapter, which dramatizes the duplicity of Bagstock and Mrs Skewton, an old acquaintance (one of the "shadows of the past"). On his way back to the hotel, he reflects on Edith's obvious reluctance (a "shadow of the future"). Dickens makes the competitiveness explicit between Bagstock and Carker, showing the latter to be the better game player. Making such a late start, as soon as the chapter is completed,

Dickens probably sends it at once to the printers to give more time to set up and run off proofs.

RH

Plan for ch.27: **(13), (14), (15), (16) & (17)**

Plan for ch.28: **(20)**

Both chapter plans are written in a similar hand with the same ink and quill. Both leave a similarly generous space for the chapter title, and, uneven in layout, have their final entry pressed up against a boundary (the next chapter number and page bottom respectively).

In ch.27, Dickens misplaces (13) and, instead of reordering, adds the emphasis of (14). Mrs Brown deepens the mystery (15). The courting couple become a picture themselves, as they view the sights (16). The "social history" (17), noted in Ws.7_2, leads to a closing tableau "Maid…like Death", the words separated so as not to overwrite the much extended top ligature of "III". He lays out and sizes the entries to show the order of events as he imagines it, assembling his ideas in a way typical of his planning method.

In ch.28, as he often does, Dickens leaves the opening material unplanned, concentrating instead on the approach to the end (Florence's return with Susan, their expectations, surprise and disorientation), and ending chapter (and number) with Edith's loving treatment of Florence, underlined for its future significance.

MS

Composition and titling of ch.27

Dickens resumes with blue ink and quill. The outing determines the shape of the day, its settings and characters (13). He uses the portrayal and viewpoint of Carker to carry the opening narrative (14). Good Mrs Brown's curses hint at what she knows of Carker's "deeper shadow"; she can also guess what is to come (15). The picture presented of Edith and Dombey, viewed from a distance by Bagstock, Carker and the mother, circumvents the difficulty of presenting directly the interaction of the unlikely couple (16). Throughout the day, any momentary contact between Carker and Edith is pregnant with their shared consciousness of the earlier meeting. As Dickens often does with backstories, he delivers Edith's history (17)—another "deeper shadow"—through dialogue, in the bitterly frank exchanges between mother and daughter that ends the chapter.

List: [8/9]

Still in blue, Dickens transfers headings for chs.24–27

MS

Composition and titling of ch.28[74]

Always aware, towards the end of a number, of the position of each chapter within his allowance of twenty-seven to twenty-eight manuscript pages, Dickens has leeway, beginning on manuscript p.21, to delay the "going home" for the printed equivalent of four and three-quarter pages out of the remaining seven and a half (383–89[419–25]). Once home, he focuses on Florence as he accelerates the narrative to its close. In the relationship between Florence and Edith, he dramatises the intensity of latter's "kindness" that will later strengthen Dombey's jealous resentment and lead to Edith's determination to protect Florence—understated, but implicit in the underlining of the final entry "Edith kind to Florence" (20).

RH

Titles of chs.26, 27 & 28: **(6), (12) & (19)**

Alignment, underlining and size of the rounded hand may be a reaction to the strain of composition, though Dickens often finds it difficult to write legibly "after convulsions of Dombey" (L5:59–60). Similarity suggests that all three titles are entered at the same time. Writing in black, with unusual slow deliberation, he spreads their entry to fill the space left for them, thus completing the record of the worksheet.

Proofs

Dickens returns to town for the day on 27 May to correct the proofs (none are extant). Differences between manuscript and text show that all chapters are only lightly corrected.[75]

Worksheet for No.10

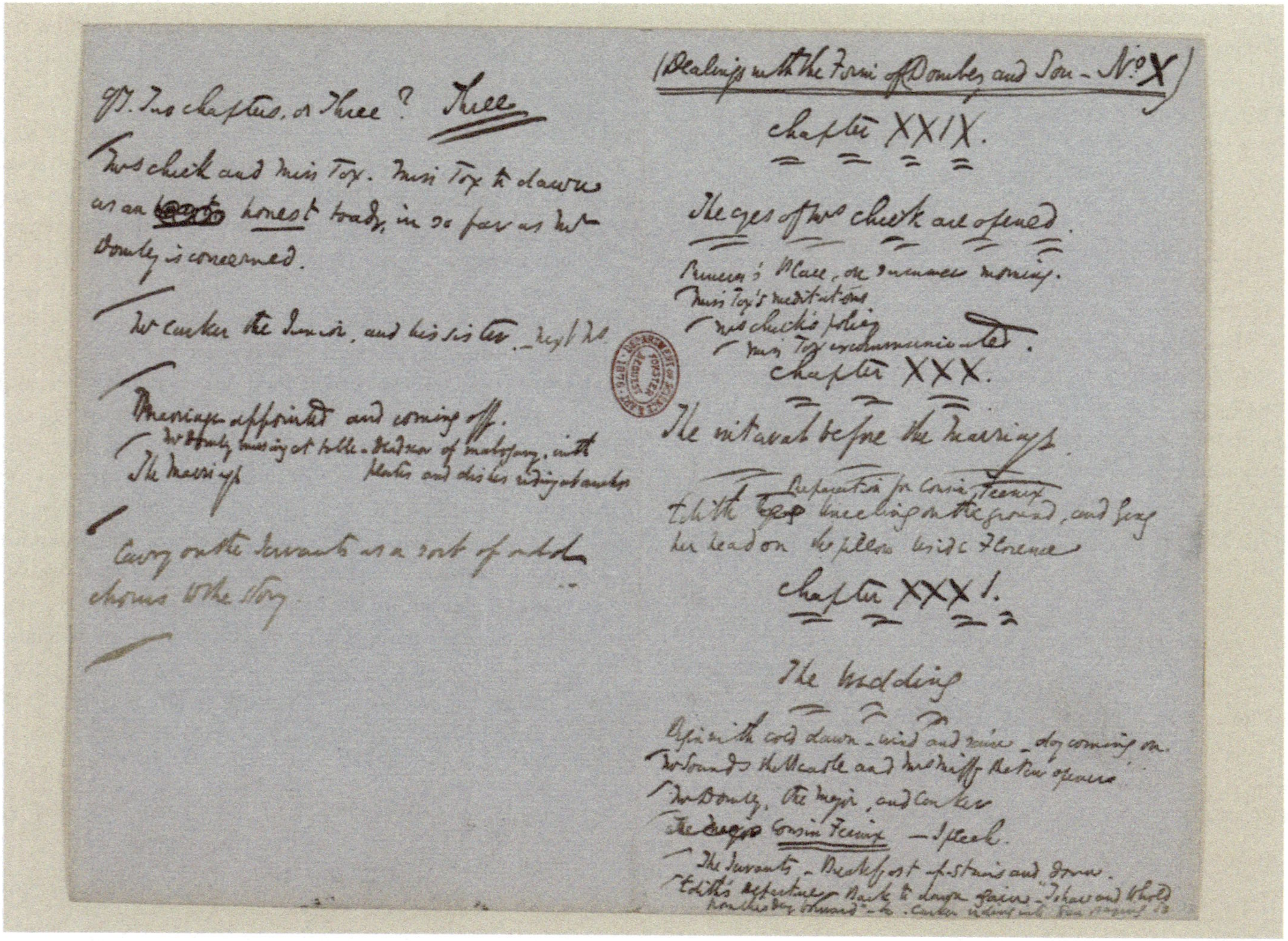
Qy. Two chapters, or Three? Three

Mrs Chick and Miss Tox. Miss Tox to dawn as an honest toady, in so far as Mr Dombey is concerned.

Mr Carker the Junior, and his sister. – Next No.

Marriage appointed and coming off.
The Marriage

Carry on the servants as a sort of odd chorus to the story.

(Dealings with the Firm of Dombey and Son – No. X)

chapter XXIX.

The eyes of Mrs Chick are opened.

Princess's Place, one summer morning.
Miss Tox's meditations
Mrs Chick's policy
Miss Tox excommunicated.

chapter XXX.

The interval before the marriage.

Preparation for Cousin Feenix
Edith kneeling on the ground, and laying her head on the pillow beside Florence

chapter XXXI.

The Wedding

Opening with cold dawn – wind and rain – day coming on.
Mr Sownds the Beadle and Mrs Miff the Pew opener
Mr Dombey, the Major, and Carker
Cousin Feenix – Speech.
The Servants – Breakfast up-stairs and down.

Image No.2012FE1497 (reduced): Forster Collection, National Art Library, Victoria and Albert Museum (2015).

Transcription of Ws.10

(1) q[y]. Two chapters, or Three ? Three

(2) M[rs] Chick and Miss Tox. Miss Tox to dawn as an ~~honest,~~ honest toady, in so far as M[r] Dombey is concerned.

(3) M[r] Carker the Junior, and his sister. – next No.

(4) ~~T~~(?)Marriage appointed and coming off.

(5) M[r] Dombey musing at table - Dead sea of mahogany, with plates and dishes riding at anchor

(6) The Marriage

(7) Carry on the Servants as a sort of odd chorus to the story.

(Dealings with the Firm of Dombey and Son – N[o:] X) (8)

Chapter XXIX. (9)

The eyes of M[rs] Chick are opened. (10)

Princess's Place, on summer morning. (11)

Miss Tox's meditations (12)

M[rs] Chick's policy (13)

Miss Tox excommunicated. (14)

Chapter XXX. (15)

The interval before the Marriage. (16)

Preparation for Cousin Feenix (17)

Edith ~~lying~~ kneeling on the ground, and lying her head on the pillow beside Florence (18)

Chapter XXXI. (19)[20]

The Wedding (21)

Begin with cold dawn - wind and rain - day coming on. (22)

M[r] Sownds the Beadle and Mrs Miff the Pew opener (23)

M[r] Dombey, the Major, and Carker (24)

~~The Major~~ Cousin Feenix — Speech. (25)

The Servants - Breakfast up-stairs and down. (26)

Edith's Departure – Back to dawn again - "To have and to hold from this day forward"- &c - Carker riding into town, saying so (27) (28)

Commentary and order of entry (Ws.10)

Dickens begins on 13 June and by the 21st has finished ch.30 and sent it to the printers. "Bidden tomorrow to the marriage of a friend of mine", he begins ch.31 the next day (L5:96). On the 24th he hopes to finish in time for a celebratory dinner, but is interrupted, and has "to sit down at my desk again, and give the finishing dig at Dombey in a vicious despair" (L5:98). The speed of his work confirms Forster's comment that "the interest and passion of the story, when both became centred in Florence and Edith Dombey, took stronger hold of him than any of his previous writings, except only the close of the *Old Curiosity Shop*" (*Life* 482[K:9462]).[76] On 30 June, No.10 for July 1847 is published.

RH

Preliminary headings: **(8), (9) & (19)**

Dickens positions the two chapter number headings so that twice the space is allocated to the first chapter, making the last chapter the shorter one (just as he may have done initially for Ws.7).

LH

Plan for the number: **(1); (2)→ch.29, (3)→(ch.33); (4) & (5)→ch.30; (6)→ ch.31**

Dickens considers the two-chapter arrangement, looking for the shorter closing chapter in (2) or (3). However, at entry (4), he may begin to write "T[he marriage(?)]", apparently stopping his hand, when on reflection, he realises that the marriage might fall easily into two, the wedding preparations (4) and the wedding itself (6). So he converts the opening down stroke of "T" to the first stroke of "Marriage" and finishes with "appointed and coming off". He adds the next entry "The Marriage", re-aligning it and emphasising the change with a slash between the two entries. The addition forms a new middle chapter. He decides to open with the shorter chapter and close with the wedding. Mrs Chick's cruel pretense of shock at Miss Tox's disappointed hopes (2) can then become a prelude to the marriage arrangements of the middle chapter. Miss Tox's dawning honesty promises further development.

Adding the insertion (5)—Dombey's "musings at [...] the dead sea of mahogany"—reveals the priority that this moment has in Dickens's creation of the new chapter; the reverie gives a rare insight into Dombey's deepest feelings towards Florence.

LH and RH

Outcome of (2)

With a full quill, he replies with an assured "Three" underlined twice.

Change to chapter number headings: **(15) & (20)**

Dickens converts the number heading of ch.30 to 31 (20) and inserts a number heading for the new ch.30. The change is revealed by the misalignment of the added 'I' and its underline; the 'I' may also cover the stop that initially followed "XXX" (see the facsimile of Ws.10 above, and cf. Ws.7 p.71).

MS

Composition and titling of ch.29

Dickens enters a title at the start, then during composition revises it for the first time (see 'Appendix D', ch.29 p.185).

RH

Title and summary of ch.29: **(10), (11), (12), (13) & (14)**

Dickens copies in the title with its first revision. In an orderly set of similar phrases, he enters a summary note for each section.

MS

Second revision to the title of ch.29

When Dickens provides Browne with the lettering of the first illustration "The eyes of Mrs Chick are opened to Lucretia Tox", he returns to the manuscript to revise the title for ch.29 a second time, presumably to avoid repeating the wording of the lettering. He does not copy to the worksheet, perhaps considering it not worth recording. The chapter goes at once to the printers.

RH

Plan for ch.30: **(18)**

Leaving a gap for the title, Dickens begins by entering the end plan, the text of the chapter's final tableau of Edith and Florence, revising it as he does so (18).

MS and RH

Composition and titling of ch.30: **(16)**

Dickens enters a title at the start of composition, later revises it, then copies the revision to the worksheet (see 'Appendix D', ch.30, p.186). He develops Edith's protectiveness of Florence, the satire of false feeling and aristocratic affectation in Mrs Skewton's preparations at Brooke Street and, through Dombey's reverie after dinner alone at the table, his apprehension and guilt over Florence (5).

RH

Memo: **(17)**

Dickens later inserts entry (17), overwriting slightly one of the title's underlines and defining it as a separate entry with a diagonal slash. The "preparation" refers to the paragraph on "Brooke-street, Grosvenor-square" ($410^{449–50}$). Already identified in ch.21 as Mrs Skewton's nephew, and Edith's cousin (286^{309}), Feenix is linked to the Brook Street house, being "one of the Feenix brood", in preparation for his role here as 'father' of the bride, and later as head of the family.[77]

Plan and titling of ch.31: **(21), (22), (23), (24), (25), (26), (27) & (28)**

The most inclusive through plan thus far covers one full day, dawn (22) to dawn (28). When Dickens re-allocates the wedding speech to Feenix, he enlarges his conception of the character as a ditherer in language as well as action (25). Another day brings the ritual of the wedding of another ill matched couple, and Carker's mockery of the marriage vows to "have and *hold*" [editor's italics], as he rides to the City (cf. chs.22 and 24).

MS

Composition and title of ch.31

Dickens draws together the first half of the novel using many retrospective references. All are present at the wedding that can be, including Good Mrs Brown (also given a small part in the very detailed illustration). Making the climatic finale the longest chapter is in contrast to most previous numbers; the notable exception is ch.22, which—like ch.31—began as the second chapter in a two-chapter experiment (for chapter length, see 'Appendix A', p.165).

List: [9/10]

Dickens transfers the headings for chs.28–31 to the List. He begins by giving the title of ch.29 to ch.28, forgetting the omission of "Alterations" in [8/9]. He corrects the error and completes the headings up to and including ch.31, marking the end of the first half.

LH

Outcome: (3)

The thread associated with John and Harriet, crucial to the plotting of the novel, is postponed again, this time to No.11 (cf. Ws.8_7 p.75).

Memo: **(7)**

Probably entering (3) and (7) at the same time—the corrosion of (3) matches that of (7)—he adds a note on using household servants as "a sort of odd chorus", a reminder to voice their reactions in the second half, as he did in the first half (cf. the other forward-looking lower left-hand memos in Ws.6_9 p.63, Ws.7_5 p.71 and Ws.8_{10} p.75). He finishes with a flourish, perhaps of exasperation (see opening biographical detail).

Proofs

Dickens is determined that the last two chapters of No.10, the climax of the first half of the novel, should start at the top of the page, without leaving empty spaces. In the proofs he instructs "Mr Jones" to begin chs.30 and 31 on a new page, and to delay both, if more text is needed for ch.30, to achieve the layout that he wanted. His instructions show his concern for page design, a dislike of gaps without function, and his commitment to giving readers what he feels is their due.

Worksheet for No.11

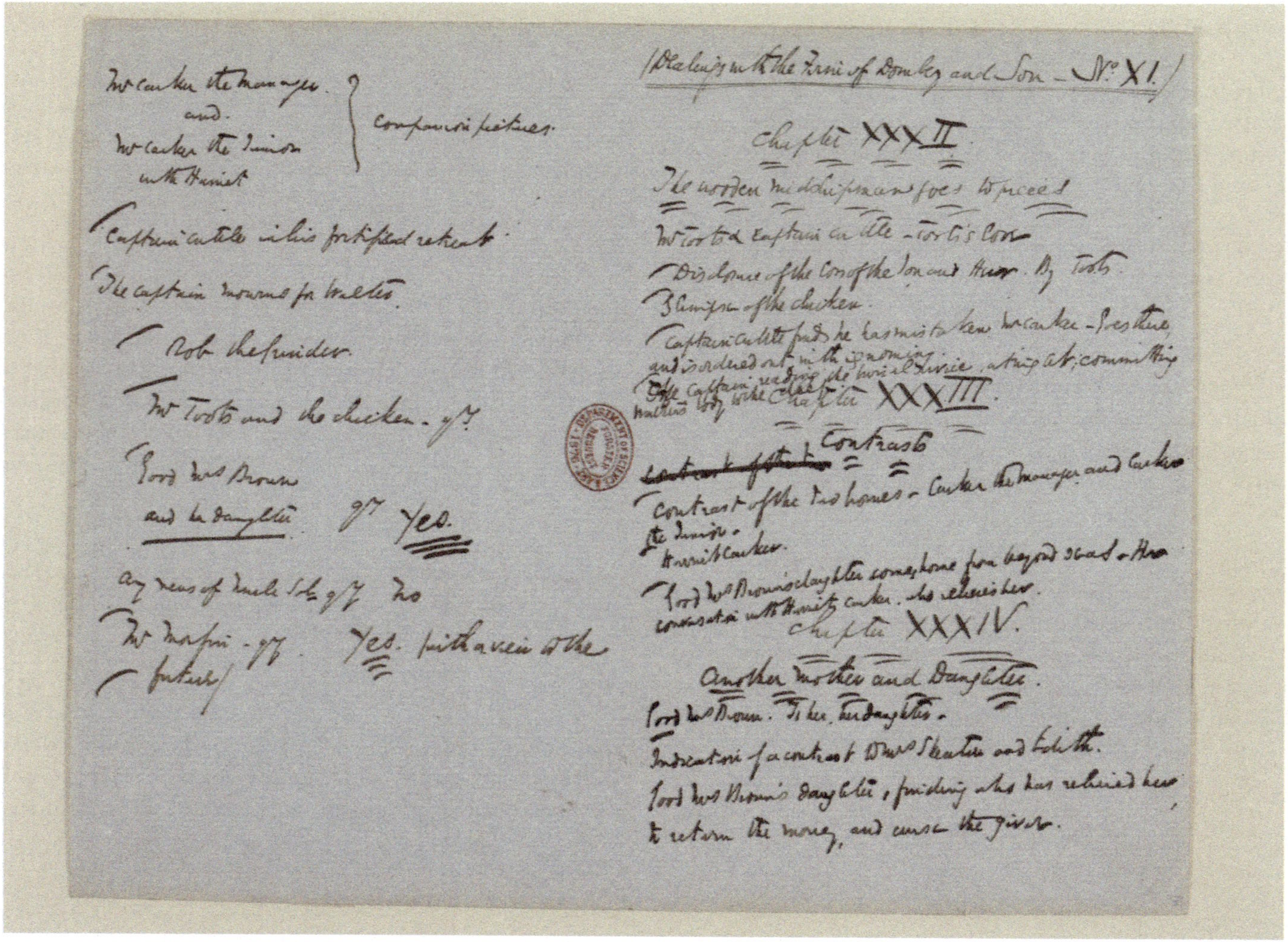

Image No.2012FE1501 (reduced): Forster Collection, National Art Library, Victoria and Albert Museum (2015). © Victoria and Albert Museum, London.

Transcription of Ws.11

(1) M[r] Carker the Manager.
and.
M[r] Carker the Junior
with Harriet — Companion pictures.

(2) Captain Cuttle in his fortified retreat.

(3) The Captain mourns for Walter.

(4) Rob the Grinder.

(5) M[r] Toots and the chicken - q[y].

(6) Good M[rs] Brown
and her daughter q[y] Yes.

(7) Any news of Uncle Sol_ q[y] No

(8) M[r] Morfin - q[y] Yes. (with a view to the
future)

(Dealings with the Firm of Dombey and Son – N[o:] XI.) (9)

Chapter XXXII. (10)

The Wooden Midshipman goes to pieces (11)

M[r]Toots & Captain Cuttle – Toots's love (12)

Disclosure of the loss of the Son and Heir. By Toots. (13)

Glimpse of the Chicken. (14)

Captain Cuttle finds he has mistaken M[r] Carker - Goes there
and is ordered out with ignominy. (15)
The Captain reading the Burial Service, at night, committing
Walter's body tothe deep. (16)

Chapter XXXIII. (17)

Contrasts (18)

~~Contrast of the two~~

Contrast of the two homes – Carker the Manager and Carker (19)
the Junior - (20)
Harriet Carker. (21)

Good M[rs]Brown's daughter comes home from beyond seas – Her
conversation with Harriet Carker, who relieves her. (22)

Chapter XXXIV. (23)

Another Mother and Daughter. (24)

Good M[rs] Brown. To her, her daughter - (25)

Indication of a contrast to M[rs] Skewton and Edith. (26)

Good M[rs] Brown's daughter, finding who has relieved her (27)
to return the money, and curse the giver.

Commentary and order of entry (Ws.11)

Most of Dickens's July letters are taken up with organising and rehearsing Ben Jonson's *Every Man in his Humour* and three farces, to be put on for charity by his largely amateur company of writers and artists, in Manchester on 26 July and in Liverpool on the 28th. The play has similarities in characterisation and plot to *Dombey* (see Schlicke 185–87).[78] Comparatively early, on 2 July, he begins working on the number, with its parallels, contrasts and intrigues "taming a spider or two […] weaving a small web of my own" (L5:96 and 111). He finishes shortly before going north with company (plus wives) on Sunday 25 July (first class, booked by him). On 31 July, No.11 for August 1847 is published.

RH

Preliminary headings: **(9), (10), (17) & (23)**

Dickens returns to his earlier entry routine (see Ws.2–6).

LH

Plan for the number:

(1)→ch.33; (2), (3), (4) & (5)→ch.32; (6)→ch.34; (7)→ch.32; (8)→ch.33

Most previous worksheets begin the number plan with a note that relates to the opening chapter of the number. Entry (1) is a notable exception. Relating to the middle chapter, it shows Dickens's interest, at this stage, in contrasting parallels, and in the portrayal of Carker. The two new settings are "companion pictures", a mockery of a pair of family portraits. The queries added to the last four entries (5)–(8) confirm that all are waiting a decision. The sifting process, evident midway through the previous quarter, occurs here and in the next five worksheets, because Dickens is now preparing not just for No.15 but also for the crises and revelations of the last quarter. He advances three of the four waiting intrigues, thus maintaining suspense in the Dombey and Edith storyline and increasing the reader's anticipation of their return.

RH

Plan for ch.32: **(<u>11</u>), (12), (13), (14), (15) & (16)**

The "Wally & Co" narrative has often, in the first half of the novel, taken up the final chapter position of each number. It appears there in Nos.1, 3, 6 and 8 (and in No.9 is displaced entirely by the main plot). In contrast, he now opens with Cuttle's hopes dashed by the news of Walter's loss at sea, followed by his humiliating encounter with Carker, juxtaposing grief and disappointment.

Uniformity of layout and hand in title and description suggest that they are entered at the same time. Yet the title in MS is apparently delayed. Perhaps, on this occasion, Dickens having entered the title in the worksheet has some reservations later about his choice.

He takes special care over the chapter. The number plan has more entries than usual concerned with a single chapter (see entries (2)–(5) in preparation for ch.32); the chapter description is also a lengthy plan. He blends the material of both number and chapter plans—a subtle process that incidentally confirms the planning intent of the description. The combination helps him achieve an extraordinary coherence, combining comedy, pathos, dramatic conflict and a muted close. Other indications of planning are: (1) he is unsure of the space the plan needs, hence the cramped final entries (2) he re-orders somewhat in composition; the glimpse of the Chicken comes earlier than the plan implies, and (3) he prepares for the closing text.

MS

Composition and titling of ch.32

Despite the title being given in the worksheet, Dickens leaves a narrow gap for the title, perhaps waiting to see how he might develop the metaphor in the text and improve on the worksheet allusion. He inserts the title during or after composition.

In a long carefully crafted chapter (thirteen MS pages), he opens with bad weather, deepening Cuttle's depression and foreshadowing Toots's news. He approaches his plan with exuberant comic invention—the recapitulation (the signal and spy-hole defence against Mrs MacStinger), the clash of the Game Chicken's sporting jargon, Toots's confusion of names and person—eventually modulating to Cuttle's history of Walter and Floy and Toots's news of the loss of Walter's ship. He relieves the intense pathos of Cuttle's elegy with Toots's response, the dramatic irony of the discovery of Carker's trickery, and Cuttle's own solemn consolatory enactment of an imaginary burial at sea.

RH

Plan for ch.33: **(19), (20), (21) & (22)**

Deletion, and re-entry further down, shows Dickens forgetting then remembering to leave sufficient space for the title (incidentally confirming that the description is entered before the title). He maximises the remaining space by tilting the entries. Harriet's meeting with Morfin is not mentioned, though it is implied by "with a view to the future" (8), a revealing entry that confirms Dickens is carefully preparing for the intrigue of Morfin and Harriet in the fourth quarter.

Plan for ch.34: **(25), (26) & (27)**

There is a marked similarity of hand and quill between this description and that of ch.33, which makes it likely, given the strong links between the two actions, that Dickens enters his outline plan for ch.34 at the same time as that of ch.33. The elided wording "to return" suggests intention and therefore planning, as does the re-ordering of "Indication of contrast" (see below). The gap that Dickens leaves for a delayed title entry now tends to be smaller than previously, a sign of his determination to leave more room for chapter planning.

MS

Composition of ch.33

Dickens writes in black ink, leaving a blank line for the title.

Composition and titling of ch.34 and titling of ch.33

Finding a limited supply of bright blue, he uses it to title and compose ch.34. At some point while using the ink, he turns back to MS p.12 to insert the title of ch.33. The "Indication of contrast" (26) is re-ordered and reshaped to end the number.

By closing with an earnest direct address that rhetorically questions Edith and her mother, and through them, the reader, Dickens encourages us to sustain his fictional world into the next instalment.

List: [11]

Using the same bright blue quill-and-ink as he employed in ch.34, Dickens transfers the headings for chs.32–34 to the list, misnumbering ch.34 as ch.24.

RH

Titles of chs.33 and 34: **(18) & (24)**

LH

Outcomes: (5), (6), (7) & (8)

Dickens returns to black ink to complete the record of the worksheet, entering the titles of chs.33 and 34 together, then moving to the left-hand half to reply to its queries. He answer the first two (5) and (6) with a heavy triply underlined "Yes", the next (7) with a "No" and the last (8) with a similar "Yes", the ink apparently thinning (and corroding), as he goes. The three replies show that Dickens is indeed "weaving a web of his own", establishing a preparatory link between Harriet and Alice, which like the link of Harriet and Morfin looks forward to the last quarter. Similarly, the negation of "Any news of Uncle Sol" (7) may suggest that he also anticipates the explanation of Sol's protracted silence and its neat tie-in with the MacStinger thread (762–63[844–45]).

Proofs

Dickens finds that he has calculated his length accurately. Apart from the only longer addition—the sentence on Rob's sou'wester (453[498])—his and Forster's changes add little to the overall wordage.

Worksheet for No.12

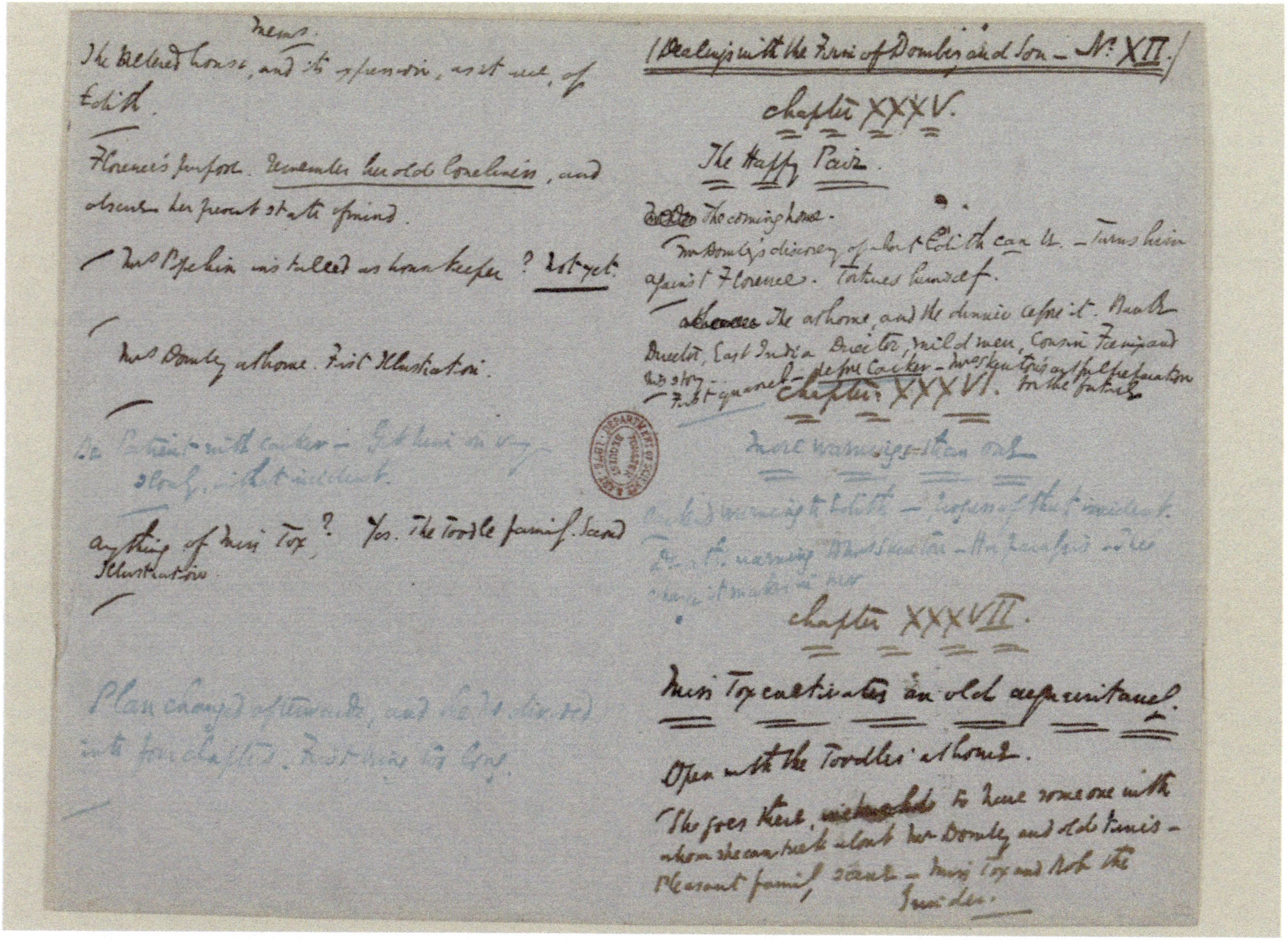

Image No.2012FE1502 (reduced): Forster Collection, National Art Library, Victoria and Albert Museum (2015). © Victoria and Albert Museum, London.

Transcription of Ws.12

(1) Mems.

(2) The ~~h~~altered house, and its expression, as it were, of Edith.

(3) Florence's purpose. Remember her old loneliness, and observe her present state of mind.

(4) Mrs Pipchin installed as housekeeper? Not yet.

(5) Mrs Dombey at home. First Illustration.

(6) Be Patient with Carker – Get him on very slowly, without incident.

(7) Anything of Miss Tox? Yes. The Toodle family. Second Illustration

(8) Plan changed afterwards, and the No divided into four chapters. First being too long.

(Dealings with the Firm of Dombey and Son – No: XII.) (9)

Chapter XXXV. (10)

The Happy Pair. (11)

~~Mr Do~~ The coming home. (12)

Mr Dombey's discovery of what Edith can be. – Turns him against Florence. Tortures himself. (13)

~~At home~~ The at home, and the dinner before it. Bank Director, East India Director, mild men, Cousin Feenix and his story – First quarrel – before Carker – Mrs Skewton's artful preparation for the future (14) (15)

Chapter XXXVI. (16)

More Warnings than one (17)

Carker's warning to Edith – progress of that incident. (18)

Death's warning to MrsSkewton - Her paralysis - The change it makes in her (19)

Chapter XXXVII. (20)

Miss Tox cultivates an old acquaintance. (21)

Open with the Toodles' at home. (22)

She goes there, ~~in her old~~ to have someone with whom she can talk about Mr Dombey and old times – Pleasant family scene – Miss Tox and Rob the Grinder. (23)

Commentary and order of entry (Ws.12)

Dickens was "still behindhand in my month's work" on 17 August, being "delayed by other business", settling bills and accounts of the July productions (L5:150 & 137). He feared that he might have lost "an important chapter", probably ch.36 (later 37), when his portmanteau fell off the cab on the way to his newly vacated house in Devonshire Terrace on 22 August. He rejoices "Thank God! the MS. of the chapter wasn't in it. Whenever I travel [...] I always carry it in my pocket" (*Life* 465$^{K:9727}$).[79] While in town 23–27 August, he corrects the second proofs of ch.35 and writes ch.38 (L5:151–53). On 31 August, No.12 for September 1847 is published.

RH

Routine headings: **(9), (10), (16) & (20)**

Progressive corrosion in the chapter number headings—with movement to the right—confirms that they are entered together.

LH

Preliminary: **(1)**

Initial plan for the number: **(2) & (3)→ch.35** (later 35 & 36); **(4); (5)→ch.35** (later 35 & 36)

Dickens looks forward and back. The more luxurious the house is, the more degraded Edith feels (2). He does the same for Florence, contrasting the earlier account in Nos.6 and 8, with her new hopefulness that Edith will help her secure her father's love (3). Having decided to keep Pipchin in the narrative, Dickens is waiting for the right moment to install her as housekeeper (4). The second half of entry (5) confirms the first subject for illustration, and is perhaps a reminder to give Browne early notice of such a visually busy occasion as the "at home". Dickens makes no note of the material of ch.36 (later 37) in the number plan, which suggests that he already has in mind how to develop the encounters between Edith and Carker; the relationship's progress is implicit in the later instruction to himself to "Be patient with Carker" (6). For much the same reason, he makes no mention of his intention for Mrs Skewton.

Additional plan: **(7)→ch.38**

At the start, Dickens had plans for the development of Miss Tox, which he later discarded (see '**Outcomes**' p.48). In ch.29, he retains her as "an honest toady" (Ws.10_2 p.83), later cooling her infatuation of Dombey to a "platonic" concern for his welfare. At this point, probably in anticipation of her supporting role in the fourth quarter, Dickens is looking to remind the reader of her story. Though uncertain at first of the means, he resurrects her relation with the Toodles (see (7) and cf. Ws.2_8 p.43), thus also keeping the family in the narrative. By economic re-use of characters and by complicating their narrative threads "weaving a small web of my own" (see Ws.11 p.88), Dickens draws attention to the continuing connection between different groups, strengthening the unity of the novel.

RH

Plan and titling of ch.35 (later 35 and 36): **(11), (12), (13), (14) & (15)**

Dickens is sure of the title, entering it at the start. The first deletion and correction (12) shows him deciding, on second thoughts, to include an opening link to the earlier number, always of concern but usually not planned for, though here included, perhaps on account of the gap created by the intervening No.11. Once more, the grouping of entries and the order of detail anticipate the narrative structure. Although Dickens notes the result of a key moment in the development of Dombey's inner conflict, the preceding 'handkerchief' scene is unmentioned. Like other disturbing scenes between father and daughter, it lives on so vividly in his imagination that it needs no annotation. Instead he notes its outcome (13). The second correction (14), heightens the drama; the failure of the celebratory dinner intensifying the hostilities of the 'at home' and what follows. He adds a note of the first quarrel, of Carker witnessing it—underlined for its significance and later use—and of the mother, who, by constructing a false version of it, attempts to absolve herself of any responsibility for it (15).

MS

Composition and title of ch.35 (later 35 and 36).

Composition and titling of 36 (later 37)

RH

Plan and titling of ch.37 (later 38): **(21), (22) & (23)**

Dickens postpones the summary of ch.36 (later 37)—written later in blue—and instead, still in black, works on the plan for ch.37 (later 38). One reason for doing so, as soon as he could, may be the necessity of sending Browne a second subject. He sees that it could serve as an instructive parallel to the first, another of the many contrasting pairs.

Similarity of hand and progressive corrosion indicate that all entries are made on the same occasion. Confident in his choice, he titles at once. "Open" suggests planning intent and the hesitation of "~~in her old~~" confirms it (22). The deletion shows that, on reflection, Dickens feels that Miss Tox would betray her good intentions, if she were to dress down for the occasion. The change makes her patronage appear less deliberate (23).

LH

Outcomes: (7) & (4)

Dickens confirms the visit to the Toodles and their family "at home" as the subject for the illustration, and postpones the installation of Pipchin as housekeeper (cf. Ws.13_3 p.95 and 14_2 p.99).

RH

Title and summary of ch.36 (later 37): **(17), (18) & (19)**

Hand and layout suggest title and summary are entered together. The two entries describe two "Warnings", each followed by a "progress". Dickens begins Carker's entrapment of Edith in (18) and in (19) uses the mother's illness to expose her guilt.

Proofs

Still in faint watery blue, Dickens divides the proofs of ch.35 "being too long" in two, creating ch.36 and titling it "Homecoming" (Horsman 1974, 'Introduction', pp.xlv and xlvi).

LH and RH

Comment: **(6)** and additional blue underline to (15)

Dickens, using the gap left between (5) and (7), inserts the reminder to slow his progress (6) and repeats the underlines to (15) to emphasise the importance of Carker witnessing the clash. These entries suggest that Dickens, projecting the stages of the couple's break-up, may already be looking towards a crisis in No.15 to end the third quarter.

MS

Composition and title of ch.38 (numbered correctly)

Dickens continues to use faint blue, perhaps a degree more watery than before. In composition, he re-orders the plan, tying in the subplot to his theme—Rob's 'charity' education trains him to deceive. He retitles to reflect his expansion of what is planned (see 'Appendix D', ch.38, p.186). He revises his initial plan (22), opening instead with Miss Tox and her motives. He also enlarges the drama beyond a "pleasant family scene", with the family's and Miss Tox's reactions to Rob's deceit.

LH

Comment: **(8)**

Leaving all number headings as they are, Dickens simply notes the division of ch.35 "the first being too long". The faint blue entries begin with the proofreading of ch.35 and finish with entry (8), beneath which a final watery blue slash marks the worksheet's end. Consecutive uses of a faint blue ink suggest that for some reason, Dickens is obliged to use a poor ink. Arriving at his recently vacated Devonshire terrace house on August 22, he seems to have sufficient black ink to finish ch.36 (later 37) but then, with only a few days left to plan and compose ch.38, he uses a faint watery blue. Perhaps this ink was left behind by his tenant.[80]

MS

Correction to the number heading of ch.36 (later 37)

Dickens alters the heading of ch.36 to 37 by adding a "I" in black ink. Perhaps he is at the printers, delivering chs.36 and 38, when he made the change.

List: [12]

In black, Dickens enters number headings for chs.35–38, titles chs.35 and 36 from his memory of proofing but, overlooking the revision he made in the manuscript (perhaps not yet returned from the printers), enters the worksheet title for ch.38.

Worksheet for No.13

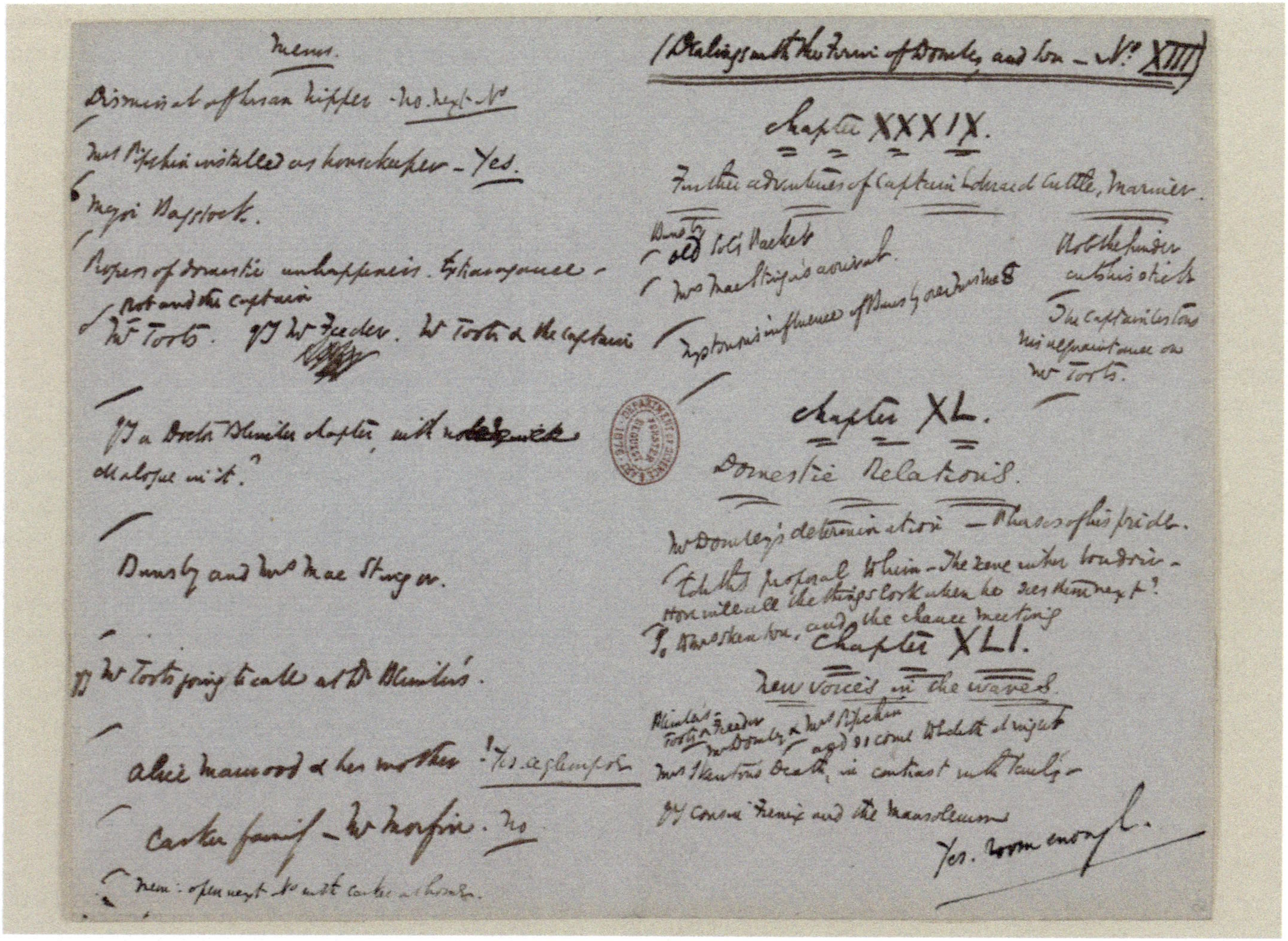

Image No.2012FE1507 (reduced): Forster Collection, National Art Library, Victoria and Albert Museum (2015). © Victoria and Albert Museum, London.

Transcription of Ws.13

(1) Mems.

(2) Dismissal of Susan Nipper - No. Next N°

(3) Mrs Pipchin installed as housekeeper – Yes.

(4) Major Bagstock.

(5) Progress of domestic unhappiness. Extravagance –

(6) Rob and the Captain

(7) (8) Mr Toots. q^y Mr Feeder. Mr Toots & the Captain ~~(No)~~

(9) q^y a Doctor Blimber chapter with no~~body in it~~ dialogue in it?

(10) Bunsby and Mrs Mac Stinger.

(11) q^y Mr Toots going to call at Dr Blimber's.

(12) Alice Marwood & her mother? Yes. a glimpse

(13) Carker family – Mr Morfin. No.

(14) Mem: open next N° with Carker at home.

(Dealings with the Firm of Dombey and Son – N°: XIII) (15)

Chapter XXXIX. (16)

Further Adventures of Captain Edward Cuttle, Mariner. (17)

Bunsby old Sol's Packet (18)

Mrs MacStinger's arrival. (19)

Mysterious influence of Bunsby over M^rs Mc S (20)

The Captain bestows his acquaintance on Mr Toots. (21)

Rob the Grinder cuts his stick (22) (23)

Chapter XL. (24)

Domestic Relations. (25)

Mr Dombey's determination – Phases of his pride. (26)

Edith's proposal to him – The scene in her boudoir - (27)

How will all the things look when he sees them next?

So to Mrs Skewton, and the chance meeting (28)

Chapter XLI. (29)

New Voices in the Waves. (30)

Blimber's – Toots ^Feeder (31)

Mr Dombey & Mrs Pipchin and so come to Edith at night (32) (33)

Mrs Skewton's Death, in contrast with Paul's – (34)

q^y Cousin Feenix and the Mausoleum (35)

Yes. Room enough. (36)

Commentary and order of entry (Ws.13)

Dickens writes the number, despite the street noise, during the final month of his regular annual summer stay in Broadstairs. On 12 September, *Dombey* becomes "very importunate". He is hard at work on the 19th. He hesitates to commit to the year's Christmas story "The Haunted Man","Dombey takes so much time, and requires to be so carefully done, that I really have serious doubts whether it is wise to go on with the Christmas book" (*Life* 466[K:9743]). On 30 September, No.13 for October 1847 is published.

RH

Preliminary headings: **(15), (16), (24) & (29)**

Dickens enters the part title and the chapter number headings—all penned with a free flowing quill or heavier hand than elsewhere.

LH

Preliminary: **(1)**

Initial plan for the number: **(2), (3), (4) & (5)→ch.40**

Dickens begins with four possibilities for the main storyline, heading them "Mems" (perhaps entering them here before the usual preliminaries). The four entries are identifiable as a group by similarity of hand and quill and by its corrosion. Judging from the resulting text, they can be expanded as follows. Dickens is concerned to isolate Florence ready for No.15. He arranges for Pipchin's re-employment as a slight to Edith's position (3), *before* Susan confronts Dombey (2). He wants to keep Bagstock (4) in the story, now his part as marriage arranger is over (cf. "Anything of Miss Tox" Ws.12₇ p.91), and plans the next stage of the failing marriage (5).

Additional number plan: **(6), (7) and (8)→ch.39; (9)→ch.41; (9) and (10)→ch.39; (11)→ch.41,**

With a hand distinct from the initial entries, Dickens decides to develop "Mr Toots" (7), hesitating between a meeting with Feeder or with Cuttle (8)—two storylines that will eventually separate to form the basis of ch.39 and ch.41.

Firstly, he adds Feeder—perhaps playing with the notion of avoiding dialogue at Blimbers (9)—then, negating the Feeder connection, links Toots to Cuttle (8), and finally, in the insertion (6) with a small slash beneath "Rob", links Rob to Cuttle. The thread will lead on to Bunsby and MacStinger (10).

Secondly, planning to take Toots back to the school (11), he re-instates the Feeder connection by deleting the negation in (8).

Further number plan: **(12)→ch.40; (13)**

In a distinctively larger hand, Dickens adds two further items before he begins composition. He considers an appearance for Alice and her mother, which he later contrives during ch.40 (12). Finally, he enters (13)—the connection of Morfin to Carker's brother and sister—not as a query but as a statement, a reminder that he needs to prepare for the thread that will foreshadow the Firm's failure and ensure Dombey's livelihood after his ruin.

RH

Plan for ch.39: **(18), (19), (20), (21), (22) & (23)**

Layout shows Dickens assembling a chapter plan with the number plan, and adding to it. Leaving a gap for the title, he anchors the narrative with two incidents, the opening of the packet (19), and the arrival of MacStinger (20). The Bunsby insertion (18) made in connection with (19) leads to the "mystery" of her submission (21); what her submission conceals is revealed in ch.50. He prefaces the incidents with two additions—both beginning to corrode—Rob's preparation for leaving (22) and Cuttle's consent to befriend Toots (23).

MS and RH

Composition and titling of ch.39: **(17)**

The title, inserted in the manuscript during composition, is copied to the gap left for it in the worksheet.

RH

Plan for ch.40: **(26), (27) & (28)**

Leaving a gap for a title, Dickens plans for three sections: Dombey's state of mind that leads to the decision to subdue Edith (26); Edith's proposal in response, his rejection of it, and his intuited sense of an impending change, as he looks back on the opulent disorder of her bedroom (27); and lastly, the departure of Mrs Skewton (with Edith Florence) for Brighton and the apparently coincidental encounter on the Downs (28). The "So to" of (28) warns of a transition that needs careful management (skilfully done, it is more than "a glimpse" (550–54[606–10])).

MS, RH and LH

Composition and titling of ch.40: **(25)**

Dickens titles at the start and copies the title to Ws. He adds Bagstock (4) to the departure scene with the explanation "he had come to take his leave of the ladies" (see (4) and 547[603]). As with Miss Tox (Ws.12$_7$), he reminds the reader of the Major's existence, drawing him into the story at this point in preparation for his later role.

Outcome: (3)

He completes the left-hand item (3) with a bold "Yes", Dombey having announced his intention to employ Mrs Pipchin, in connection with Carker's various 'services' (see 542[598] and cf. 578[638]).

RH

Plan for ch.41: **(31), (32), (33), (34) & (35)**

Layout reveals a planning procedure comparable to that of ch.39. Leaving a gap for the title, Dickens enters the episode of Mrs Skewton's death with its query as to the involvement of Feenix (34) and (35). Then he assembles—always preserving the title gap—a list of the names of those characters involved in two scenes prior to the death: the plan for Toots's visit to his old school (31) and a scene between Dombey and Mrs Pipchin (32), which later redundant is set aside.[81] The directive "and so come to" (33) warns him of another difficult transition, from the Toots reunion (or the dropped Pipchin scene) to Edith's final words to her dying mother (see paragraph beginning "Mr. Toots", where Dickens uses the "waves" as a bridge passage (559–60[617])).

List: [13]

Dickens transfers the headings for chs.39 and 40 and the number heading for ch.41, probably before starting ch.41, and certainly before he titles it.

MS and RH

Composition and titling of ch.41: **(30)**

A false start and its revision show Dickens working on a title suggestive of the contrasting parallel to Paul's death ('Appendix E' p.189) . He squeezes the final version into the gap left for it in worksheet. Assisted by the Brighton setting and Toots's visit to Blimbers (11)—joined by Florence and Diogenes—he once more finds pathos in retrospection. He does not attempt to avoid all dialogue at Blimber's but certainly restrains it (9). With about one manuscript page in hand, having omitted (32), he has space for the burial arrangements.

LH and RH

Outcomes: (2), (12) & (13)

In the same smallhand, the replies are probably made together. Entry (2) postpones Susan's dismissal to No.14; (12) confirms the "glimpse" in ch.40; (13) notes the intention to link Morfin to Harriet and John; (9) and (11) are answered in the plan and text of ch.41.

Memo: (14)

Dickens gives himself a reminder of the start of the next number.

Outcome: (35)

Entry (36) confirms the bleak ending with an irony and a final Shakespearian flourish.[82] With thirty-six separate entries, Ws.13 is the most elaborate of the single worksheets. More than the midway sheets of the first two quarters, e.g. in Ws.3 or Ws.8, the left-hand half is crowded with potential business and the right-hand with detailed plans. Florence though present in chs.40 and 41 is not mentioned in the worksheet (cf. Ws.11).

Worksheet for No.14

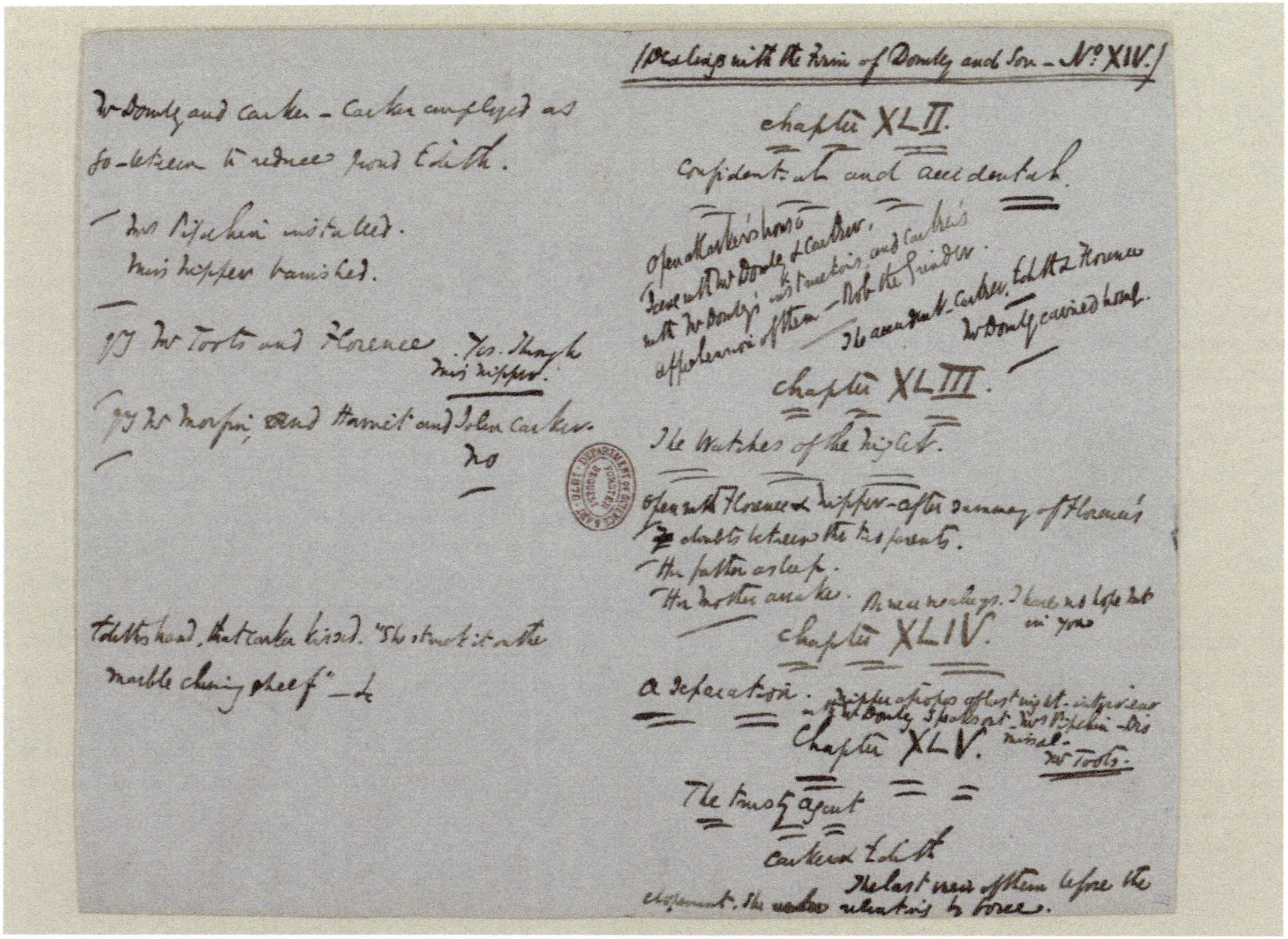

Image No.2012FE1503 (reduced): Forster Collection, National Art Library, Victoria and Albert Museum (2015). © Victoria and Albert Museum, London.

Transcription of Ws.14

(1) Mr Dombey and Carker – Carker employed as go-between to reduce proud Edith .

(2) Mrs Pipchin installed .

Miss Nipper banished .

(3) qy Mr Toots and Florence . Yes . Through Miss Nipper.

(4) qy Mr Morfin, and Harriet and John Carker .

No

(5) Edith's hand, that Carker kissed. "She struck it on the marble chimney shelf" – &c

(Dealings with the Firm of Dombey and Son - No: XIV.) (6)

Chapter XLII. (7)

Confidential and accidental . (8)

Open at Carker's house (9)

Scene with Mr Dombey &Carker , (10)

with Mr Dombey's instructions and Carker's apprehension of them – Rob the Grinder . (11) (12)

The accident - Carker, Edith & Florence

MrDombeycarried home.

Chapter XLIII . (13)

The Watches of the Night . (14)

Open with Florence & Nipper – after summary of Florence's (15)

~~F~~ doubts between the parents . (16)

Her father asleep . (17)

Her Mother awake. (18)

Be near me always. I have no hope but in you (19)

Chapter XLIV. (20)

A Separation . (21)

Nipper à propos of last night - interview with Mr Dombey Speaks out - Mrs Pipchin - Dismissal - (22)

Mr Toots.

Chapter XLV. (23)

The trusty Agent (24)

Carker & Edith (25)

The last view of them before the elopement. She ~~relen~~ relenting by force . (26)

Commentary and order of entry (Ws.14)

The family returns at last to Devonshire Terrace on 1 October. "In harness" (L5:220) to Dombey from the second week until the 24th—a feasible deadline with the printing offices only an hour away—Dickens finds the number, concerned entirely with the main plot, both challenging and absorbing. He is unable to promise even a couple of hours to a close friend, compelled as he is to give it uninterrupted attention. On 15 October he writes "so late am I [...] I cannot spare those two hours" (L5:174). He postpones the Christmas story, a sure sign of his commitment to *Dombey* (L5:175). On 31 October, No.14 for November 1847 is published.

RH

Preliminary headings: **(6), (7), (13) & (20)**

Dickens enters the part heading and three chapter number headings with their underlines. The chapter number headings are progressively corroded, confirming that they are entered together.

LH

Plan for the number: **(1)→ch.42; (2)→ch.43; (3) & (4)**

In entry (1) Dickens lines up Dombey and Carker; one works round to his go-between proposal while the other schemes. In entry (2) he meets his timetable for Pipchin and Nipper (cf. Ws.$13_{2\ \&\ 3}$ p.95). He plans to have Pipchin established as housekeeper in time for the drama of Susan's confrontation with Dombey. The involvement of Toots will end his hope of Florence but also prepare for his role as messenger in recalling Susan (3). Finally in (4), the note for Morfin to meet Harriet is repeated, reflecting Dickens's determination to include the meeting, well in advance of the denouement. He writes that he is "forced to creep carefully over the ground I am laying for the No. after this one" (L5:174). As in the penultimate number of the second quarter, he is concerned with main plot and its climax in the next number.

RH

Plan for ch.42: **(9), (10), (11) & (12)**

Dickens slopes the line to avoid the title gap above and the heading below. The directive "Open" (9) shows his planning intent. Group (10) summarises Dombey's purpose and Carker's reaction. The last item "Rob the Grinder" is probably a reminder to detail Rob's promotion to livery, which becomes a topic of conversation to Carker's advantage. Dombey's injury and treatment (11) and (12) gives Carker access to Florence and Edith, and many opportunities later to get to Edith alone.

MS & RH

Composition and titling of ch.42: **(8)**

Dickens inserts the title into the manuscript during composition and copies it to the worksheet. He re-orders the final item of (10), bringing Rob into the opening recapitulation. In conversations with Edith, Carker plays on what is unspoken. When he brushes her hand with his lips, her reaction shows that she knows its meaning. Despite revulsion, she dwells on it for the opportunity it may give ($578–79^{638–39}$).

LH

Memo: **(5)**

Dickens copies in the text of Edith's decisive moment of self-harm. He signals its special significance by isolating it in the bottom half of the left-hand page (cf. Cuttle's watch (Ws.6_9 p.63) and the servant chorus (Ws.10_7 p.83)). He does have other uses for the space, e.g. a last minute chapter plan (Ws.7_6 p.71), a checklist of potential business (Ws.8_{10} p.75), a memo on how to open the next number (Ws.13_{14} p.95), and two retrospective self-justifications (Ws.12_8 p.91 and 15_6 p.103). In the fourth quarter, except for curtain call of Ws.19&20, the lower left-hand is not needed.

RH

Plan for ch.43: **(15), (16), (17), (18) & (19)**

After "Open […] Nipper" Dickens writes "F", perhaps intending "Florence's doubts between the parents" as the next entry. Then deleting "F" he adds "– after […] parents.", thus re-ordering his initial plan, (16) now preceding (15). The change shows his concern to keep plans in the order of the narrative as he imagines it (cf. Ws.12$_{12 \& 14}$ p.91). His focus on Florence continues in (17) and (18), noting her visit to Dombey's room, then to Edith's. He plans to close on Edith's plea (19), alluded to in the cancelled ending of ch.45 (see 'Proofs' below).

List: [13/14]

Dickens transfers the title for ch.41, the headings for ch.42, and the number heading of ch.43 probably before he starts writing ch.43, and certainly before he titles it.

MS and RH

Composition and titling of ch.43 (leading to the creation of ch.44): **(14)**

Dickens revises the title of ch.43 during composition, copying the final version to Ws.14. He follows the salient points of the plan, but goes beyond it when he develops Susan's reactions to Florence's mistreatment. At the planned endpoint (19), Dickens writes on into the second day. However, before he is far into Susan's story, by cutting and pasting what he has just written, he creates a new chapter, inserting number and title of ch.44 at the top of MS p.17. It ends with Susan dashing Toots's hopes of Florence, from the night-coach, on the way to her brother's farm. The final scene echoes other farewells, furthers Toots's attachment to Susan, and prepares for her return.

MS

Composition and titling of ch.45

The title is entered at the start. Dickens winds back the narrative to Edith's preparations for her visit (595[654]), then on to later that evening. By angrily making Carker's duplicity explicit, she becomes allied with him against Dombey, calling attention to her helplessness by absent-mindedly pulling feathers from her fan. Overwhelmed by the threat to Florence, she consents to a second kiss—on the hand she had so deliberately punished—and to further visits.

RH

Chapter number, title and summary for ch.45: **(23), (24), (25) & (26)**

Similarity of hand and quill suggest that number, title and description are entered together. The summary is unusually short, even for a final chapter, consisting of subject and explanation of why Edith gives way, ~~relen~~ relenting by force", together with the comment "The last view….". Dickens creates a deliberate narrative gap, partly to delay revealing Edith's motives until the "tremendous" final scene, partly to leave other meetings to the reader's imagination.

Title and summary of ch.44: **(21) & (22)**

Dickens copies in the title (21) under the number heading for ch.44 and adds its short but inclusive summary (22). For reasons why ch.45's entries come before those of ch.44, see endnote 83. He enlarges slightly his lettering of "Toots" and ends with a celebratory double underline.[84]

List: [14]

Dickens transfers the title of ch.43 and the headings for chs.44 and 45. His entries completing the record for Nos.14 and 15 are more frequent than any others, reflecting his involvement in the crises (see p.178).

Proofs

Overrunning by a third of a page, the last three paragraphs are cut by Forster. For the cut, see endnote 85, or Horsman 1974, p.605 n.1, or the end of ch.45 in ebook 821.[86] By alluding to her earlier pleas, the final "I have no hope left" emphasises Edith's isolation and her earlier "black fore-shadowings" (579[638] and 587[647]). To Carker's perception of the "graces of her face and form" in ch.42 (577[636]), Dickens adds in ch.45 her vulnerability, "pluck[ing] off the feathers [of her fan]" and later "lay[ing the soft trembling] plumage of the beautiful bird against her bosom" (600[662]). While Edith lies sleepless on her bed, Carker lies in his, "musing […] with a dainty pleasure" on her enticing strength and weakness—the reader's last view of them before they elope.[87]

Worksheet for No.15

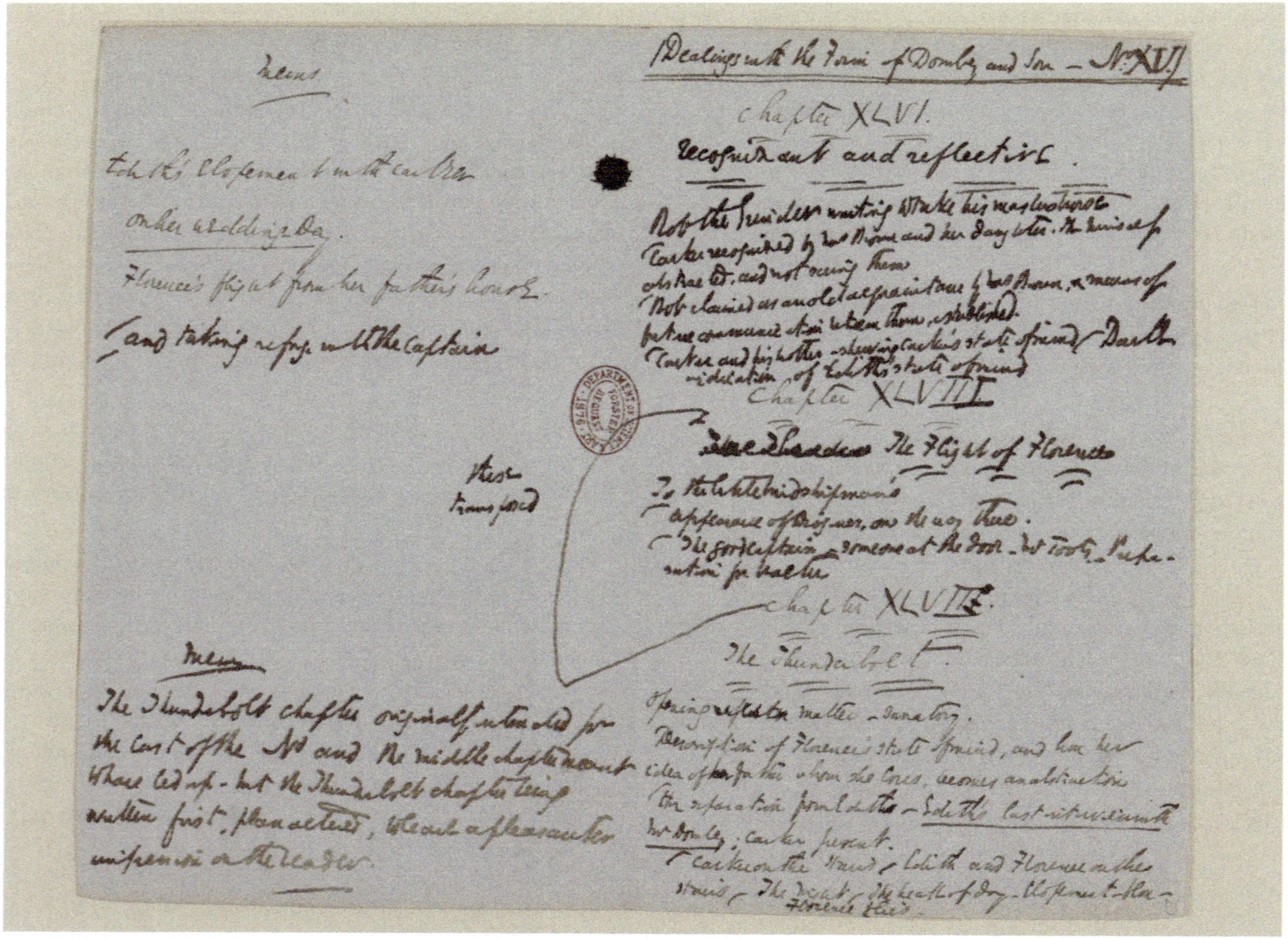

Image No.2012FE1487 (reduced): Forster Collection, National Art Library, Victoria and Albert Museum (2015). © Victoria and Albert Museum, London.

Transcription of Ws.15

(1) Mems.

(2) Edith's elopement with Carker

On her wedding-Day .

Florence's flight from her father's house.

(3) and taking refuge with the Captain

(4) these transposed

(5) Mem

(6) The Thunderbolt chapter originally intended for the last of the N° and the middle chapter meant to have led up – but the Thunderbolt chapter being written first , plan altered , to leave a pleasanter impression on the reader .

(Dealings with the Firm of Dombey and Son – N°: XV.) (7)

Chapter XLVI. (8)

Recognizant and reflective . (9)

Rob the Grinder waiting to take his mastershorse (10)
Carker recognized by M[rs] Brown and her daughter. He himself abstracted, and not seeing them (11)
Rob claimed as an old acquaintance by M[rs] Brown, & means of future communication between them, established. (12)
Carker and his brother –shewing Carker's state of mind / Dark indication of Edith's state of mind (13) (14)

Chapter XLVIII. (15) (16)

~~The Thunder~~ The Flight of Florence (17) (18)

To the little Midshipman's (19)
Appearance of Diogenes, on the way there . (20)
The good Captain - someone at the door - M[r] Toots - Preparation for Walter (21)

Chapter XLVII~~I~~ . (22) (23)

The Thunderbolt . (24)

Opening ~~reflection~~ matter – sanatory . (25)

Description of Florence's state of mind , and how her idea of her father whom she loves , becomes an abstraction (26)
Her separation from Edith – Edith's last interview with M[r] Dombey ; Carker present . (27)
Carker on the stairs / Edith and Florence on the stairs / The Night / The break of day - Elopement -blow – Florence flies . (28) (29) (30) (31)

Commentary and order of entry (Ws.15)

Busy with his commitment to the opening and running of Urania Cottage, Dickens probably again begins late, working first on ch.48 (later 47).[88] He writes on 18 November of "some terrible circumstances taking place in Mr Dombey's family" (L5:197). On the 19th, he intends "to make the first two chapters as light as I can" (*Life* 483[K:9481]). On the 23rd, he is still "in the whirlwind of finishing a No with a Crisis in it" (L5:200). On 30 November, No.15 for December 1847 is published.

RH

Preliminary headings: **(7), (8), (15) & (22)**

Part heading (7), corroding and in a different hand, may have been entered with that of Ws.14. In contrast, the chapter numbers for chs.41–43 are entered with a distinctive thin line—as usual moving right, as he goes down the page.

LH

Preliminary: **(1)**

Initial plan for the number: **(2)→ch.48** (later 47)

In the same fine hand as (1), (8), (15) (22), Dickens sums up the crisis of the main storyline.

RH

Plan for ch.48 (later 47): **(24), (25), (26), (27), (28), (29), (30) & (31)**

Dickens continues to use the same thin line for all entries (see above). Title and plan, uniform in hand and layout, are entered together. He hesitates over how to describe the planned digression and substitutes "matter" for "reflections" (25), implying that the digression is to be more fact than opinion. In (26), he traces the alteration in Florence's feelings for her father and in (27), notes Edith's distancing herself from Florence—the two ideas central to the narrative prior to the dinner and Edith's final interview with Dombey in Carker's presence. Lastly, he delineates four moments in the accelerating action: Carker's secretive departure on the first night (28), Florence's meeting with Edith on the stairs (29), the second anxious night (30) then, at daybreak, Dombey's discovery of the elopement, his violence, and Florence's rush into the streets (31). There are no positive indications of planning, apart from the corrected deletion. However, noting sequences appears to be an aid to narrating successive transitions, like the movements of Cuttle in ch.60. The parallel with the planning of ch.31 in the degree and amount of detail suggests that it too is a plan. Initially intended as an important closing climax, it is also carefully through-planned.

MS and Ws.6a

Composition and titling of ch.48 (later 47)

Florence's age

Either before composition or soon after the digression on man and nature, Dickens breaks off to calculate Florence's age when Edith elopes (see Ws.6a p.67). The title is entered as he begins ch.48 (later 47), early in the narrative incorporating details of the timeline (see in Ws.6a, p.69). A long chapter, completed late, it goes at once to the printers, but, because it is not the opening chapter, he does not number its pages. The compositor pencils in the temporary MS page numbers (one to fourteen).

List: [15a]

Dickens enters number headings only for chs.46 and 47, and gives the number heading and title of ch.48 (later 47), thus establishing that "The Thunderbolt" is written first (before both chs.46 and 47) and initially intended to be the last—all entered with the same fine line as the worksheet entries so far p.178.[89]

LH

Additional plan: **(3)→ch.47** (later 48)

Dickens changes to a quill with a broader heavier line. The contrast of the two quills supports the view that he writes the "Thunderbolt" chapter before ch.46 (see 'Comment' below).

MS and RH: (9)

Composition and titling of ch.46

Dickens inserts the title during composition, and transfers it later to the worksheet.

RH

Summary of ch.46: **(10), (11), (12), (13) & (14)**

Dickens outlines the main events that prepare for the denouement (10), (11) and (12). The theatrical "recognition" is by Alice, who is seeing Carker for the first time since her transportation, whereas her mother has watched him on many other occasions. The final two entries record the angry exchange with John, which clarifies Carker's true feelings (13) and reveal more of Edith's motives with hints of her intentions (14), the latter added partly at Forster's suggestion, to offset cuts made to No.14 (see 'Proofs' in Ws.14, p.101). Edith is to give herself to Carker, then commit suicide (*Life* 484[K:9485] and 410[449], 617[682]).[90]

MS

Composition and titling of ch.48

On reflection, Dickens decides to rearrange the order of the chapters. He numbers and titles ch.48 correctly. When manuscript of ch.47 (still numbered 48) is returned to him, the pages are lightly numbered in pencil '1' to '14' to preserve their sequence. Dickens can use the numbering (with that of ch.46, which finishes on p.8) to begin ch.48 on what would be the next page p.23. As usual, he paces his text as it approaches the end of the instalment.[91]

RH (and LH)

Summary of ch.48 (initially numbered ch.47): **(4)**, (16), **(17)**, **(18)**, **(19)**, **(20)**, **(21)**, (23)

Dickens's first thought, as shown in (17), is leave the chapter number as 47 and title the chapter "The Thunder[bolt]", retitle the chapter below, and mark only the descriptions for transposition. Midway through the title, he takes a shorter route. He deletes "The Thunder[bolt]", enters "The Flight of Florence" and its description, and marks the whole for transposition (4), adding Roman 'I' to ch.47 (16) and deleting 'I' from ch.48 (23).

The summary notes three contrasting events. "To the little Midshipman's" repeats Florence's first frightening experience of the city (19), with Diogenes (instead of Walter) taking the role of protector and lessening her fear of its dangers (20). Entry (21) notes the confusion of events that both mocks Cuttle's playful attempt at mystery and prepares for the recognition of Walter—a 'weak' final curtain replacing the 'strong' one that was initially intended in ch.48 (later 47).

List: [15b]

Dickens corrects the title of ch.48, and enters the titles of chs.46 and 47, completing the unusually broken-up record for Ws.14 and 15 (see comment in 'Appendix C' p.178).

LH

Comment: **(5) & (6)**

The repetition of "Mem" (5)—see (1) above—shows some concern to set the record straight. Dickens explains that he wrote "The Thunderbolt" first of three, intending to make it the last chapter (and end with a strong final curtain) and that a middle chapter (not in fact written) would lead up to it. Instead "The Thunderbolt" chapter becomes the middle chapter, and he writes a "lighter" final chapter "to leave a pleasanter impression on the reader".[92] Like other final entries, entry (6) has a diminishing ink supply and progressive corrosion, and finishes with a flourish.

Worksheet for No.16

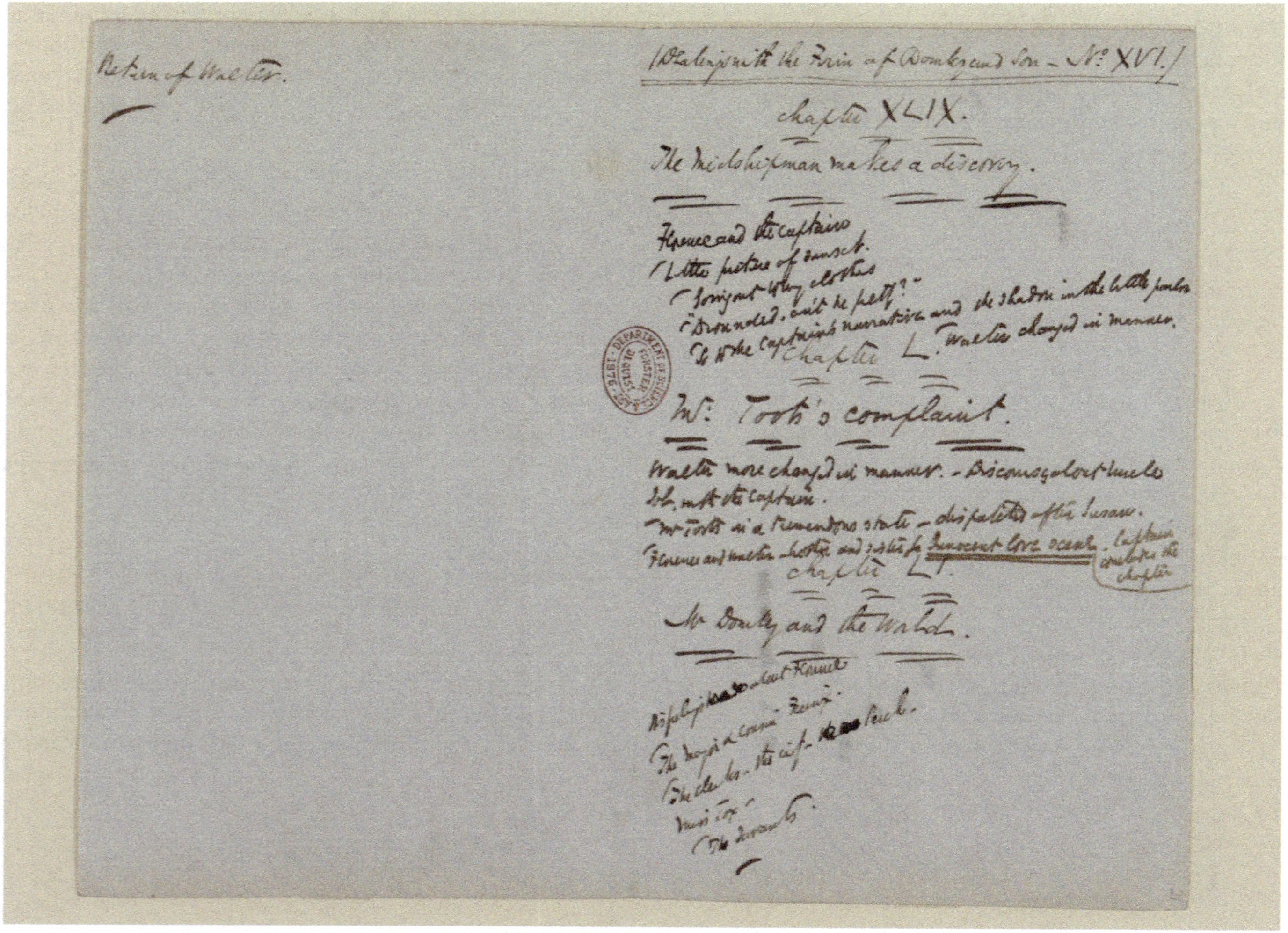

Return of Walter.

(Dealings with the Firm of Dombey and Son — No. XVI.)

chapter XLIX.

The Midshipman makes a discovery.

Florence and the Captain

chapter L.

Mr. Toots's complaint.

Walter more changed in manner.

Mr Toots in a tremendous state

Innocent love scene.

chapter LI.

Mr Dombey and the World.

Transcription of Ws.16

(1) Return of Walter .

(Dealings with the Firm of Dombey and Son – N$^{o:}$XVI.) (2)

Chapter XLIX . (3)

The Midshipman makes a discovery . (4)

Florence and the Captain (5)

Little picture of sunset. (6)

Going out to buy clothes (7)

"Drownded , an't he pretty?" (8)

So to the Captain's narrative and the shadow in the little parlor (9)

Walter changed in manner. (10)

Chapter L. (11)

M^{r}: Toots 's Complaint . (12)

Walter more changed in manner. - Discourses about Uncle Sol, with the Captain . (13)

Mr Toots in a tremendous state – dispatched after Susan . (14)

Florence and Walter - brother and sister&c Innocent love scene - Captain concludes the chapter (15)

Chapter LI. (16)

Mr Dombey and the World . (17)

His feelings ~~towards~~ about Florence (18)

The Major & Cousin Feenix . (19)

The clerks - the city - ~~the ser~~[?] Perch - (20)

Miss Tox -

The Servants . (21)

Commentary and order of entry (Ws.16)

On 10 December, Dickens is "pursuing Dombey under difficulties […] in a state of imbecility [suffering from winter flu]" (L5:207). By the 21st he is a few pages from the end of ch.50 (MS p.22), writing the "innocent love scene [that] ought to be one of the prettiest things in the book" (*Life* 483[K:9484]). He has only a day or so left for the final chapter: "Tomorrow [the 23rd] I shall be forced to imprison myself the whole day long, finishing Dombey" (L5:212). On 31 December, No.16 for January 1848 is published.

RH

Preliminary headings: **(2), (3), (11) & (16)**

LH

Plan for the number: **(1)→ch.49**

Dickens evidently feels that number planning is not needed to unravel the few entanglements of the romance plot. From now on, the remaining number plans are brief and not added to, except in the final double number.

RH

Plan for ch.49: **(5), (6), (7), (8), (9) & (10)**

Contrast of hand and layout between plan and title suggests that Dickens leaves a gap for the title to be added later. The plan lists six salient points in narrative order. The first, more general, introduces the over-arching relationship between the nurturing Captain and the abused and rejected Florence (5). The next two, (6) and (7), are leading episodes that aid her recovery, preliminary to the creation of a home. In entry (8), the protective Cuttle, in his childlike way, seeks to soften the shock of Walter's return. "So to" (9) indicates a narrative turning point that may need preparation as a story within a story. With some authorial self-mockery, Dickens relates how Cuttle tells the story and into it, Walter appears. Entry (10) notes the start of a change in Walter's feelings for Florence.

MS and RH

Composition and titling of ch.49: **(4)**

A false start in the manuscript shows that Dickens unsure of a title leaves a narrow blank line and inserts the title later, just as he does if unsure of a title, when planning a chapter ('Appendix E' p.190). Delay gives him an opportunity to reflect on what might be appropriate for the chapter, as he writes it. He eventually devises a teasing title in keeping with the chapter's light tone, probably added to MS and worksheet after he has finished it, but certainly before he updates the List.

RH

Plan for ch.50: **(13), (14) & (15)**

Dickens leaves a gap for the title. The differences of alignment suggest that the plan is compiled in three stages. Entries (13)–(15) lose density towards the end of each line, while tilted entries (14) and (15) are each progressively corroded—suggesting re-dipping and separate entry. In entry (13), he notes the change in Walter that effectively hinders the resolution of the romance. His "discourse", a longwinded contribution to the Sol plot, is partly an avoidance of what preoccupies him (other distractions will be added in composition). Entry (14) leads to the reunion of Susan and Florence, prepared for by the involvement of Toots in their separation. In (15) three items map the close: the sibling pretence—the first of a number of misunderstandings to be cleared away—the doubly underlined item "an innocent love scene", and lastly and most corroded, the celebration of Cuttle the nurturing protector, whose presence and authority (now usually referred to as the Captain) make the relationship proper.

MS and RH: (12)

Composition and titling of ch.50

Dickens enters a title and later revises it, copying the final version to the worksheet. Like that of ch.49, the final title is more oblique and less descriptive ('Appendix D' p.187). The plan is much extended by various two-handed dialogues, and by the presentation of Florence, who—isolated, unhappy and unwell—takes the lead in sorting out the lovers' misunderstandings during "the little love of Florence and Walter", of which Dickens was rather proud (L5:223). He needs to resolve the romance plot quickly, in order to leave sufficient real and narrated time for her child to be born after the marriage, and for the Firm to fail before her reconciliation with the ruined Dombey.

List: [16]

Dickens copies in the number heading and title for ch.49. Making the entries for ch.50, he misremembers the title, then corrects it. Finally, he enters the number heading for ch.51.

RH

Plan and titling of ch.51: **(17), (18), (19), (20) & (21)**

Entry (18) is shaped to avoid the broken underlines of the title that is entered at the start. The first correction "~~towards~~ about" shows Dickens emphasising Dombey's attempt to distance himself from his daughter to avoid thinking about her (cf. 682[754]). The second correction "the ~~ser~~(vants?) Perch" shows him planning to re-position the servant chorus to the end of the chapter. In composition, reactions to the elopement are added to and re-ordered further (see below).

MS

Composition of ch.51

Dickens transfers the title from the worksheet (see above). By way of an introduction to what he has planned, he begins with a family visit from Mrs Chick. Dombey reveals his attitude to Florence in his rebuff to her enquiry after her niece (18). Despite hiding "the world within from the world without", Dombey accepts the representations of Bagstock and Feenix; they speak for polite society (19). Dickens adjusts the plan further by re-ordering the responses in (20). He begins with the comment of the "true", the loyal Miss Tox, in conversation with her former teacher Pipchin, goes on to the response of the clerks and of Perch, and ends as planned with the servant "chorus" (687–89[760-63]).

Proofs

Writing on to MS p.28 for just half a dozen lines, Dickens appears to have calculated his allowance precisely. The only deletion, near the end of ch.51, is a telling piece of 'low' mimicry, which he may have deleted not wishing to gratuitously offend his more genteel readers.[93]

His terse comment to Forster on the first of the two plates that came with the proofs, "Shadow plate, poor" (*Life* 483[K:9484]), shows his resignation to being occasionally let down by what he considered clumsy or inaccurate illustration. Compare this with his reaction to Browne's illustrations for No.2 that "made his legs curl up" and to the first plate for No.3 that was "frightfully and wildly wide of the mark" (*Life* 478[K:9375 & 83]).

Worksheet for No.17

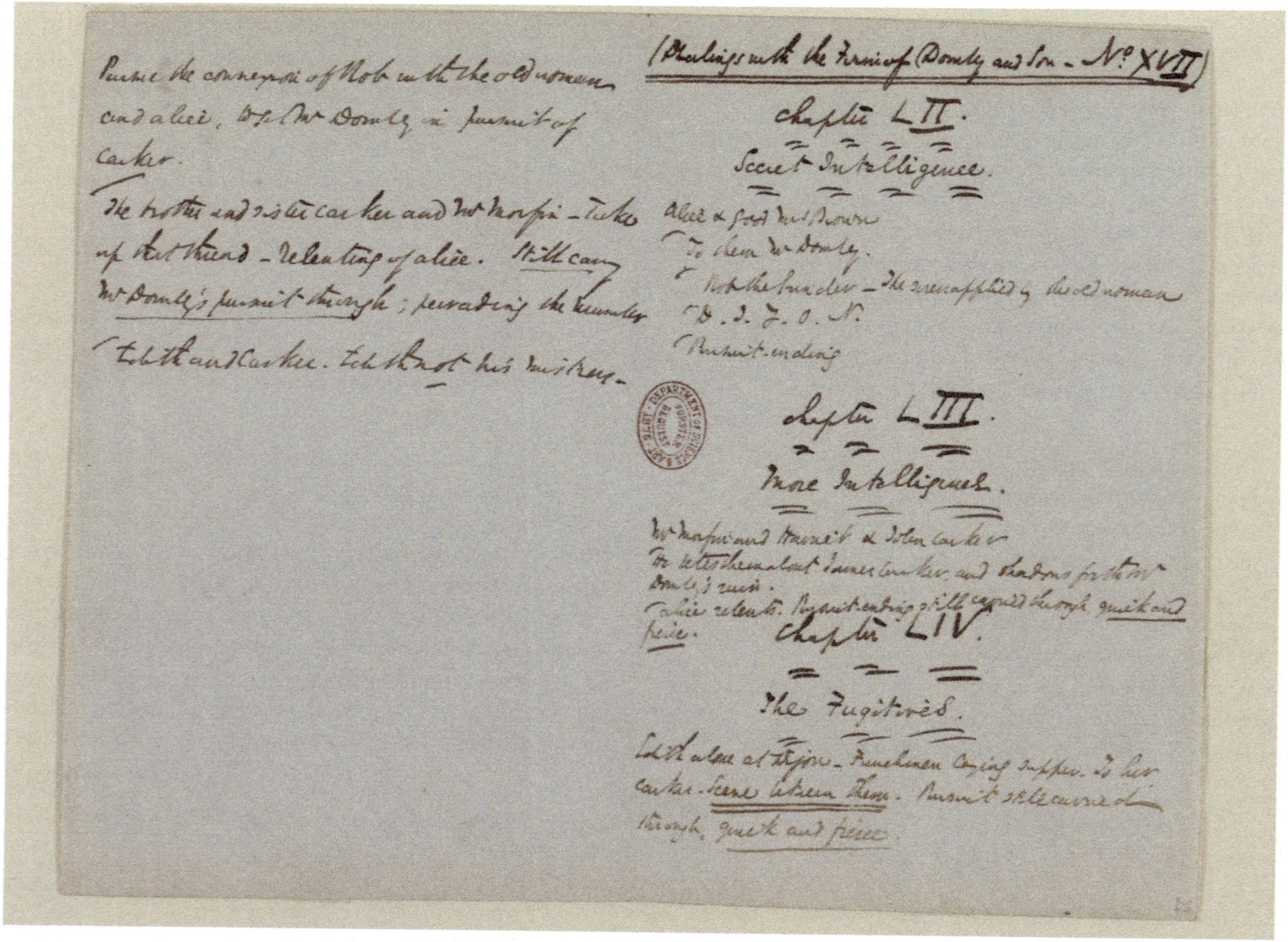
Pursue the connexion of Rob with the old woman and Alice. Use Mr Dombey in pursuit of Carker.

The brother and sister Carker and Mr Morfin – Take up that thread – relenting of Alice. Still carry Mr Dombey's pursuit through; pervading the number

Edith and Carker. Edith not his mistress –

(Dealings with the Firm of Dombey and Son – No. XVII)

Chapter LII.

Secret Intelligence.

Alice & good Mrs Brown
To clear Mr Dombey.
Rob the Grinder – His news applied by the old woman
D. I. J. O. N.
Pursuit-ending

chapter LIII.

More Intelligence.

Mr Morfin and Harriet & John Carker
Do letters them about James Carker, and shadows forth Mr Dombey's ruin.
Alice relents. Pursuit-ending still carried through quick and fierce.

Chapter LIV.

The Fugitives.

Edith alone at Dijon – Frenchmen laying supper. To her Carker – Scene between them. Pursuit still carried on through, quick and fierce.

Transcription of Ws.17

(1) Pursue the connexion of Rob with the old woman and Alice, to get Mr Dombey in pursuit of Carker.

(2) The brother and sister Carker and Mr Morfin – Take up that thread – Relenting of Alice. Still carrying Mr Dombey's pursuit through ; pervading the number

(3) Edith and Carker. Edith not his mistress –

(Dealings with the Firm of Dombey and Son - No: XVII) (4)

Chapter LII. (5)

Secret Intelligence. (6)

Alice & Good Mrs Brown (7)

To them Mr Dombey. (8)

Rob the Grinder – The screw applied by the old woman (9)

D. I. J. O. N. (10)

Pursuit-ending (11)

Chapter LIII. (12)

More Intelligence. (13)

Mr Morfin and Harriet & John Carker (14)

He tells them about James Carker, and shadows forth Mr Dombey's ruin. (15)

Alice relents. Pursuit-ending still carried through, quick and fierce (16)

Chapter LIV. (17)

The Fugitives. (18)

Edith alone at Dijon – Frenchmen laying supper. To her Carker. Scene between them. Pursuit still carried through, quick and fierce. (19)

Commentary and order of entry (Ws.17)

Dickens's monthly pattern of commitment to the "relentless savage" continues. He tries to begin No.17 on 10 January, "Sniffing, and wheezing, and hating myself"..[with a cold].."a second Edition of my former one, and the most ridiculously intense" (L5:229 and cf. Ws.16 p.108). He finishes on the 24th, the day he usually keeps clear of engagements, expecting to "revise them [the proofs] at the printers [...] before five or six or seven o'Clock this evening" (L5:237–39). On 31 January, No.17 for February 1848 is published.

RH

Preliminary headings: **(4), (5), (12) & (17)**

Dickens enters the part heading and the chapter number headings with a consistently heavy stroke. Similarity of hand suggests that he may enter the remaining part headings at the same time, as well as $Ws.18_{2\,\&\,5}$ and $Ws.19\&20_2$ (see pp.115 and 119).

LH

Plan for the number: **(1)→ch.52; (2)→ch.53; (3)→ch.54**

Dickens's style of notation changes. He writes evenly across the whole page, without hesitation. Entries correspond closely to each chapter. Entry (1) advances the intrigue prepared for in ch.46 of No.15, where the pursuit is primed by Dombey's "intelligence of a singular kind", an incident described later by Mrs Brown (686^{759} and $691–2^{764}$). In (2) the "thread" has at least three strands: Harriet and John, Harriet and Morfin, and Harriet and Alice. Dickens develops all three storylines, moving on from Harriet's first meeting with Morfin in ch.33 ($Ws.11_8$ p.87). In (3) he finally decides, on reading Jeffrey's reaction to No.15 that Edith, while shaming Dombey by appearing to become Carker's mistress, should refuse to be so, which in Forster's opinion makes for a "more bitter humiliation for her destroyer" (*Life* $483^{K:9482}$).[94]

MS

Composition and titling of ch.52

Dickens enters the title as he begins composition, the "singular intelligence" of ch.51 (686^{759}) becoming "secret intelligence". He employs the common method of pursuit narratives, in which a clue from the past gives impetus to future action. The pace of narration is slowed by dialogue. Rob's basic ability to read and write, so useful in the service of Carker, is now used against him. Rob pieces together the fragments of Carker's note that names the town where Edith is to meet him, which he now spells out in Dombey's hearing.

RH

Summary and title for ch.52: **(<u>6</u>), (7), (8), (9), (10) & (11)**

Writing with a fine hand and an ink liable to corrosion, Dickens explains how Dombey gets what is needed to begin the chase; he enters the title and names of those involved in the scene, giving its purpose, the order of events, method of interrogation and its outcome.

MS

Composition and titling of ch.53

Dickens inserts a title during composition, and later revises it. Winding back the narrative to early morning of the previous chapter, he lingers over Perch's delivery of Dombey's letter of dismissal and John and Harriet's reaction to it, in preparation for the next visitor.

John Carker introduces Morfin to Harriet, unawares uncovering the name of their benefactor, in the manner of a theatrical discovery. Morfin manoeuvres so that he can confide some of his own history to Harriet alone, forewarning her of James' deceptions and the threat they pose to the Firm.

Some evenings later, Harriet's reverie of Carker's ghost foreshadows his death. Another face at the window announces the final visitor Alice, who by telling her story explains her actions and the reason for her visit. Dickens is preparing for the final twist in the Alice thread to be given dramatically, as part of the ongoing relation of Harriet and Alice (see Ws.19&20, ch.58, p.121).[95]

RH

Summary and title for ch.53: **(13), 14), (15) & (16)**

Dickens enters the title. From a chapter full of incident and information, he selects the names of the principal actors (14) and a few salient points, laying bare "the management of the manager" (his running heading, in the 1867 edition, for the page that reveals James's wrongdoings). Harriet becomes involved in the life of the repentant Alice. Her change of heart, though it comes too late to affect the outcome, adds to the urgency of the chase (16).

MS and RH

Composition and titling of ch.54

Dickens enters the title, briefly sets the scene, and then slows the action with the waiters' business. The confrontation is visualised as theatre, a "tremendous scene" (*Life* 484[K:9486]), employing the codes of melodrama that he knows so well—the arrested tableaux, large gestures, emotive speech, explanations of past mysteries and sudden action. A libidinous Carker, clinging to the fantasy of delicious "Sicilian" days, hesitates while the imperious Edith taunts him with her "good account". She explains her actions, and clarifies her motives to him, and to the reader. A violent outcome is circumvented by the concurrence of the ringing bell, Dombey's voice amid the hubbub, and Edith's exit—pointedly prepared for earlier in the chapter—followed by Carker's hurried escape.

RH

Summary and title of ch.54: **(18) & (19)**

In this passage, the corrosion is more marked. After the first item, the ink begins to thin, causing the progressive corrosion of the title and summary that follows. The order of entry is confirmed by similarity of hand and alignment. Although the chapter is almost as long as the previous one, the summary is laid out as a paragraph with stops, instead of a list with slashes—Dickens's alternative method for a final, usually shorter, description. Like a stage manager's order of business, the summary enumerates the reveal, the waiters' preparation, the next entry, the scene, and the continuing pursuit. Omitting any details of the climax, Dickens simply double underlines, for its importance, the "Scene between them" (19).

List: [16/17/18]

Changing his previous practice somewhat, he leaves updating the List until he can give ch.51 its title and complete all the headings for the No.17, and the number heading of the first chapter of the next number, the last single number. He is gradually catching up with the manuscript, so that he can complete the record up to the double number.

Proofs

The proofs of the number are lost. However, differences between the manuscript and the published part show the probable extent of the corrections. In ch.54, Dickens takes special care over Edith's speeches, making many minor improvements.

The only longer deletion reveals how clearly she understands Carker's ploys to get power over her. The deletion—worth retaining, though Dickens may have thought it too blunt an explanation—comes in the paragraph beginning "I can" and after "Hear it":

'You—being the villain I have spoken of—approached me, first with your entreaties for permission to remain one minute; then, with your condolences and protestations; then with your regrets that I was destined to be a curse upon the head of my adopted daughter' (Horsman 1974 notes, p.727 n.1; not in ebook 821).

Worksheet for No.18

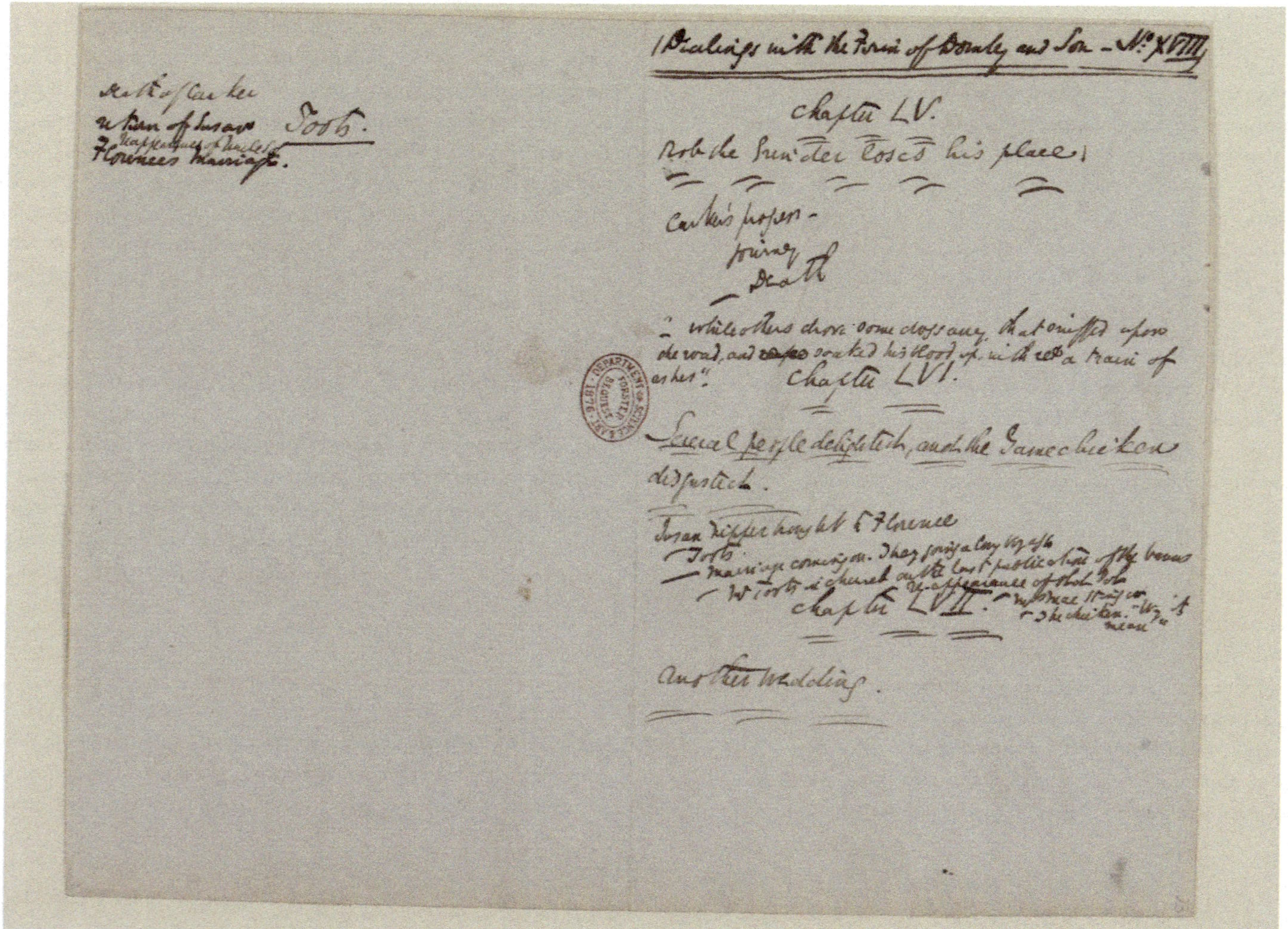

Image No.2012FE1492 (reduced): Forster Collection, National Art Library, Victoria and Albert Museum (2015). © Victoria and Albert Museum, London.

Transcription of Ws.18

(1) Death of Carker

(2) (3) **return of Susan** Toots .

(4) Reappearance of Uncle Sol

(5) **Florence's Marriage.**

(Dealings with the Firm of Dombey and Son - N°: XVIII) (6)

Chapter LV. (7)

Rob the Grinder loses his place . (8)

Carker's progress – (9)

journey

Death

"– while others drove some dogs away that sniffed upon the road, and ~~sup~~(?)soaked his blood up, with ~~it~~ a train of ashes". (10)

Chapter LVI. (11)

Several people delighted, and the Game chicken disgusted . (12)

Susan Nipper brought to Florence (13)

Toots . (14)

Marriage coming on. They going a long Voyage (15)

Mr Toots in church on the last publication of the banns (16)

re-appearance of Old Sol (17)

Mrs Mac Stinger (18)

The chicken. "Wy its mean" (19)

Chapter LVII . (20)

Another Wedding . (21)

Commentary and order of entry (Ws.18)

On 17 February, Dickens is "deep in No.18". On the 24th he excuses himself to a close friend that he "shall be very busy finishing Dombey, in a few days." So once again, what Dickens called "that most fraudulent month" February—despite the advantage of a leap year—helps create a difficulty (see L1:510 and cf. Ws.6 p.64). Though he does not underwrite the number, as he did in 1847, he does overrun his usual deadline, which probably means his attendance in the office to correct proofs as they become available. By happy accident, the last two chapters (MS pp.9–28) would have been comparatively easy to set up—having more dialogue and cleaner copy, with fewer long corrections—compared to the opening ch.55—descriptive of Carker's sensations as he flees overwhelmed by irrational fear and panic—which was probably set up and proofed separately earlier in the month. On 29 February, No.18 for March 1848 is published.

LH and RH

Initial number plan: **(2)→ch.56; (5)→ch.57**

Preliminary headings: **(6), (7), (11) & (20)**

The part heading (6) and the two events central to the number (2) and (5) were probably already entered (see "preliminary headings" p.112). Dickens now adds the chapter number headings (7), (11) and (20).

LH

Additional number plan: **(1)→ch.55; (3) & (4)→ch.56**

Contrasts of hand and layout shows how Dickens brings together materials for the number, assembling them in the following order: (2) and (5)—entered earlier—then (1), (3) and (4). He places "return of Susan" at the heart of the number, and, at the same time, positions "Florence's Marriage" at the end. The death of Carker is then entered in a smaller, lighter hand, but still carefully aligned with the other two.

Dickens had very probably already decided to relieve the suspense ending of the No.17 with an immediate return to Carker's desperate journey and death. Always alert to readers' responses, he was gratified to overhear of discussions of what might follow ch.54 and "hugged myself in private" (L5:249).

He adds "Toots" to the right of the summary list, and finally inserts the "Reappearance of Uncle Sol", moving the "Sol" downwards to avoid overwriting the start of Toots' entry. In adding character and incident to the page, Dickens is also visually laying out the order of the chapters and the narrative. The underlining of the enlarged lettering of "Toots" denotes as usual emphasis and recurrence. Toots has still to work through his feelings for Florence, before he can discover his attachment to Susan (hinted at in chs.22 and 44).

RH

Titling and end plan for ch.55: **(8) & (10)**

Deletion with correction suggest that Dickens begins, as earlier, by devising the wording of a closing text and positioning it as close as possible to the heading beneath. Always preserving the title gap, he may then add (9) a "mem" of Carker's "progress", how he travels and how his feelings change. Finally, happy in the choice of a deliberately misleading title, Dickens enters it, tight against the underlines above, with its underlines midway between the title and "Carker's progress".

MS

Composition and title of ch.55

Dickens transfers the title from the worksheet during composition. The journey is in two stages, by horse and carriage at night in France, and by train in England the next day. Carker struggles to come to terms with exposure and disappointment, "progressing" from guilt, fear, and panic to finally an irrational fascination at the violent power of the passing trains. At the finish, after a brief but graphic account of the dismemberment of Carker's body by the train—a shocking moment in a gruesome death—Dickens vivifies the closing text by embedding it in Dombey's viewpoint.

RH

Plan for ch.56: **(13), (14), (15), (16), (17), (18) & (19)**

Dickens enters seven groups, writing on a slant to avoid the title gap above and number heading beneath. He identifies, in narrative order, an action and/or character in each group. Planning intent is shown by the number of entries, the cramped entry towards the end, and the closing text—comparable to the crowded outline plans of the double number.

MS

Composition and titling of ch.56:

Layout and underlining in the manuscript suggests that the title of ch.56 is entered during or after composition. Dickens writes fluently, with less revision than usual. Toots is threaded through most of the chapter. He comes to terms with disappointment in love, accepts that Florence is "married to the man she loves and who loves her" and begins to voice his appreciation of Susan. All of the "little society" are crowded into the shop, including Polly—recalled to become housekeeper—a detail not prepared for in the worksheets, but appropriate nevertheless. Uncle Sol reappears the day before the wedding. Cuttle's prophetic dream is happily only partly fulfilled, the letters to Cuttle, sent to Brig Place, having been refused by Mrs MacStinger. Toots now more self-assured dismisses the "morally incompatible" Chicken.

RH

Titles of chs.56 and 57: **(12) & (21)**

Dickens transfers the title of ch.56 from MS and at the same time titles ch.57. Both are written with the same fine evenly corroding line.

MS

Composition and title of ch.57

Dickens enters the title at the start. The couple share memories, as they walk early one sunny summer morning, from the Dombey church through dark narrow streets to the dingy City church that Toots attends. The churches, the walk through the city, the marriage, the farewells, and the feelings of those left behind, all resonate with memories of earlier occasions.

Dickens writes that he saw "in Florence's marriage, and in her subsequent return to her father, a brilliant opportunity" (see *Life* 483[K:9485]). "Another Wedding" gives him a chance once more to revive the past. By Walter and Florence's visit to Paul's memorial and by their long walk from there to Toots's dingy City church, they revisit their feelings for Paul, and their earlier journey as children. Similarly in "Retribution", Florence's return to her father is preceded by Dombey's obsessive confused recalling of moments in his mistreatment of her.

Dickens needs no plan or record for ch.57. The pathos of the chapter, heightened by the historic present, is sustained by contrasts reminiscent of early occasions, for the reader and for those involved. The couple pass by Mr Sownds and Mrs Miffs, walk through the city and take their leave in a procession of friendly farewells.

Proofs

To the proof of ch.57, Dickens adds a second mention of the sound of man with a wooden leg (Horsman 1974 p.769 n.3), a reminder of another reality that could find "nothing entertaining there" (769[852]). At the second proofing of ch.56, Dickens extends Cuttle's reaction to the letters that went astray, adding about twenty lines, from "What do you mean" to "and sat down." The change has the effect of softening Cuttle's responsibility for the mistake (Horsman 1974, p.762 n.2).

List: [18]

Dickens titles ch.56 beginning "Some people pleased" presumably from memory, but soon corrects the error (underlines confirm that the change is a running correction). He completes titling to the end of the number but does not go on to give the number heading of ch.58. The usual reminder of the next chapter number is unnecessary, as he goes to Brighton to begin work on the double number soon after proofreading ch.57 (see the commentary on Ws.19&20 p.120).

Worksheet for Nos.19&20

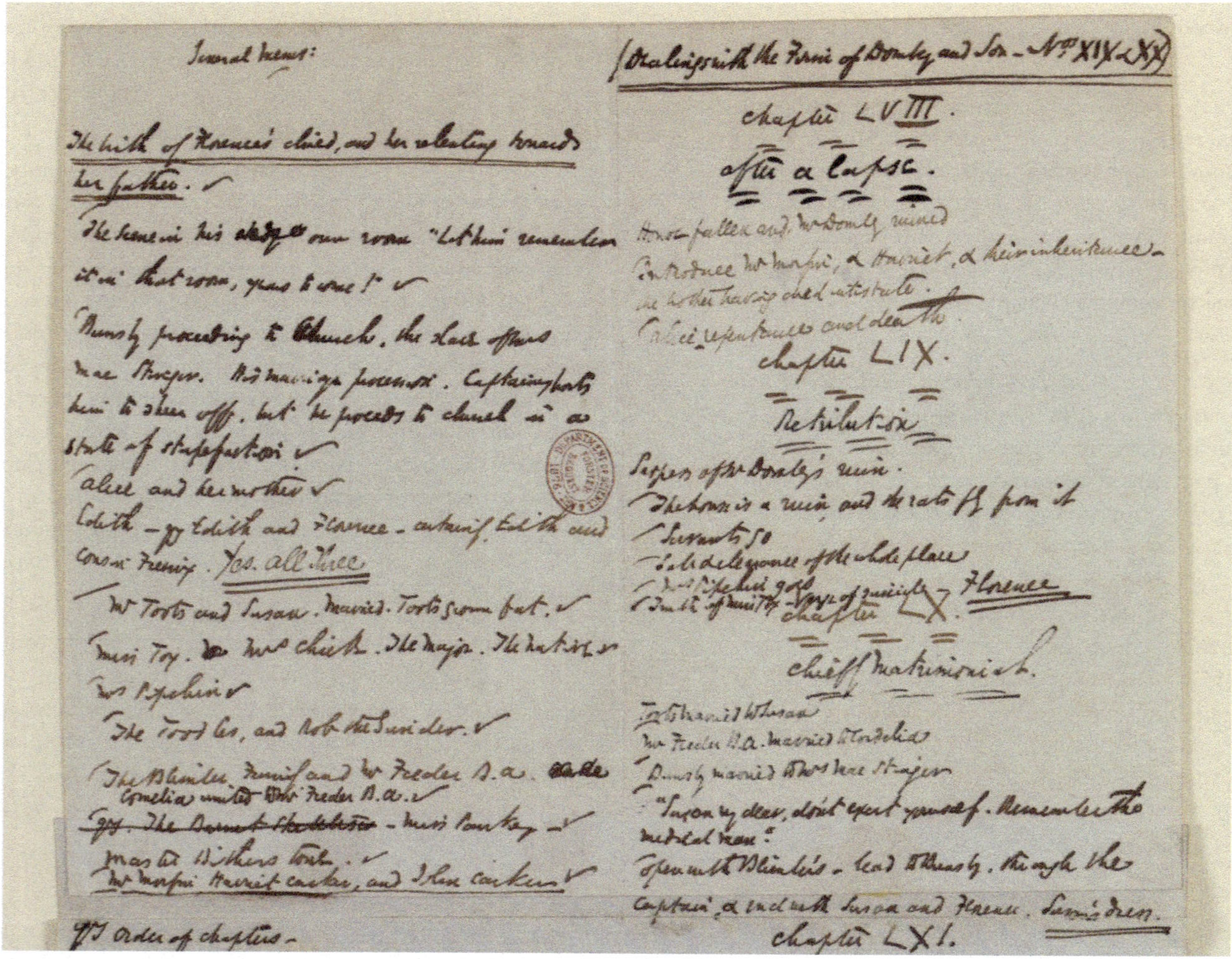

Image No.2012FE1509 (reduced and cropped): Forster Collection, National Art Library, Victoria and Albert Museum (2015). © Victoria and Albert Museum, London.

Transcription of Ws.19&20

(1) **General mems:**

(2) **The birth of Florence's child, and her relenting towards her father.** ✓

(3) The scene in his ~~study~~ own room "Let him remember it in that room, years to come!" ✓

(4) Bunsby proceeding to church, the slave of M[rs] Mac Stinger. His marriage procession. Captain exhorts him to sheer off, but he proceeds to church in a state of stupefaction. ✓

(5) Alice and her mother ✓
Edith – q[y] Edith and Florence - certainly Edith and Cousin Feenix. Yes. All Three

(6) M[r] Toots and Susan. Married. Toots grown fat. ✓

(7) Miss Tox. ~~M[r]~~ M[rs] Chick. The Major. The Native. ✓

(8) M[rs] Pipchin ✓

(9) The Toodles, and Rob the Grinder. ✓

(10) The Blimber Family and M[r] Feeder B. A. ~~And~~
Cornelia united to M[r] Feeder B. A. ✓

(11) ~~qy. The Barnet Skettleses~~ - Miss Pankey – ✓
Master Bitherstone. ✓

(12) Mr Morfin, Harriet Carker, and John Carker ✓

(Dealings with the Firm of Dombey and Son -N[os:] XIX&XX) (13)

Chapter LVIII. (14)

After a lapse. (15)

House fallen and M[r] Dombey ruined (16)

Introduce M[r] Morfin, & Harriet, & their inheritance – the brother having died intestate. (17)

Alice – repentance and death. (18)

Chapter LIX. (19)

Retribution (20)

Progress of M[r] Dombey's ruin. (21)

The house is a ruin and the rats fly from it (22)

Servants go (23)

Sale &clearance of the whole place (24)

M[rs] Pipchin goes (25)

Truth of M[rs] Tox – Verge of suicide – Florence (26)

Chapter LX. (27)

Chiefly Matrimonial. (28)

Toots married to Susan (29)

M[r] Feeder B. A. married to Cordelia [sic] (30)

Bunsby married to M[rs] Mac Stinger (31)

"Susan my dear, don't exert yourself. Remember the medical man." (32)

Open with Blimber's – lead to Bunsby, through the (33)

[See below for how the added leaf Ws.19&20a is attached to Ws.19&20.]

Commentary and order of entry (Ws.19&20)

On 29 February, Dickens goes down to Brighton to "finish the story" (L5:257). In an indication of the importance that he gives to the double number, he makes an early escape from the interruptions that come with his London life, "scarcely writing any letters", and only returning "for a few hours at a time" to Urania Cottage on 6 and 7 March. He returns to Devonshire Terrace on the 16th "from the necessity of being near the printers", perhaps to proofread the first two chapters the following day (L5:262), and remains there to finish the number. On the 21st, he expects to be "lingering over [Dombey], with a great desire to carry my care of him and his to the last [...] until – I think – Thursday night [the 23rd]" (L5:263). On 31 March, Nos.19&20 for April 1848 are published.

LH

Initial plan for the number: **(2)→ch.59**

Number plan heading: **(1)**

Dickens has perhaps already entered (2)—with (13) on the right-hand page (see Ws.17 p.112). Entry (2) is a reminder to motivate Florence's wish to be reconciled to her father by the birth of her child. Still using the thicker free-flowing quill, he heads the mems "General" because of the plan's scope, forward and back (cf. Ws.3_L, 'Outcomes' p.48).

Additional plan: **(3)→ch.59, (4)→ch.60**

Entry (3) notes the setting of Dombey's breakdown and the memory that begins the flood of memories (see 795^{882} and cf. 96^{101}, $253^{272–73}$ and 500^{551}). In entry (4), a strong contrast to (3), Cuttle meets the hapless Bunsby being led off to be married. "His" emphasizes the comic contrast to other marriage processions.

Further plan: **(5), (6), (7), (8), (9), (10), (11) & (12)**

Dickens plans to sum up the fortunes of most named characters by a final action and/or description. In recalling them, he groups them together, where possible in preparation for an incident or closing scene: in entry (5) with Alice and her mother, Edith and Feenix, and perhaps Edith and Florence; in (6) with Susan married to Toots (grown fat); in (10) with the Blimbers and Feeder (married to Cornelia); and in (12) with three characters underlined for their part in the last twist of the Carker story. Other groupings (7), (9) and (11) reflect their contribution to earlier episodes—he queries the inclusion of the Skettles, presumably as less germane (but see below "Proofs" p.125). In (8), the fierce Mrs Pipchin stands alone. Throughout, density, corrosion and size often vary from one item to another, reflecting the many pauses in the hand. Nevertheless, Dickens scrupulously defines each group with a slash, carefully keeping, for example, the slash that defines group (12) distinct from its underline.

RH

Preliminary heading: **(13), (14), (19) & (27)**

Dickens has probably already entered the part heading (13) with (2) on the left-hand page. With an ink more liable to corrosion, he enters three chapter number headings, as for a single number.

Plan for ch.58: **(16), (17) & (18)**

Dickens leaves a gap for the title, then in a lighter, corroding and smaller hand, notes: Dombey's bankruptcy, John and Harriet's anonymous gift to Dombey (funded from Carker's estate, arranged by Morfin), and Alice's deathbed repentance. "Introduce" confirms the intent of an outline plan much extended in composition.

MS

Composition and titling of ch.58

Dickens is concerned to give the reader a sense of time passing, to make the timeline of the Dombey thread more obviously consistent with Florence's marriage and the birth of her first child. After titling, then heavily revising and re-writing the first paragraph (see 'Appendix E' p.191), he elaborates the reactions to bankruptcy. He develops Perch the gossip and social drinker, then, through Morfin, brings in Harriet and her determination (with John) to use part of their inheritance from James to help Dombey (12). Harriet, having brought Alice out of the city to convalesce, comforts her as she dies, nursed by the morose Wickam (now well established as a carer). Mrs Brown's revelation that Alice's father was the brother of Edith's father begins the long cadence to Alice's death (5).[96] (Ch.58 takes up MS pp.1–10, or just over eleven printed pages).

RH

Plan for ch.59: **(21), (22), (23), (24), (25) & (26)**

Leaving a gap for the title, Dickens sums up his subject (21); the "Progress" covers both persons and things, the exoduses and the auction. In (22) he notes the varying end-of-paragraph refrain that will mark the successive departures of servants (23), of auctioned goods (24), and of Mrs Pipchin (25), in contrast to the return of the loyal Miss Tox. The important part Polly will play in the drama—here unmentioned—is perhaps devised during composition. Dombey transformed by his memories is brought to the "Verge of suicide", when he is rescued by the forgiving and penitent Florence (26). There is no intrinsic evidence of planning other than the omission of the title and some irregularity of layout. However, the description, as it is in black, must precede the use of greeny blue, which begins with the composition of ch.59 and ends with the titling of ch.62 (assuming as seems likely that all uses of greeny blue ink are consecutive). Dickens presumably brought a supply of black with him when he came to Brighton. That supply of black running out, he falls back on a greeny blue ink that happens to be available at his lodgings (cf. the use of watery blue ink in Ws.12 p.93).

MS

Composition and titling of ch.59

The chapter is written in a greeny blue ink. Ingenious transitions, extensions and additions to the plan suggest that it has been frequently rehearsed. Dickens closes the first paragraph with the refrain (22), adding its varied repetition to the end of each section (23), (24) and (25). He includes a last appearance for Mrs Chick (7) and Mrs Pipchin (9). With her husband's consent (inserted at proofing), Polly takes over as housekeeper, supported—to Bagstock's astonishment (795[882])—by the tender Miss Tox, now Rob's new employer (7) and (9). After Dombey's breakdown and rescue by Florence, he devises a retrospective coda, compressing a final departure scene into the last paragraph, in which Polly locks up the ironically signed "desirable Family Mansion" before returning to her home and children. (Ch.59 takes up MS pp.11–22, almost fourteen printed pages). Dickens writes that he saw "in Florence's marriage, and [...] return to her father, a brilliant opportunity", perhaps referring to how both, in different ways, reveal the power of memory to heal and transform (see the top of right-hand column of p.117).

RH

Having completed ch.59, still in greeny blue, he makes at least one entry in each of the five chapters. The greeny blue entries are probably consecutive (like the watery blue entries of Ws.12). The order of entry suggests that he may have kept the greeny blue to write ch.59, but having insufficient to complete any other chapter, uses his supply for other entries (mostly chapter titles, see below).[97]

Title of chs.58 and 59: **(15) & (20)**

Dickens copies the titles in the manuscript to the worksheet.

Titling and plan for the first section of ch.60: **(28); (29), (30) & (31)**

Dickens still greeny blue enters the chapter's title (28) and the plan for the marriages of the three couples, named in (29), (30) (31), in the order of their occurrence.

[Probably after writing ch.59 and certainly before making the last three entries in greeny blue, Dickens wafers a half-foolscap leaf Ws.19&20a to Ws.19&20. See the 'Introduction to Ws.19&20a' below p.123].

Facsimile of Ws.19&20a

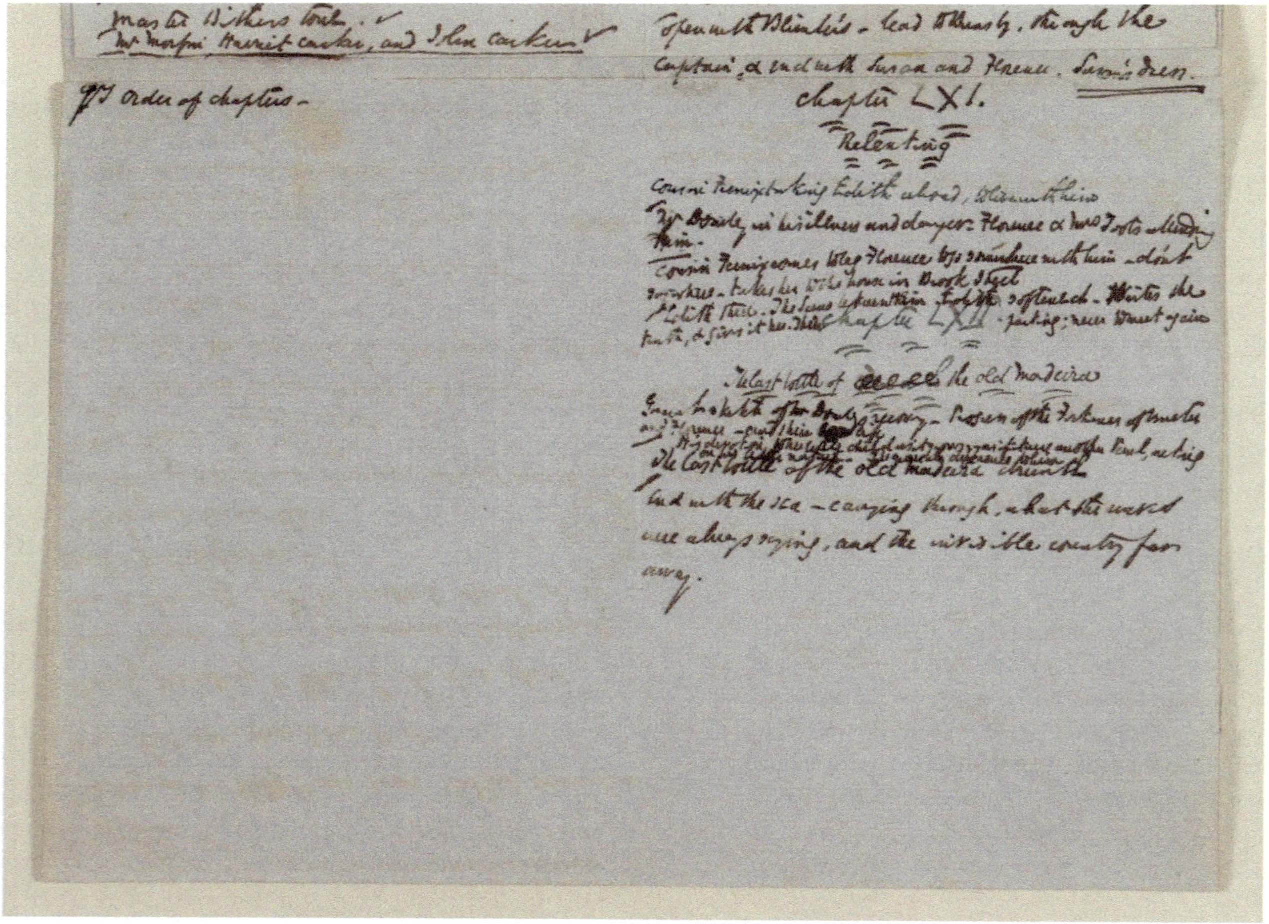

Image No.2012FE1509 (reduced and cropped): Forster Collection, National Art Library, Victoria and Albert Museum (2015). © Victoria and Albert Museum, London.

Transcription of Ws.19&20a

Mr Morfin, Harriet Carker, and John Carker ✓

qy Order of chapters –

[Introduction to Ws.19&20a

The compression of the later entries in the list of named characters on the left-hand half of Ws.19&20, especially (10)–(12), suggests that Ws.19&20a was not attached to Ws.19&20 until after those entries are made. Assuming the entries in greeny blue are consecutive, the attachment is probably made after the plan for ch.59 and just before or during the change to a greeny blue ink.

Dickens adds another leaf of roughly the same size (identified as Ws.19&20a). He does this by first wafering a slip of foolscap to the back of Ws.19&20, so that the slip hangs down below its bottom edge. He then wafers the additional leaf onto the exposed slip, leaving a narrow gap between the bottom of Ws.19&20 and the top of Ws.19&20a, an arrangement probably intended to strengthen the join between two half-foolscap sheets.]

Open with Blimber's – lead to Bunsby, through the Captain, & end with Susan and Florence. Susan's dress. (33)

Chapter LXI. (34)

Relenting (35)

Cousin Feenix taking Edith abroad, to live with him (36)

Mr Dombey in his illness and danger - Florence & Mrs Toots attending him. (37)

Cousin Feenix comes to beg Florence to go somewhere with him - don't say where - takes her to the house in Brook Street (38)

Edith there. The Scene between them. Edith softened - Writes the truth, & gives it to her. Their - parting; never to meet again (39)

Chapter LXII. (40)

The last bottle of ~~Final~~ the old Madeira (41) (42)

General sketch of Mr Dombey's recovery - Progress of the Fortunes of Walter and Florence - and their ~~life~~[?]life (43)

His devotion to her little child as it grows, - as if it were another Paul, acting on his better nature - The general deference to him

The last bottle of the old Madeira drunk (44)

End with the sea – carrying through, what the waves were always saying, and the invisible country far away. (45)

Commentary and order of entry in Ws.19&20a (with some entries made to Ws.19&20)

RH

Plan for the first section of ch.61: **(36)**

Leaving space for number and title, Dickens gives the ending of Edith's story; she is to settle in Italy, "under Feenix's protection" (825^{916}).

He is perhaps still undecided about the meeting with Florence (5).

Chapter number heading and titling of ch.62: **(40) & (41)**

He enters the chapter number heading and the title "Final".

Plan for the second section of ch.60: **(32) & (33)**

From now on writing in black—having returned to Devonshire Terrace on the 16th (see L5:262)—Dickens crossing to Ws.19&20 enters a final speech tag for the much-married Toots (32), then in entry (33), reminds himself of the order of the narrative, defined by person and place—its transitions carried by Cuttle. Crossing back to Ws.19&20a at "Captain", he notes as a coda Susan's re-adoption of her old dress in service (33), a gesture that conveys her unchanged loving attachment to Florence. The various directives and assembled entries in chs.60 and 61 confirm planning intent.

MS

Composition and title of ch.60

Dickens copies the title "Chiefly Matrimonial" to the worksheet (28). The initial transitions are managed through Toots, then after the arrival of Cuttle's letter, through Cuttle as planned. Cuttle encounters Bunsby, a slave in the marriage procession; he tries and fails to dissuade him. Managing the coincidences with some self-mockery, Dickens dwells on this, the final wedding scene. It inverts romance and patriarchy for broad comic effect, in a last object lesson to the unworldly and unchanging Cuttle. To inquire after Dombey's health, Cuttle makes his way to the Gays' "out of London" home, where he re-joins Toots and Susan ($816–17^{906}$). (Ch.60 takes up MS pp.23–30, or just over nine printed pages).

LH

Further plan

Entering "^{qy} Order of chapters –" at the top of the left-hand half Dickens perhaps considers transposing chs.59 and 60.

Outcomes: (2)–(12)

He checks all of the left-hand entries in Ws.19&20, ticking all groups except for (5), where he only ticks "Alice [...] mother" and (11), where he deletes "qy [...] Skettleses" but ticks "Pankey" and "Bitherstone" mentioned in chs.59 and 60 (793^{879} and 805^{893}).

List: [19&20]

He enters the headings for chs.58–60 once ch.60 is finished (p.179).

RH

Number heading for ch.61: **(34)**

Plan for the second section of ch.61: **(37), (38) & (39)**

Leaving a gap for the title, Dickens adds his plan for Dombey's care and for Florence's meeting with Edith.

MS and RH: (35)

Composition and titling of ch.61

Soon after beginning to compose, Dickens titles manuscript and worksheet (see 'Appendix E', ch.61, p.191).). He follows the sequence of the plan from entry (37), opening with Florence's care of Dombey and his slow recovery, but—unplanned and perhaps an afterthought (cf. Toodles in 'Proofs')—adds the presence of Walter, who consents to Florence's making a visit with Feenix to London and reassures her on the way. At Brook Street, Feenix takes her to the unsuspecting Edith.

When Edith's resolve not to deny adultery wavers in the face of Florence's love, Feenix intervenes and—as senior spokesman for the family name, who takes responsibility for the meeting—urges Edith "to set right whatever she has done wrong", which she does by giving Florence the written account she has already prepared (826[917]). The development of Feenix ends with his epilogue, still speaking in his own characteristic style—perhaps also a humorous pastiche of the author's own fondness for Shakespearian quotation and cadencing blank verse rhythms. (Ch.61 takes up MS pp.31–38, or just over eight printed pages).

Cutting and pasting from "and tenderness at once." to the end of the chapter (827-28[918-19]), Dickens rewrites the chapter's final paragraphs, so that he can on end on MS p.38—aware that it would leave four clear pages for ch.62. He calculates that forty-two manuscript pages is the equivalent of about forty-eight printed pages, i.e. three printers sheets, which leaves the fourth sheet for extra pages (see "Green covers", p.9).

LH

Outcome: (5)

Dickens adds "Yes. All three" (with double underlines) to the three unticked items in (5).

RH

Plan and titling of ch.62: **(<u>42</u>), (43), (44) & (45)**

Dickens deletes the earlier title "Final" (41), substituting (42) "The last bottle of the old Madeira" (its third broken double underline beneath "Fin" may be accidental 'run-on'). He assembles his ideas, dividing the notes into three sections: the first, Dombey's recovery and Walter's good fortune (43), the second, the drinking of the last bottle of Madeira (44), and the third, a closing allusion to sea, waves and shore (44). Then he expands (43) by adding "and Florence – and their life" and inserting (44) "His devotion to her little child as it grows [...] The general deference to him".

MS

Composition and titling of ch.62: (**<u>41</u>**)

Dickens reinstates the initial title, probably to avoid a repetition of the wine detail of the text, with which he now opens and which he later repeats. The refrain is inserted twice in MS (verso) with a "white line" to mark the passage of time, during which Florence has a second child.

Despite the care with which he planned the chapter, during composition he re-imagines the order of his plan and expands its content. The opening dramatises the "general deference" to Dombey. He reduces the "sketch" of Dombey's recovery to a brief mention, "a storm that has passed". He adds an explanation of Dombey's acceptance of the annuity, Morfin's marriage to Harriet and the new partnership of "Gills and Cuttle". Walter's success is reported (at second hand) through Toots, who bursts in to announce the birth of his little girl. Finally, Dickens holds back Dombey's devotion to little Paul, which is evident to all, for a final scene of the children running free. It prefaces another tie, hinted at earlier, but only presented at the end, his intense relation to the granddaughter, known to no one but Florence, who can appreciate its significance. (The chapter takes up MS pp.38–42—with a quarter of the page unused—or four and a half printed pages).

List: [19&20a]

When he has completed ch.62, Dickens enters the headings for chs.61 and 62 on the back of the last leaf of the List p.180.

Proofs

Additions

Dickens carries on the "care to him [Dombey] and his to the last" (L5:263). He works in a mention of the following: young Mr Skettles (living abroad with his father now a diplomat); Mr Toodles giving his approval for Polly's return to the Dombey mansion; Miss Tox for one last time; and at the very last moment, he arranges for Forster to make good his omission of Diogenes (*Life* 484[K:9490]).[98]

Cuts

The additions to the text may have meant that Dickens had to cancel the last two paragraphs (see Horsman 1974, 'Introduction', p.xxxvi). However, he may also have other reasons: among them, perhaps, doubt at the implications of the final plea that it is better to die a young Paul than live an aged (and unredeemed) Dombey. The cancellation, creating closure on the "untold story", adds weight to the final blank verse cadence "and smooths away the curls that shade her earnest eyes".[99]

Section 6. Overview

This final section surveys aspects of the worksheets that are noted in the commentaries. It examines the following:

- preliminary entries, particularly the decision on the number of chapters
- chapters titles, when and where they are revised
- chapter descriptions as plans
- chapter descriptions as summaries
- changes in number and chapter plans as the novel progresses
- planning and the double number.

Preliminary entries and the number of chapters

Having perhaps prepared a few blank worksheets and selected a quill of lesser quality than those he uses for the manuscript, Dickens heads the right-hand page of a worksheet with the novel's title and instalment number, bracketing and double underlining them, the line extending—because he uses the longer title of the novel—from the midway fold to the page's edge. He comes then to the chapter number headings. These he will make distinctive by using slightly larger letters, with a heavier hand for the Roman numeral, and by underlining them with a pattern of broken double underlines. Completing them marks the end of the routine entry into his month's work. First however, he has to decide on the number of chapters.

The three-chapter norm

It is clear from the worksheets that Dickens's preferred strategy is for three chapters to a number. This choice is apparent throughout, even in the final double number where he initially lays out its first worksheet for three chapters, independently of the second sheet, to which he later allocates two more chapters. Whereas the distinction between left and right-hand arises from his concern for the part's relation to the story and the chapter's relation to the part, the number of chapters is determined by the fixed length of each instalment. Given thirty-two pages of print, Dickens finds a number of factors act together to make a three-chapter structure the optimum arrangement.[100]

 https://doi.org/10.11647/OBP.0092.08

For the sake of all readers of the monthly issue, Dickens wants to vary the shape, tone and substance of the number, an intention that coincides with the regular practice in all "green covers" of including two contrasting narrative threads. In the first half of *Dombey and Son*, he usually starts each number with a chapter on Dombey's story followed by a contrasting subplot, whereas in the second half he often begins the number with one or other of the subplots, using them to pace the action of the main plot. There is a comparable contrast in his and/or Browne's choice of subject (and its treatment) for the two illustrations. They are, with the one exception (No.4), chosen from two different chapters. The effect of both illustrations varies somewhat depending on whether they are viewed in the part or single-volume issue. Within the green cover they are presented to the reader in a way that invites inquiry, inserted between the first section of advertisements and the text, not physically separated and tied to a particular page, as in the single volume publication (see endnote 128).

In a typical opening chapter, once the story is under way, partly to remind the reader of previous numbers, and partly to engage new readers, he revisits the relevant storyline by inventive backward looking re-description, as he slowly manoeuvres the narrative towards the principal development that he has in mind for the chapter.[101] The opening chapter of No.4, for example, is ten pages long, but begins with a four page preamble containing a striking recapitulation of Mrs Pipchin, Berinthia and Paul, followed by Dombey's arrival and the prickly conversation with Mrs Pipchin about his son's progress, all of which prepares for the main business "Paul's introduction to a new scene", where the six year old is to be "taken in hand" by Dr.Blimber.[102]

The element of recapitulation varies greatly but it is always present even in those chapters that open in the middle of an encounter, e.g. in ch.20 that begins No.7. However, most initial as well as middle chapters—ch.18 (later ch.17) fills both of those positions in No.6 at different stages of its production—are extended less by retrospection and more by Dickens's characteristic relish the opportunity to extemporise, what he later called "elbow room [and] open places in perspective", i.e. a pleasurable sense of distance from the pre-defined close that gives him licence to invent.[103] In ch.26 beginning No.9, he makes the typical combination of retrospect and prospect explicit in the title "Shadows of the past and future", but leaves it implicit in the text, playing with the reader's expectations of the Janus-faced qualities of storytelling.

As we shall see, the inclusion of two principal storylines, a tendency to write a longer opening chapter, a dislike of very long chapters, and his preference for shorter closing chapters, all help to make a two-chapter number, even when planned for, difficult to achieve. The first departure from the thee-chapter norm occurs in the four-chapter number that opens the novel.

The four-chapter numbers

Composing No.1, Dickens allows himself to write freely, to "plunge" into the story that had been growing in his imagination during the previous six months. Although there is no chapter planning in the worksheet, the number plan supplies the names of most principal characters of the first four chapters, briefly describing them, roughly in the order of their appearance, with the omission of Miss Tox. She figures, however, in the "outline of [...] immediate intentions" (see first paragraph of endnote 42) and is prominent in the pre-format entries of Ws.2_8 and 3_5. Even when Dickens reaches the end of ch.3 on page thirty-two of the manuscript—coincidentally, a reminder of the boundary of every instalment at the thirty-second page of print—he goes on to write into a fourth chapter, introducing his main contrasting narrative thread "Wally & Co". The final chapter runs on to page forty-two in the manuscript. Following chs.1, 2 and 3, it becomes almost eight printed pages (for the editor's calculation of chapter length, see the 'Key' to 'Appendix A' p.167).[104]

Dickens anticipates four chapters in the worksheet. He enters the initial number entry for ch.4 by turning the sheet over to enter the chapter number heading (and later the title) on the under (verso) side of the leaf. These are the only two verso entries in all of the worksheets (apart from those in the exceptional separate leaf Ws.6a). Similarity of hand and style of the four chapter number headings makes it very likely that all four headings are entered on the same occasion. (Conversely, the dissimilarity of the chapter headings of ch.4 (recto) from ch.4 (verso) shows that the latter's number heading is added later).

During composition, Dickens appears to use the right-hand side of the worksheet as a trial page, where he can devise, revise, and finalise (by broken underlines) the titles of the first three chapters (see 'Appendix D', chs.1–3, p.181, for more detail). The chapter descriptions of the chs.1–3, entered together, are probably an afterthought, a summary note of the content of each chapter added to an otherwise uninformative title. By the time of those entries, after squeezing the headings of ch.4 on to Ws.1 (recto), there is no space for a summary note on ch.4.

From both manuscript and worksheet, it is clear that Dickens from the beginning of his work on No.1 intended the opening number to be a four-chapter number. However, his stance towards the number boundary is uncharacteristically relaxed. He apparently dampens his awareness of the constraints of fixed length serialisation, in order to reassure himself—after a break of two years—of his own powers of invention. When he considers how to solve the problem created by the overrun, he always preserves the four-chapter structure, perhaps unwilling to disturb the existing chs.1–3 by adding the equivalent of six printed pages (thus making them up to thirty-two). Instead he prioritizes the greater variety of character and action possible in four chapters.[106]

In the next of the four–chapter instalments, No.12, Dickens writes a long opening chapter, which he divides in two when he sees it in print in the proofs. The manuscript shows that he may have anticipated the possibility of division of ch.35 during its composition.[105] The change, not registered in the right-hand half of the worksheet, is only noted when he adds a retrospective explanation on the left-hand half, in the same distinctive faint blue ink that he had just used to write the closing ch.38. An alteration in the presentation of ch.35, made after composition, the four-chapter number follows from his judgment of the readers' experience and expectations, that they might find the opening chapter—at just over seventeen printed pages—too long (Ws.12$_8$ p.91).

In No.14, Dickens plans for three chapters. However, his imaginative engagement with the material unbalances the plan. The opening ch.42 fills ten dense manuscript pages, which becomes over eleven and a half pages of print, as Carker at last moves centre stage. Then, during the writing of ch.43, he overruns what was probably his planned endpoint "Be near me always. I have no hope but in you" (Ws.14$_{19}$ p.99).

Writing on into the day after Dombey's accident, Dickens begins by motivating Susan's reckless action with her outrage at Florence's treatment. A page or more into this section, he decides to use the dawn of the second day as a chapter break. Perhaps anticipating what threatens to be another overlong chapter, he cuts off the bottom third of page sixteen of the manuscript, replacing it with a heavily revised slip containing the last three paragraphs, from "Not when you lie asleep near me, sweet" to the end. Then at the top of the following page, he inserts the number heading and title of ch.44.

In the new ch.44, Dickens embarks on what he may now view as a pressing issue, Susan's clash with Dombey (and Pipchin) and her subsequent departure. This is a crucial addition to Florence's isolation, best made well before 'The Thunderbolt' of the next number. The confrontation across classes, enlivened by the antipathy of the characters involved, leads to its extension. As he reaches manuscript p.23, he realizes that there is now only four, or at most, five manuscript pages left for the final chapter, the crucial encounter of Carker and Edith and the reader's "last view of them before the elopement" (Ws.14_{26} p.99).

On manuscript, after "I say, Susan! Miss Dombey, you know", he cuts the page and pastes on a slip containing a re-written fair copy that probably reduces the turn taking, shortens the dialogue, and leaves a blank half page. He deletes the page number "23" replacing it with "22½". Despite gaining this extra half page, however, he learns at proof stage that ch.45 has to be shortened, which Forster does by excising the final three paragraphs.[107] The deletion is perhaps the most damaging of all the cuts to the novel made at proof stage (see endnote 85).

To sum up, in No.1, Dickens accepts Forster's advice to include the principal counter plot "Wally & Co" in the first instalment. The ensuing difficulties could only have been avoided by planning to limit the scope of the first three chapters (for the sake of the fourth chapter), which his "headlong plunge" into his story probably precluded. In No.12, the long chapter, which later has to be divided, arises from the freedom he gives himself in the opening chapter of a number, and from his initial decision to override the distinctiveness of the two halves. (He probably senses the unity of each half as he was writing, when he reached the point where he later divided ch.35.) No.14, the last of the four-chapter numbers, is largely a result of the narrative expanding as Dickens is caught up in the drama of the moment in a number full of incident, but especially in ch.42 and again in the second half of ch.43 (the newly created ch.44).

Between writing the No.3 and No.4, he composes the second preface to the Cheap Edition of *Pickwick Papers*. In the preface, he recognises from his past "experience and study" the need for planning, not just in his conception of the novel's unifying themes but also in the shape and substance of the instalment and its relation to the whole. Nevertheless, in the four-chapter numbers, it is his continuing predilection in the heat of composition to protect "invention" against "planning" that brings in its train compromise and loss. Taken together, the planning and composition of these four-chapter numbers are a nice demonstration of the fluctuating tension between his chosen mode of publication and his extraordinary imaginative powers.

In Ws.12_8 p.91, instead of updating the right-hand record, Dickens adds a comment in the left-hand page "the No. [is] divided into four chapters. First being too long", revealing an overriding constraint—the reluctance to submit the reader to an over long chapter, which, in practice, means any chapter that fills more than half of the number. As we shall see, it was this reluctance in particular that helped undermine his attempt at a two-chapter number.

The two-chapter experiment

The worksheets reveal Dickens's growing interest in formal innovation. We have seen in Ws.5 and 5a how he intensifies the pathos of Paul's death that closes the first quarter by a carefully planned innovation in narrative method. In No.10, the number that finishes the second quarter and the first half of the novel, he is interested in testing the feasibility of a climactic two-chapter number.

However, No.7 becomes for a short time at least Dickens's first two-chapter instalment. He begins the opening chapter on 10 March 1847. On the same day, he sends the long description of Dombey's first meeting with Edith to Browne, as the subject of the number's first illustration. As soon as he completed ch.20 (later 20 and 21)—well over half of the number, and probably finished by the 18th—he sends it to the printers. The compositors perhaps take at least two days to set up and run off the proofs of eighteen pages of print. In the meantime, he is writing the next chapter, initially numbered ch.21 in the manuscript. Receiving the proofs on 20th, he will be at least half way through though the chapter. With no plans for another chapter and his deadline only two or three days away, he will by now be aware that the narrative has become the closing chapter of a two-chapter number.

It is also possible that Dickens planned No.7 as a two-chapter number from the start, entering the number heading for ch.20 and ch.21, as he does later for Ws.10. When he divides the proofs of ch.20, he may have adjusted the number headings in the worksheet by inserting the number heading for a new ch.21 and converting the number heading of the initial ch.21 to 22 in the same way he converted the number heading of ch.21 to ch.22 in the manuscript. Evidence from hand, ink and layout, however, is inconclusive. Whether No.7 was planned as a two-chapter number or simply became a two-chapter number from the pressure of the approaching deadline, he would certainly have the experience in mind, when he next considers testing its formal advantages.

In No.10, when Dickens marks up the right-hand half with its preliminary entries, he appears initially to contemplate a two-chapter number to the same pattern as No.7 with a long opening chapter, very probably devoted to an extended main storyline, followed by the usual shorter closing chapter. He spreads the chapter number headings, giving ch.29 twice as much space as ch.30. Moving to the left-hand and assembling three subjects that need his attention, he is uncertain how to proceed. Despite his early doubt about the arrangement shown in (1), he outlines two possible chapter subjects for the final shorter chapter, the dashing of Miss Tox's romantic hopes (2) and the introduction of the Harriet Carker thread (3). However, as he starts to enter (4), he sees the possibility of dividing the marriage material between (4) and (6); separating the preparations from the wedding itself gives him room to expand on both occasions. Despite the division, the interval before the marriage and the wedding itself remain closely connected, so that Mrs Chick's delivery of the news of the marriage to the shock of the tender Miss Tox could, without loss and with some gains, be placed at the start of the number, delaying the event, raising expectation and easing the transition to the wedding climax.

Dickens can now answer his initial query with an emphatic "three". Returning to right-hand side, he converts the two-chapter headings to three by adding a number heading for a new ch.30 halfway between ch.29 and the initial ch.30, and by converting the latter to ch.31. He manages the conversion by adding a "I" (perhaps covering the stop after the Roman "XXX") and attaching a pair of underlines to the additional "I", both of which he misaligns.[108]

He abandons the attempt at a two-chapter number, partly because of the way his longer storylines naturally break in two, and partly out of concern for his readers, not wishing to subject them to more than sixteen unbroken pages of print. His reservation about chapter length becomes explicit later when he divides ch.35, finding that at over seventeen pages of print, it had become "too long" (see Ws.12$_8$ p.91).

There are two notable exceptions to his aversion to longer chapters, ch.14 (Paul's farewell to the Blimbers) and ch.56 (the preparations that clear the way for Florence's wedding). Both chapters are well over seventeen pages of print in the part issue (see 'Appendix A' p.165). In the opening ch.14, as the action moves steadily forwards, the manuscript shows many passages written with fluency and without revision. Likewise in ch.56, as he moves the Florence/Walter romance forward (and disposes of Sol Gills' return), Dickens focuses particularly on Toots, with evident pleasure in his presentation, lingering over Toots's interaction with Florence, Cuttle, Susan and the Chicken. However, the lengthening of both chapters—apart from the pleasure Dickens has in creating them—may also be a deliberate ploy, to prepare for the unusually short final chapter that ends each number. "What the waves were always saying" and "Another Wedding" are only four and six pages respectively. The concentrated poignancy of ch.16 is more effective being short. Similarly, the pervasive retrospective pathos of ch.57 is enhanced by the simplicity of its short journey narrative. For that reason, perhaps, it is the only later chapter without plan or summary (Ws.18 p.115).

Chapter titles: When and where they are entered and revised

Importance of chapter titles in the worksheet

Although Dickens probably does not know at the start exactly how the division between the left- and right-hand halves will function, he clearly expects to use both together as a basic record of the contents of each instalment. Number and chapter plans vary in length and detail, whether plan or summary, with the progress of the novel, but chapter titles—with the single exception of ch.36, see below—are always recorded. Moreover, he gives titles prominence on the page by their lettering and layout and, from Ws.4 onwards, avoids obscuring them with the details of revision. When he writes Ws.6a—to resolve the issue Florence's age before Dombey's return to the family table in No.15—he appears to use worksheets with their chapter titles (along with their descriptions) as a key to the content of the more distant instalments among his growing pile of back numbers.[109]

Overall, titling in the worksheets is accurate, apart from Ws.12. In that instance, Dickens simply reminds himself, in a retrospective comment on the left-hand page that "Plan changed afterwards, and the N° divided into four chapters" ($Ws.12_8$ p.91). Consequently, there are some uncorrected chapter number entries and one omission "Housewarming", the title of the new ch.36 following the late division of ch.35. Apart from this complication, there are only two wrongly titled chapters in the worksheets, those of chs.29 and 62. In the case of ch.29, he may well have felt that the slightly different wording did not merit correction (the complicated history of ch.29, see 'Appendix D' p.185). As for ch.62, at that late point, updating the record would seem unnecessary.

After the publication of No.5, Dickens begins to compile a cumulative list of chapter numbers and titles, which he calls his "List of Chapter Headings". Because the record for each instalment is usually updated towards the end of its composition, the List is wholly accurate except for three differences: the order of chs.17 and 18 and the wording of the title for ch.2 and ch.38. The act of completing the List would confirm for him the final version of the title, its number and relative position. Moreover, as an alternative to leafing through a pile of worksheets, Dickens may have intended the List as a basic overview. It differs from the worksheets in that it shows the position of each chapter title relative to all past chapters, and the changes of hand in the List from ch.17 onwards give a rough indication of the relation of the chapters to the instalment in which they are published.

This emphasis on chapter titles in the worksheet and List may seem too obvious to be significant, but it is in keeping with the care with which Dickens chooses and revises them (see 'Appendix D'). Like the titling of the novel itself or the naming of characters, chapter titles can be strikingly suggestive or oblique, intended to give readers the pleasure of uncovering meaning as they read, thus drawing them into the story. However, they also serve as important signposts in his memory of the narrative.

Titling during composition

Dickens soon finds that, because of the close relation between the substance of each chapter and the choice of title, it is often better to delay titling—and revising—until some way into composing the chapter. From Ws.4 onwards, if he is at all uncertain about a title, he tends to work on the task during composition. The content of the chapter occasionally indicates the interval during which a choice is probably made. For example, Dickens entertains the "association" of the onset of bad weather with Cuttle's despair, after the opening exchanges with Rob, at the start of the evening narrative (439[481]). However, the title of ch.32—"The Wooden Midshipman goes to pieces"—is a wordplay that gets its full force later in the chapter, when Cuttle is alone, imagining the wreck near the chapter's end (452–53[497]). The title is inserted between Dickens's treatment of the "outward influence" of the stormy weather and Cuttle's contemplation of the fragments of his hopes "as they floated past him". The postponed title entry in the manuscript is confirmed by the contrast of hand between the title and the opening text.

Late entry of titles in manuscript is most obvious when Dickens uses a different coloured ink. For example, ch.33 is written in black with the interpolated title written in blue, presumably entered while he is composing the following chapter in the same blue ink. Similarly, the first part of ch.26 is in black whereas the later part is in bright blue, the same ink used for the title when he later inserted it. There are also in the manuscript occasional revealing false starts to chapters, many of which are given in 'Appendix E' p.189. The false start of ch.58 shows him titling at the start. The false start of ch.61, on the other hand, shows a title being inserted after writing just the first line, while that of ch.49 shows how he might leave a chapter untitled, then, dissatisfied with the opening, turn the leaf over and begin again, returning later to insert the title.

Other less obvious indications of late title insertion in manuscript are overwriting (ch.19) or shaping the title entry so as to avoid the surrounding text (ch.23), or a marked alteration in the title's hand and/or the quill quality (chs.5, 19, 24 and 32), or, most commonly, a cramping of the title, having left insufficient space for it (chs.19, 26, 39, 43, 46, 49, 56 and 61).

A cramped title entry in manuscript, however, has to be assessed with caution. Dickens comes to depend on his count of the manuscript pages as a measure of his progress in preparing text. Once well into the novel (from about No.4), he is careful to keep both the space between words and between lines as narrow and regular as possible, by making most corrections interlineally, but also by minimising the space reserved for titles. Consequently, a cramped title entry in the manuscript, e.g. in chs.39 and 42, can give a misleading appearance of being inserted. In the worksheet, similarity of hand and ink is needed to confirm that they are indeed entered as he writes, and conversely dissimilarity to confirm later insertion.

Titling before composition

Of course there are occasions when there is no reason to delay titling. Dickens confident in his choice may title in the worksheet before he begins to compose, particularly in those much rehearsed and carefully planned-on-the-page climaxes to each quarter. Such assurance in titling may occur when the substance of the title is particularly ironic, e.g. ch.35 "The Happy Pair", or strongly predictable, perhaps at a climax or towards the denouement, e.g. ch.48 (later 47) "The Thunderbolt" or ch.54 "The Fugitives".

Titling at the start of composition in manuscript can usually be recognised by orderliness of hand and layout. In a false start for ch.51, for example, he lays out the chapter number with its title "Mr Dombey and the World", writes the opening of the first sentence, and unhappy with wording, turns the leaf over and begins by entering the title again (for more on the titling in ch.51 in the worksheet, see below in 'Timing of title entry', p.141). Such titles have few or no corrections, lineation is evenly spaced with title and text in the same hand, and corrections carefully shaped to avoid its underlines. Despite Dickens's concern over wordage in the manuscript (and space in the worksheet), they are nevertheless sometimes written with a slightly larger bold hand, e.g. chs.31, 35, 47 and 51.

Revising chapter titles in the manuscript

After titling in manuscript at the start or during composition, Dickens may still return to revise his choice. The timing and the purpose of revision varies. He may insert a revision after writing just a paragraph, or several pages, or occasionally after the chapter is finished. In revising, he often rewords, making association and implication more apt, e.g. the title for ch.30 "Before the Wedding" eventually becomes "The Interval before the Marriage". Sometimes, he is seeking to avoid wording elsewhere, e.g. the lettering for an illustration (ch.29) or the wording of a refrain in the text (ch.62). However, when he rethinks the title entirely, the revision may focus the reader's attention on a particular episode or allusion (in place of more usual inclusive titling), e.g. the title of ch.30 Relatives and Friends" becomes "Father and Daughter" and that of ch.41 "The sea shore" becomes "New Voices in the Waves" (see 'Appendix D' p.186).

All the titles in manuscript are as published, with the exception of ch.35, which was divided into two and re-titled at proofing. That, however, does not mean that the manuscript has all the revisions that were devised in the course of titling. Eight chapters have a revision that does not appear in manuscript (chs.2, 3, 8, 23, 36, 38, 56 and 62). In these eight chapters, revision is made in the worksheet (chs.2, 3, 8, and 62), in the "List of Chapter Headings" (chs.23 and 56), or in both worksheet and List (ch.38), or in proof (ch.36)—but not in manuscript.

Memory, speech-making and planning

When Butt and Tillotson assert that the chapter notes 'always serve to summarise the contents and put Dickens in the mood of the last monthly number when beginning upon another', they underestimate the writer's powers of recall, as well as his involvement in his own narrative (Butt and Tillotson, p.27). If he needed to be reminded of what was in the last number, it would more probably be in connection with some small detail, in which case he would surely consult his own copy of the number, having presumably received the customary complimentary copy soon after publication. For more distant chapters, he may rely on the worksheets alone, and if he requires more detail, use them as guides to chapter and page in the back numbers (see 'Outcome' in the commentary on Ws.6a p.69).

Dickens's memory, notably visual as well as aural and kinetic, was remarked on by many of his contemporaries, and has been confirmed by later research. There are 'numerous comments of his contemporaries [...] and in his own works'.[110] He could learn a part in a play or prepare a speech in a morning. He could recall and repeat a speech verbatim that he had given a week after giving it. He could 'read' from his own works to thousands, without much reference to the text, except in so far as he needed to, to preserve the appearance of reading. Among contemporary testimony, two accounts in particular throw light on the relation between memory and note-making.

Prior to the writing of *Dombey and Son* Dickens had avoided systematic preparatory planning on the page, preferring to rely on memory. Writing to Gaylord Clark, the editor of an American literary monthly, by way of explanation for his delay in sending an extract from his current novel (probably *Nicholas Nickleby*), he explains how difficult it was to find "an entire scene capable of segregation". To account for this interdependence of the part and the whole, he describes his habit of 'planning-in-the-head' as opposed to 'planning-on-the-page':

> I never commit thoughts to paper until I am obliged to write, being better able to keep them in regular order, on different shelves of my brain, ready ticketed and labelled, to be brought out when I want them.[111]

The reflection partly explains his reluctance to notate plans at the time of writing (1839). The shelving and ticketing analogies describe the retaining of a thought, sensing its association with other ideas, and using the association to recall it when needed. Such a process suggests an unusual degree of control over remembering, as well as confidence of recall, both of which help account for the allusiveness of much of his later note-making, when he came to try its advantages.

A second report comes from George Dolby, Dickens's personal manager during his later reading tours in the 1860s. It is an anecdote about how, according to Dolby—and there is no reason to doubt the account, Dolby being a reliable witness in other respects—Dickens might prepare for an important speech:

> He told us that, supposing a speech was to be delivered in the evening, his habit was to take a long walk in the morning, during which he would decide on the various heads to be dealt with. These being arranged in their proper order, he would in his 'mind's eye', liken the whole subject to the tire of a cartwheel – he being the hub. From the hub to the tire he would run as many spokes as there were subject to be treated, and during the progress of the speech he would deal with each spoke separately, elaborating them as he went round the wheel (Dolby, *Charles Dickens as I knew him*, 273–74).

The wheel analogy, like the shelving model, explains how he orders his thoughts, remembers and then extends each topic, but retains its position in the whole, as he performs his speech and adapts it to his audience. Similarly, once his use of the worksheets is well established, chapter descriptions that are plans become so many salient ordered points, requiring expansion in many different ways. The main task in narration, as in performing a speech, becomes one of fleshing out his notes, including of course whatever comes to him during composition. But here the similarity begins to break down. Dickens may have a quite comprehensive vision of a chapter, even if it is a rather long one, well before he puts pen to paper. A single entry in a plan may be his brief reminder or 'mem' of what already exists in considerable detail in his imagination, to which he may add further entries, each with their imagined narrative potential, as well as other matters already noted in the number plans. The relation of the items in chapter plan to each other and to the preparatory number plan is also more complex. Like "the stock of the soup", they may intermingle or coalesce.

The early half-formed routines of Dickens's use of the earlier worksheets were disrupted by a series of misfortunes. The number plans for both Nos.7 and 8 have only a few short entries (Ws.$7_{3\&4}$ and Ws.$8_{1,2\&5}$ pp.72 and 76) and no chapter descriptions, whether plans or summaries. However, despite adversities, in the case of No.7 during his "dream" of work from 10 to 23 March, he found time to give Browne an extended description of the subject of the first illustration. He may have already written the outline of Mrs Skewton's character and Edith's psychology in Ws.7_2, and perhaps written part of the first half of ch.20, but he had certainly not begun to compose the second half, which later became ch.21. The only mention of the material of the chapter in Ws.7 is the number plan note added some time later to the outline above: "These to be encountered in Leamington" (Ws.7_3).

Nevertheless, a letter to Browne shows how fully imagined is Dickens's picture of the scene at the heart of that unwritten chapter. He is "very late with my number, which I have only begun this morning [10 March 1847]" emphasising that the illustration is "very important to the book":

> I should premiss that I want to make the Major, who is the incarnation of selfishness and small revenge, a kind of comic Mephistophelian power in the book; and the No. begins with the departure of Mr Dombey and the Major on that trip for change of air and scene, which is prepared for in the last Number. They go to Leamington, where you and I once were. In the Library, the Major introduces Mr Dombey to a certain young lady, whom, as I wish to foreshadow, dimly, said Dombey may come to marry, in due season. She is about thirty—not a day more—handsome, though haughty-looking—good figure—well dressed—showy—and desirable. Quite a lady in appearance, with something of proud indifference about her, suggestive of a spark of the Devil within. Was married young. Husband dead. Goes about with an old mother who rouges, and lives upon the reputation of a diamond necklace and her family.—Wants a husband. Flies at none but high game, and couldn't marry anybody not rich—Mother affects cordiality and heart, and is the essence of sordid calculation—Mother usually shoved about in a Bath chair by a page who has rather outgrown and out-shoved his strength, who butts at it from behind, like a Ram, while his mistress steers herself languidly by a handle in front—Nothing the matter with her to prevent her walking, only once sketched (when a Beauty) reclining in a Barouche, and having outlived the beauty and the barouche too, still holds on to the attitude, as becoming her uncommonly. Mother is in this machine in the Sketch. Daughter has a parasol.
>
> The Major presents them to Mr Dombey, gloating within himself over what may come of it, and the discomfiture of Miss Tox. Mr Dombey (in deep mourning) bows solemnly. Daughter bends. The Native in attendance, bearing a camp stool and the Major's great coat. Native evidently afraid of the Major and his thick cane. If you like it better, the scene may be in the street or in a green lane. But a great deal will come of it: and I want the Major to express that, as much as possible in his apoplectico-Mephistophelian observation of the scene, and his share in it.
>
> *Lettering.*
> *Major Bagstock is delighted to have that opportunity*
> (L5.34–35 and cf. 280–85[305–08]).

Giving Browne a choice of settings—indoors or out—confirms that Dickens has yet to compose the scene. Some of the information that he provides appears earlier in the first half of ch.20, but most will appear in the second half of ch.20 (later ch.21). Dickens's rapid broken bursts of description are delivered with such energy that he seems to be stirring the characters into life. He identifies with each participant in turn, telling Browne about their motives and history, while giving a glimpse of their appearance and actions. He supplies significant details for each character, which Browne might work into in his sketch of the moment when the Major introduces the participants to one another. Despite the fullness of the description, he has to write a second letter to bring Browne's sketch of the Native into line with his vision of him incongruously got up in "European" rather than native costume, a detail not mentioned earlier.[112]

The "lettering" for the illustration—like a "label" or "ticket" kept in order on different shelves, or a "spoke" in the turning "wheel" of a memorised speech—calls up a memory and, by association, the whole of which the memory is a only part. That whole probably includes most of the following: Edith's first marriage, the loss of her child, her first husband's link with Bagstock as Colonel in his regiment, the Native's dress and earrings, the meetings that follow the first encounter, and the chapter's deliberately truncated ending as Edith displays her final genteel accomplishment, accompanying herself on the piano, singing in her "deep and rich voice" the song that Florence sang, and Paul crooned, as she carried him up the stairs to bed (289–91[313–15] and cf. 96[101]).

The three accounts above, given at the start and end of Dickens's career, and during the writing of *Dombey and Son*, demonstrate his extraordinary visual and verbal memory and the deliberate training with which he cultivated his ability to recall. They help explain not only the allusiveness and omissions of his planning, but also his concern, despite hiatuses, to find, on many occasions, fixed points that secure the course of a plan's progress.

Chapter descriptions as plans

Terminology

Butt and Tillotson, arguing from mainly *David Copperfield* and *Bleak House*, rightly conclude that chapter descriptions, whether they are plans or summaries, always act as records (Butt and Tillotson, p.27). However, because all plans can be viewed as records, they consistently set aside the number and variety of Dickens's chapter plans. In the chapter devoted to *Dombey and Son*, they seldom identify and discuss a chapter description as a chapter plan. When they describe the crucial right-hand entry Ws.5_4 "his [Paul's] illness [to be] only expressed in the child's own feelings", they refer to it as 'the decision recorded in the number plan', presumably using 'number' to mean 'instalment' and 'plan' to mean 'worksheet' (Butt and Tillotson, p.100).[113] Even in the double number, where Dickens's planning intent in the chapter descriptions is generally agreed, they treat their own quotation from a chapter plan as something akin to a summary, describing how 'the movement of chapter lx is *traced* [editor's italics] in the notes' (Butt and Tillotson, p.111).

The first scholars to give a general account of Dickens' working notes, Butt and Tillotson led the way for later commentators, many of whom have also emphasised the recording function of the notes. To test the validity of this emphasis with regard to *Dombey and Son*, this edition sets aside assumptions and begins with terminology. It uses 'worksheet' for the leaf, i.e. for the left and right-hand half as a whole, 'chapter description' as the general term for entries that Dickens makes after each chapter heading, and 'summary' and 'plan' as subordinate terms that distinguish between types of chapter description. Ridding key terms of ambiguity turns out to be an important first step.

The point at which Dickens enters his chapter descriptions does indeed vary. Many descriptions are made before composition (and must therefore be plans), and some afterwards (and therefore are summaries). This variation in function with alteration in timing is accompanied by other differences.

The following account looks first at the descriptions whose features mark them as plans. It divides their distinguishing features into those that are inherent in their wording and appearance and those that involve a comparison with the text of the novel. First, we examine intrinsic indications of planning.

Directives

When Dickens writes "Introduce" (Ws.4_{19} p.51), "Open" (Ws.12_{22} p.91), "Begin" (Ws.10_{22} p.83) and "End with" (Ws.19&20a_{45} p.123), it seems reasonable to assume that the instruction to himself can only mean that the description is a plan, outlining his intentions for the chapter, and similar to his use of directives in number planning, e.g. "connect Carker with Edith, before the wedding , and get in Florence" (Ws.$9_{2\,\&\,3}$ p.79).

Queries

Queries are indicators of planning, like directives, though much less frequent. Only three occur in the chapter descriptions. The first is answered with a qualified negative "Not yet" (Ws.5_{9} p.57), the later ones with an emphatic positive (Ws.$13_{35\,\&\,36}$ p.95). In number plans, on the other hand, interrogatives and their answers are frequent. The contrast between number and chapter plan, in this respect, points to a difference between the different stages in planning that they represent, the one more open and fluid and the other more closed and defined. However, both involve self-questioning that is unlikely to occur in a summary.

Elisions

Elision can sometimes imply intention, such as "Back to dawn again" (Ws.10_{28} p.83). On other occasions, similar phrases—without an implied directive—may be read as ways of ordering a summary, especially if they are short and to the point. Like a stage direction, they may announce a new arrival joining character(s) already on stage, e.g. "To her, a daughter" (Ws.11_{25} p.87). However, preceded by 'so', elided directives regularly signal a narrative shift that requires preparation "So to Mrs Skewton" (Ws.13_{28} p.95) and "So to the Captain's narrative" (Ws.16_{9} p.107). As the plans for the double number demonstrate, anticipating and managing narrative transitions is an important part of Dickens's craft as a story-teller (see for example "lead to Bunsby, through the Captain" Ws.19&20_{33} p.119).

Variation in layout

Layout of a description can also give an indication of planning, particularly in the case of those descriptions that are obviously accumulated, with some entries—judging from the hand—made at different times (Ws.$5_{8\text{-}11}$ p.57) and (Ws.$9_{13\text{-}17}$ p.79). The gathering together of ideas over time is particularly obvious where it is accompanied by changes of ink, for example in Ws.19&20$a_{36\text{–}37}$ p.123.

Listing is a characteristic of both plan and summary. However once assembled, a planning list often has a distinctive irregularity, a sudden change of positioning, or of hand, or of both together. It may have additions, inserted or tacked on, at the beginning, in the middle or at the end. This sort of accretion gives some assembled plans their distinctive layout, e.g. ch.15 (Ws.5) or ch.27 (Ws.9). Listing can also lead to frequent use of Dickens's idiosyncratic diagonal slash, to separate and order the entries. Moreover, because the pressure on space is greater in planning—being essentially more unpredictable than summarising—there is a greater tendency to vary orientation in order to use space more economically.

The worksheet attachment Ws.5a demonstrates how Dickens can use layout to help him shape narration. Initially, he appears to use the attachment—without entry (6)—in the composition of ch.14. Its layout—focused on Paul's experience of illness—maps the child's thoughts and speeches into an imagined narrative, while the hand and alignment suggests their emotional weight (see the facsimile and transcription of Ws.5a). Then the attachment, with the addition of (6), may be used in the same way, for the composition of ch.16. In composing both chapters, Dickens looks to incorporate the wording (and the expressiveness) of the attachment into his narrative as he writes. The reader of the finished text of chs.14 and 16 may see beneath their surface the tracery of these early plans (see the commentary on Ws.5a p.61).

Revisions

Chapter descriptions, which appear for other reasons to be plans, often contain deletions followed by revisions. In Ws.16, for example, Dickens makes a change to emphasise the distance between father and daughter, deleting "his feelings ~~towards~~" and adding "about" (Ws.16$_{18}$ p.107). Such alterations may appear small, but—apart from what they us about Dickens's stylistic judgement—they are also the immediate second thoughts of the sort that might be expected in planning. A few deletions with revision involve substantial change during planning, e.g. in the approach to the ending of ch.14 "~~News of Paul's illness No~~" (Ws.5$_{5}$ p.57) or to the choice of speechmaker at the wedding (Ws.10$_{25}$ p.83).

A special instance of revision sometimes occurs in the preparation of a text to close a chapter. In his plan for the end of ch.55, Dickens revises the sensational horror of Carker's death by deleting "sup(ped)", thus omitting any suggestion of dogs drinking his blood (Ws.18$_{10}$ p.115). Then in the text, with characteristic subtlety, he embeds the whole within Dombey's perceptions (743^{823}). Compare this alteration with the summary note that describes the tableau of Edith and Florence together at the end of ch.30 (Ws.10$_{18}$ p.83). When he deletes "lying" for "kneeling", he may be adjusting his vision of the scene, rather than merely making a running correction (cf. 420^{461}).

In summarising, Dickens seldom needs to delete an entry, or any part of it. The many early summary notes, usually a word or phrase describing an aspect of the chapter, contains only one isolated deletion "~~Miss T~~", which seems to show him hesitating over the scope of notes of this sort, not correcting the summary itself (see Ws.1$_{16}$ p.39). Apart from the deletion in ch.12, where he accidentally begins with the dinner scene—corrected to the "Internal economy of Blimber's" (Ws.4$_{15\,\&\,16}$ p.51)—the only deletion in subsequent summaries, a running correction, occurs in Ws.14. At the end of the chapter giving the reader's "last view of them [Carker and Edith] before the elopement", he hesitates over how to suggest Edith's mixed motives, deleting "~~relen~~" but then continuing "relenting *by force* [editor's italics]" (Ws.14$_{26}$ p.99).

Planning for transitions

Dickens's planning for transitions in the narrative varies. Generally he leaves it to the invention of the moment, often changing the scene, for instance by moving the narrative focus from one character to another, e.g. the use of Bagstock in ch.26. However, if the transition is particularly awkward—perhaps rather abrupt or frequent—he may plan for it in the worksheet. The most explicit example occurs amid the crowded ch.60, partly prepared for by Ws.19&20. The narrative focus is like a baton handed from one character to the next. Having followed his own direction to "Open with Blimber's" during Feeder's marriage to Cornelia, Dickens shifts the focus of the narrative to Toots by his arrival there with Susan, his wife (Ws.19&20$_{29}$ p.119). Afterwards, he follows the couple to their hotel where they receive a letter from Cuttle, in response to which they leave at once to meet its writer (810^{898}). Dickens can now "lead to Bunsby, through the Captain" (Ws.19&20a$_{33}$ p.123).

Of course, such a multiplication of plotlines, or "threads" as Dickens calls them, is a comparatively rare occurrence. However, there are instances of planning for a transition in single-number worksheets. Among them is the transition in ch.41, signalled by his characteristic pointer "*So to* [editor's italics] come to Edith at night" (Ws.13$_{33}$ p.95). Other similar instances of the cautionary "So to" can be found in the planning of ch.40 (Ws.13$_{28}$) and that of ch.49 (Ws.16$_{8}$ p.107).

For an uncharacteristic example of inevitable awkwardness in managing a transition, examine how Carker's ride home from the office is suddenly interrupted in ch.22. Coming up short in an unplanned, and unusually long, second and closing chapter, Dickens unexpectedly finds he has to extend the chapter as he approached its probable endpoint (see the added 'chapter plan' on the left-hand side (Ws.7$_{6}$ p.71) and its commentary). On this occasion, abruptness is unavoidable. Despite the attempt to disarm readers—with typical self-mockery explaining "a few digressive words are necessary" (305^{331})—they may detect a telling creak in the otherwise smooth transition. The narrative extension also detracts somewhat from what was probably his initial intention to end with the lascivious Carker, slowly riding by Dombey's house and contemplating the opportunity for advancement offered by the maturing Florence: "With dark eyes and hair, I recollect, and a good face; a very good face! I dare says she's pretty" (304^{330}).

Related to the use of chapter planning to manage awkward transitions is the planning of successive incidents to prepare for acceleration to an approaching climax. Compare for example the plan for Edith's final meeting with Florence in ch.61 (Ws.19&20$_{38\ \&\ 39}$ p.123), with the plan for the aftermath of Dombey's wedding ceremony in ch.31 (Ws.10$_{26-28}$ p.83) or the planned events leading up to the flight that ends ch.47 (Ws.15$_{28-31}$ p.103). Most of these notes would be without purpose or out of place in a summary, but in a plan they warn the author of an important sequence that requires particular narrative ingenuity.

Planning for the end

A special sort of transition is the more obvious, careful planning for the chapter's end, and the approach to the end, both of which are handled with the finesse that is characteristic of Dickens as a serial novelist. From Ws.4 onwards, when he plans chapters, he regularly defines their endings. For example in the more detailed chapter plans for Ws.5 he begins each plan by first identifying its end (Ws.5$_{5}$ p.57).

When he returns to chapter planning in Ws.9, he usually anticipates the detail of a chapter's conclusion. The procedure is especially evident in the closing chapter of the instalment; concerned to retain his reader, he designs the end to raise expectations and to linger in the reader's memory until the next month's issue.

Closing texts appear in shorter as well as longer chapter plans, whether "Dombey and Son's a daughter after all", which appears after the carefully planned ch.16, or "I have no hope but in you" in ch.43 after briefly planning the beginning and the middle, or in ch.30 where Dickens just describes, with no preliminaries, the chapter's closing tableau. Texts of endings are often revised (as in ch.30) at the planning stage, and then further changed during composition, as they are woven into the narrative, for example, at the death of Carker (see Ws.18_{10} p.115 and cf. 743^{823}). Summaries, of course, will also include material that ends a chapter, but usually as part of a list of similarly generalised items and always in less detail (see Ws.6_{17}, Ws.10_{14} & Ws.15_{14} pp.63, 83 and 103 respectively).

We come now to extrinsic indications of planning, i.e. differences between chapter description and the novel's text that have to do with the very different relationship that plans and summaries have with what Dickens actually composes. Plans differ from summaries in their relation to the manuscript in a number of ways.

Timing of title entry

A rather involved consideration is the relation in time between the entry of the title in manuscript and worksheet. Dickens's frequent practice, from Ws.4 onwards, of inserting the title in the manuscript during or after composition and, if necessary, revising it there, has an outcome for the worksheets. In the worksheet, if he intends both to plan on the page and to postpone the choice of title, he has to leave a blank space for the title between chapter number and chapter description. This sometimes results in a contrast in hand between the underlined title and the description, and some irregularity in their layout.

The contrast created by entering plan first and title later is obvious in Ws.5 and Ws.9 and 10. However from then onwards, the contrast between the two is less marked, partly because Dickens becomes more adept at estimating the space needed for the title, and partly because he may deliberately narrow the gap, if he anticipates a long plan, e.g. ch.32 in Ws.11. Title gapping in both manuscript and worksheet is also made easier by changes in the sort of title he chooses. Although throughout the novel he searches for titles that are inclusive and intriguing, after the first quarter he moves away from the longer mock-heroic title, preferring shorter ones in the second half, particularly the internally referential titles, many of which are one-liners (and easy to insert).[114]

A further complication is indicated by ch.51 (Ws.16 p.107). In that chapter, the first entry of the description has to be adjusted to prevent overwriting the title, which shows that the title is entered before the description. However, we can be reasonably certain—from the deletion of "~~the ser~~(vants)" and their move to the end of the description, from the omission of the introductory exchange between Dombey and Mrs Chick, and the later re-ordering in composition of the appearance of Miss Tox—that the chapter description is a plan, made before Dickens begins composition. So in this instance, we find that the title is first entered in worksheet, followed by the plan, then by the title in the manuscript, and finally by the composition of the text. A false start confirms that the title is entered early in the manuscript (see 'Appendix E', ch.51, p.190).

This less common procedure—titling first in the worksheet, then copying to manuscript (see 'Titling before composition', p.134)—is a reminder that Dickens is seldom methodical simply for the sake of being so. If circumstances change, as in ch.51—being so sure of his title that he can enter it first in the worksheet—he may change his practice. His general approach in this and in many other procedures is always business-like rather than systematic. Nevertheless, with the caveat to allow for the possibility of an early entry of a title in the worksheet, the relation of title entry to description entry, as revealed by layout and hand considered together, may indicate that the description precedes the title entry and that its purpose is planning.

Change of substance in composition

Many of Dickens's allusive salient-point plans are probably markers for narrative that he has already rehearsed in considerable detail. His fluent and startling inventiveness will of course open out what he has visualised in planning (see the letter to Browne, quoted above, p.136). Nevertheless, by comparing the published text with worksheet plans, it is clear that some passages are not an enlargement of a plan but additions to it. This is particularly true of early passages in opening and middle chapters—often more retrospective parts—where there is more time and space for invention independent of planning. For example in No.5, after the skilfully contrived opening reminder of the "young gentlemen" and adults involved in Paul's life at Dr Blimber's, the number continues with a lengthy exchange between Paul and Miss Blimber about his end-of-term analysis. Eventually, about a third of the way into the chapter, the narrative moves on to the invitations in preparation for the party, the first item in the chapter plan (Ws.5_4 p.57). Unlike the plan, a summary would probably include some reference to Miss Blimber's analysis and/or to the special position that Paul now enjoys at Dr Blimber's.

Change of order in composition

A summary of course aims to cover, in one way or another, however brief, the more important incidents in the order in which they occur in the text. Plans, on the other hand, are provisional. They may not only omit significant matter but also may be re-ordered at any point in composition (see for example the re-ordering of the items in the plan for ch.51 (p.107) during its composition (686-90$^{759\text{-}63}$)).

Interdependence of number plan and chapter plan

A final consideration has to do with the relation, not between chapter plan and the text that follows it, but between the chapter plan and the preceding number plan. It will be examined in connection with the development in number and chapter planning in the third quarter (see below).

Conclusion

Various sorts of evidence may indicate that a chapter description is a plan rather than a summary. The stronger, more reliable indications are:

- a choice of word(s) indicating intention
- an irregular layout suggesting hesitancy or pauses for thought
- deletions that are followed by revision, rather than by running correction
- the foregrounding of narrative transitions that require careful preparation
- the inclusion of the draft of a text to end the chapter.

Four less reliable indications all stem from the relation of the chapter plan to the manuscript. Less reliable, partly because of the difficulty of interpreting hand, quill and ink, they are:

- dissimilarity in the hand, quill or ink used for plan and for title, suggesting a gap in time between their entry
- marked irregularity of layout between plan and title, also suggestive of a gap in time between entries
- an order in the plan, which is re-ordered in composition
- omission in the plan of important material that is added in composition (or, rarely, the inclusion in the plan of material that is entirely omitted in composition).[115]

The table in 'Appendix B' summarises the entry history of each chapter title; the initial purpose of each chapter description, with a query if there are residual doubts about its purpose; and the briefest of notes on the reasons for the choice of plan or summary (see 'Appendix B' and its key, p.172). [116]

Chapter descriptions as summaries

Summaries, unlike plans, have no intrinsic defining features that enable us to identify a chapter description at once as a summary. However, those descriptions that cannot be identified with any certainty as plans—judging from the criteria in the 'Conclusion' above—may well be summaries. By examining these possible summaries, we can discover if some have features in common, which can be regarded as characteristic of Dickens's summaries.

Summaries in the first quarter

Dickens begins by using the space below chapter headings for a summary note, sometimes an expansion or clarification of the chapter title, sometimes a note of the main concern or of an important moment. In Ws.4, he expands the summary to two or three short entries, derived from successive parts of the chapter, and therefore ordered as in the text. As might be expected, the order of the summary matches that of the narrative, a characteristic (though not a defining one) of the longer summaries.

Summaries in the second quarter

In Ws.6, Dickens expands the summary further. Two of the more extended examples—the summary of the opening ch.17 (later 18) and that of the closing ch.19—are comparable in length to the plans of the first quarter. They are distinguished from them by a second feature to do with the relationship of chapter titling and description.

Dickens makes two attempts at titling ch.17 (later 18) during its composition, eventually choosing "Father and Daughter" (see 'Appendix D', ch.17 (later 18), p.184). In the worksheet for the chapter (Ws.$6_{12\text{–}17}$ p.63), although the lettering used for the title is of course larger than that used for the description, the slope of the lettering and density of the ink are the same for both. Moreover, the vertical alignment of title and description is comparable—setting aside for the moment the insertion (13) on "The state of mind of the household"—though with some slippage to the right as the arm of the right-handed author moves downwards. So it is reasonable to conclude from this uniformity of hand and layout that the final title and description are entered together, a conclusion that is incidentally confirmed by an ink smudge and the way entry (13) is inserted between title and summary (see commentary p.65). As the titling occurs during composition and is copied into the worksheet from the manuscript, and the description and title appear to be entered together, the description is very probably written after composition—and is therefore a summary.

The above line of argument rests finally on the hand and layout of title and description. In the third quarter especially, Dickens sometimes leaves a narrow gap for the title in the worksheet, enters his plan and inserts the title later with the same quill and ink that he used for the plan, obscuring evidence of the insertion. The description, appearing to be a summary, may be shown to be a plan on other grounds. For that reason, though uniformity of title and description may be typical of summaries, the feature has to be treated with caution.

Later in the second quarter, comparison of the summary of chapter twenty-nine with that of chapter seventeen (later eighteen) reveals another feature. Since the entries in each chapter summary are made at the same time, Dickens uses a similar syntax to describe them. In the case of ch.29, each entry opens with a name; in ch.17 (later 18) each entry—with the exception of entry (16)—has a similar phrase structure. Such stylistic mannerisms are more likely to be found in descriptions of what has already been narrated; they go with a tendency, being summaries, to generalise, simplify or compress.

Summaries in the third quarter

In the entanglement of Dickens's "threads" in the third quarter, most descriptions, whether plan or summary, become longer, more intricate and more detailed. He plans most opening chapters of the third quarter, including ch.32, an opening chapter that brings important developments in the counter plot, but excluding the opening ch.46 in No.15.[117] There are some contra-indications that the description for ch.32 is a summary—late titling in manuscript, the uniformity of hand and layout of title and description—but they are less persuasive than the many indications of planning (see the commentary on the 'Plan for ch.32', p.88).

Most of the summaries of the quarter can be reliably classified as such (see chs.36 (later 37), 44, 45, 46 and 48 in 'Appendix B'). The grounds for the classification vary. The commentaries on the faint blue entries in Ws.12 p.93, from the 'Title and summary of ch.36 (later 37)' onwards, show the effect of the use of this unusual ink on the order of entry in the worksheet and in the manuscript. All uses of faint blue in Ws.12, including its use in the composition of ch.38, are very probably unbroken and consecutive, i.e. involving only one colour change (from black to blue and back). A cursory look through the worksheet reveals that, because the description is in faint blue and its use is consecutive, the composition and titling of ch.36 (later 37) in black must come before the description, which is therefore a summary.

The initial purpose of the description of chs.44 and 45 is also largely established by factors extrinsic to the worksheet itself. The special circumstances affecting both ch.44 and 45 have been examined in an earlier section, concerned in part with No.14 (p.129), which shows that ch.44 is unplanned. Similarly, the commentaries on chs.44 and 45—arguing from the layout of chapter numbering, titles and descriptions, the brevity of content, and the circumstances of composition—present a strong case for treating the descriptions of both as summaries made after composition (see Ws.14 p.101).

With regard to the first two chapters of No.15 (which were written last), we know that Dickens, heavily committed to overseeing the establishment of Urania Cottage, was on 19 November "in a whirlwind of finishing a No [15] with a Crisis in it". Having finished the "crisis" chapter—with the two remaining chapters to write in little more than six days—Dickens is in a rush to complete the number. Nevertheless, he finds time for a detailed summary of ch.46, in view of its importance to the plot. He notes the crucial events in (10) and (11), in preparation for their later development, as he did, for example, in the only note on ch.22, a summary of Rob as Carker's spy (Ws.7_{16}). Then in entries (13) and (14), making up for the unfortunate cut made to ch.45, he wishes to make the motives of Carker and Edith more explicit and their later actions more plausible.[118] As part of the summary, he may memo both "states of mind", expecting to re-visit the worksheet—and, from it, the text—before advancing the action and opening out their characterization further in the final meeting of ch.54.[119]

In the description of ch.48 (formerly 47), Dickens notes three moments, one in each of the chapter's three sections, expanding the last (Ws.15_{21}) with the items that give rise to Cuttle's bewilderment. These details act as a reminder to himself and a sign to the reader of the starting point for the opening chapter of the next number. In ch.46, he inserts the chapter title after he begins composing; in ch.48 (formerly 47) he is obviously sure of the title from the outset, deriving it from (2) in the number plan. In both chs.46 and 48 (formerly 47) there is the same uniformity of hand and layout. Their substance, titling and appearance are indicative of summarising rather than planning.

Summaries in the fourth quarter

The last two single numbers of the fourth quarter, Ws.17 and 18, bring a marked change to the treatment of the worksheets. All remaining descriptions, though similar in the number of entries to the earlier ones, become less detailed. Their brevity reflects Dickens's concentration on the "pursuit" and the working out in narration of the denouement—what he calls in connection with a late scene in *Barnaby Rudge* "the Machinery of the Tale" (L2:471). All except for ch.55 and possibly ch.56 can be identified as summaries by the timing of entry and the hand of title and description (see chs.52–54 and 56 in 'Appendix B' p.171).

Conclusion

Summaries have no intrinsic or extrinsic feature that defines them as summaries. The principal task in identifying a summary is to determine the order of entry of the chapter description relative to the titling of the chapter in the manuscript. The timing of titling in the manuscript during composition has been examined in a previous section (see 'Titling during composition' p.133). If a chapter title is entered in manuscript during composition (either by insertion or with revision or both) and if the appearance of title and description in the worksheet shows they are entered together, we may tentatively conclude that the chapter description likely to be a summary. However, even if these two conditions are met, other evidence is needed to confirm it.

To sum up, examination of the chapter descriptions that are thought not to be plans reveals typical characteristics which suggest they summaries:

- similarity of entries—the entries of a summary are usually made at the same time and fluently written, which makes them similar in hand and in layout, whereas the entries of a plan, sometimes assembled over time, may be written in contrasting hand and layout
- similarity of order to that of the text—entries of a summary tend to follow the order of the text to which they refer, whereas those of a plan may be re-ordered in composition
- inclusiveness—apart from the recapitulatory and expansive matter of opening chapters, which both plans and summaries regularly omit, summaries are likely to refer to all important narrative material, whereas plans will omit all material that comes to Dickens during composition, and may include other material that he decides not to use (see Ws.13_{32} p.95).
- stylistic uniformity—on at least two occasions Dickens takes an obvious pleasure in making summary entries stylistically similar (see ch.17 (later 18) and ch.29 pp.63 and 83).

Development of number and chapter planning in each quarter

First quarter: Paul's story

Having devised the worksheet's basic format—a leaf for each instalment, folded in half vertically, then flattened down, with the left-hand half assigned to number planning and the right half to part and chapter headings—Dickens allows the issues that arise during planning and composition to guide him how he might adapt the format to his needs. Chapter planning entries in particular show how quickly planning-on-the-page develops from Ws.3 to Ws.5, once Paul becomes "a talking, walking, wondering Dombey".

The scope and method of number planning on the left-hand side is clear from the start. In Ws.1, Dickens confidently lays out his ideas for the opening and the following chapter. The first group of entries, bounded by a slash, gives the general situation and predicts the end "the boy born to die" (1), as planned in the "outline of [his] immediate intentions" (see endnote 42). The other three initial plans (3)–(5) with the insertion (2) introduce the principal characters of the first two chapters in order of appearance. The assembly as a whole carries in its sequence the shape of the narrative, just as groups (6) and (7) of the 'additional plans', though more spare, map the four sections of the final ch.4. The material of ch.3, unmentioned in the number plan (except for a note on possible lettering for the illustrations), grows out of the composition of ch.2. It introduces Susan Nipper and, through Richards, develops the character of Florence as a young child, revealing her difficult relationship with her father. It also contributes to the overrun and Dickens's dilemma in ch.4 (see 'Composition of an alternative' p.41).

With the leading characters introduced and the direction of the quarter established, Dickens has the shape of the next instalment in mind from the start. In Ws.$2_{1\text{-}3}$, the number plan moves smoothly from one episode to the next, but of course omits any reference to the closing ch.7 concerning Miss Tox and Major Bagstock, which had been written earlier as a shorter alternative closing chapter to No.1.

The number plan for Ws.3 is less orderly. In this central instalment of the first quarter, as Dickens begins to complicate both the main Dombey plot and the counter plot "Wally and Co", he considers bringing in other threads associated with Miss Tox, the Major and Carker. He has also been pondering the effect of extending the life of Paul from four to five numbers. By listing possible lines of development and querying potential ideas, the number plan determines the likely content of the number, but at the same time indicates that some of its material will be held over to the next instalment or beyond. He marks by underlining two groups of entries (4) and (7) to "stand over". Similarly, in Ws.4, he underlines two entries (1) and (4) signalling that, though important to the part under preparation, they are also to be carried forward into later numbers. Such underlining, like querying, are often used as ways of indicating that some entries may need to be attended to later.

His starting point on the right-hand side is determined by the loose-leaf nature of the worksheet. As he accumulates the worksheets, he probably expects to regularly shuffle through them to track the substance and detail of earlier numbers. The right-hand side serves first of all as a basic record of the part number, so that he can quickly re-order the sheets by their instalment, if they become disordered. After the part number, he usually goes on to enter the chapter number headings (the exceptions occur towards the end of the novel when he heads up a few sheets in advance). Titles follow as he works on each chapter.

In Ws.1, Dickens appears to use the right-hand side—in this worksheet only—to trial, revise and finalise chapter titles (probably during composition), whereas from Ws.2 onwards he usually titles and revises in manuscript, then transfers the final title to the worksheet (the only early exception is ch.8). This arrangement, if there is any doubt in his mind about the choice of title, becomes his common practice. It has two obvious advantages. In the worksheet, it leaves the record prominent, uncluttered and clear at a glance, and in the manuscript, it gives him the opportunity to devise an apt title, revising as he writes. It is an obvious first step in adapting format and improving method, which has consequences that are probably unforeseen at the time. His concern to anticipate how he is going to use the worksheets is evident in the his decision, after Ws.1, to avoid both reversing the page as in Ws.1_8, and turning the page over as in Ws.1 (verso)$_{22\ \&\ 23}$ p.37, both of which would encumber the later use of the worksheet as a record. He hurriedly re-enters the number heading and title of ch.4—without underlines or capitals—on the front of the worksheet.

The right-hand half of Ws.2, in one respect, may seem more unsettled than that of Ws.1. It has eight negated "smallhand" notes towards its right-hand edge. These appear to be pre-format jottings (see commentary, p.44). The negative, which probably applies to all eight, confirms Dickens's decision to confine number plans to left-hand page. Always excluding number plans from the right-hand page is another important step, which also affects how the worksheet is used. It confirms the importance of the number plan as a separate and distinct entity. He completes the record for Ws.2 by adding the chapter titles altogether, including that of ch.7, the alternative ch.4 held over from No.1.

As the mock-heroic style of many of the chapter titles in Ws.1 and 2 do not explicitly refer to their subject, Dickens takes one step further by way of record. He adds a descriptive note or two beneath most of the chapter titles. In Ws.3, he expands that record to include an incident from each chapter, demonstrating a theme common to all three—the power of money, what it can, cannot and should not do. He also adds to the lower left-hand side a striking simile for use later, together with other details for chs.8 and 9. These final entries in Ws.3 signal a another important development. He is adapting the worksheet format to include—for the moment on the left-hand page—striking textual detail destined for individual chapters, as yet unwritten, and probably not yet fully imagined.

The next worksheet Ws.4 widens the focus and setting of the story. Paul is first dispatched with Florence to Mrs Pipchin's, then to the Blimbers. With the substance of the instalment defined in (1), the structure of the narrative follows in (2) and (3) and the triangular relation of the father and the two children deepens in (4). However, Dickens's imagination, now preoccupied with Paul, outruns number planning. He pursues the development of the previous worksheet, evident in its final left-hand page entries, by using a separate leaf (Ws.4a) that he eventually attaches to the bottom of the left-hand page of Ws.4. This leaf concentrates on chapter planning, as in Ws.3, but with the difference that it prepares for a sequence of incidents in just one chapter, and, in its final entries, visualises a small section of text. Rehearsing part of a chapter, it may have been used as a separate sheet during the composition of a mid-section of ch.12. Its entries, like some left-hand entries in Ws.3, could just as well belong in the right-hand half.

Finally, with his course set for the climax of No.5, Dickens temporarily sets aside his previous method of number planning. He decides to present Paul's "illness only in the child's own feelings". He had anticipated as long as ago as the beginning of July that such an innovation would generate "a new and peculiar sort of interest" in the reader and involve "a little bit of delicate treatment".[120] He supports the innovation—"a difficult, but a new way of doing it"—with an additional leaf Ws.5a, in which he plans the presentation of the ailing child's inner life. The leaf, a unique chapter-cum-number plan, first serves as a map of Paul's part in ch.14, and then, with one addition (6), is also used to intensify the effect of ch.16. It is later wafered into the position of a number plan on the unused left-hand side of Ws.5, with the incidental result that no mention is made in the chapter-cum-number-plan of the meandering ch.15 (partly planned on the right-hand half by Ws.5$_{8-11}$). The early chapters plans, like many later ones, reveal Dickens's concern to plan for closure, particularly for the end—and for the approach to the end—of the closing chapter of each number.

The first five numbers are not planned as a narrative unit, but grow out of Dickens's involvement with Paul. He consults Forster, before he embarks on No.3, about extending Paul's life into No.5. Once he makes "number three a kind of halfway house between infancy and Paul being eight or nine", Paul's education can take up two numbers. Following that decision, ch.16 becomes the aim and endpoint of his story (*Life* 477[K:9358]) and the climax of the first quarter.

The notes preparing for the first quarter—assembling some materials, often roughly in chapter order, adding other possibilities, noting what is to be used or carried forward, and finally abbreviating number plans to concentrate on the planning of chapters—set a pattern, which recurs with some differences of emphasis in the next two quarters. Dickens also begins the two forward-looking procedures—querying and underlining (with a continuous single line)—that he will rely in later numbers, especially in the corresponding, less orderly, midway numbers of the second and third quarters (Ws.8 and Ws.13). As might be expected, querying disappears in the denouement of the fourth quarter, except for his hesitation over Florence's meeting with Edith and over the inclusion of the Barnet Skettles. Single underlining is also reduced there to three predictable instances; the pursuit (Ws.17$_{2,\ 16\ \&\ 19}$ p.111), Toots (Ws.18$_3$ p.115) and the legacy thread (Ws.19&20$_{12}$ p.119). However, although the single point-of-view chapter plan of Ws.5a is not used again in *Dombey and Son*, it does reveal Dickens's enduring interest in the power of focalisation to move the reader. An innovation intended to intensify empathy for the dying child, it prepares for the more sustained ironized first person narratives of childhood in his later fiction.

Second quarter: Florence alone and the second marriage

In the number plan for Ws.6 p.63, Dickens declares that he must "throw the interest of Paul *at once* [editor's italics] on Florence" (2). He knows what he plans to do, but finds it difficult to discover how to do it. There are signs of uncertainty in the changes of hand, the varied positioning of entries and the thinness of material concerning Florence. The opening ch.17 seems to preoccupy him, particularly the part that the father has in it. Dombey's hostility towards Florence has to be sufficiently fierce to make the memory of it a source of guilt, and motivate the remorse implied by (6). Yet it must not result in so painful a scene that it precludes further development of their relationship.

Knowing that he has less time—February being a short month—in Ws.6 Dickens abandons chapter planning of the sort evident in chs.13–16. He reverts to record keeping, similar to but more detailed than the one-line entries of Ws.1–3. The summary for ch.17 (later 18) is the fullest record, entered after composition (see 'Title and summary of ch.17' p.65). As in the past, he relies on "invention" rather than "planning" to carry him through each chapter. In this way, despite difficulties, he completes Ws.6, even extending the worksheet's function in one respect.

Progressive corrosion suggests that the left-hand entry concerning Cuttle's watch is a final note, added after Dickens completes the summary of ch.19. He makes the note at this point, expecting that the detail will be used and perhaps further developed later on. Similar last minute 'memo-ing'—tagging an idea by its isolated entry on the lower left-hand page—recurs in later worksheets of the second quarter, another step in the development of worksheet,

Though he seldom records how a number begins, in the opening ch.17 (later 18) he keeps a record of the start of ch.17 (later 18), inserting the household's "state of mind" (Ws.6$_{13}$ p.63). In Ws.10 a similar late entry—but another afterthought and 'memo' on the lower left-hand half—reminds Dickens to enlarge on the way the servants act "as a sort of chorus" in the second half of the novel (see Ws.10$_{7}$ p.83). He adds the qualification "sort of" because he has by then already dramatised the way members of the household interact with one another as well as intrude rather than comment on life above stairs.

By transposing chs.17 and 18 at proof stage, Dickens may wish to avoid two successive chapters on the counter plot and, at the same time, bring immediate comic relief to readers of the one-volume edition, after the pathos of the previous chapter. Although he always strives to engage his readers in an opening chapter, which the first half of ch.17 certainly does, he may also, on reflection, want to move the chapter away from that position, because of his apprehension over the effect of its final scene. The transposition incidentally reveals that he enters the monthly update of his "List of Chapter Headings" before proofs arrived (see 'Appendix C' p.176). However, when they did, he immediately realised that, quite untypically, he had overestimated the length of his copy. He rushes from Paris to London to supply more text.

The worksheet for No.7 is prefaced by the lengthy (and unique) account, in bright blue, of the circumstances and motives of Mrs Skewton and her daughter. By establishing Edith's background, it prepares for her ambivalent coolness prior to marriage. Below this prefatory account, Dickens makes just two entries in black, Ws.$7_{3\,\&\,4}$ p.71. They prepare for what was initially intended as a very long opening chapter during which Dombey, on a visit to Leamington Spa, egged on by his travelling partner Major Bagstock, begins his rush into a second marriage. He then titles and composes the number in a bright blue ink, adding the title for ch.20 to the worksheet. The final items on the left-hand side—also in bright blue, entered adjacent to ch.22—are probably a hurried plan to extend ch.22, made during its composition. He appears to have approached his prepared ending sooner than expected (see 'Additional plan' p.73, for a reconstruction of his movements and the use of bright blue).

The only entry in the chapter description space (Ws.7 p.71) notes how Carker plants his spy Rob in Sol's shop (15), a crucial plot device contrived early, on the presumption that Florence will probably go there, anxious for news of Walter. Once again surveying a completed but rather spare worksheet, he adds a final entry (5), a memo of the location of the backstory of Harriet. He anticipates her importance to the action, midway on the social scale between the rich and the destitute, and purposefully located on the great North road. She replaces her brother's part in the story, who is now for the most part redundant with the change of plan for Walter. This entry (Ws.7_5) and Cuttle's watch (Ws.6_5 p.63), the list of names (Ws.8_{10} p.75) and the reminder about the servant chorus (Ws.10_7 p.83), are all final entries noted for their later potential, probably entered as Dickens surveys a completed worksheet.

The number plan and commentary for No.8 reveal the dilemma now facing him. On the one hand, he wants to give the novel a pleasing shapeliness by postponing the courtship to No.9, and therefore the wedding to No.10. On the other hand, he knows how difficult it will be to generate a narrative centred on Florence—especially in Dombey's absence—from his experience of producing No.6. Of the ten entry groups in the number plan for No.8, only half are used to plan and compose its three chapters. Like the number plans for the other midway instalments of the first and third quarters, the plan is strategic, i.e. undertaken in the light of what is to follow (cf. Ws.3 and Ws.13). A letter to Forster adds to our understanding of his view of the impasse, and incidentally how he now construes preparation for composition as *planning* and invention, in that order:

> I have only just begun [No.8]. I have been trying for three or four days, but really have only just begun. I am particularly anxious not to anticipate in this No. what I design for the next, and consequently must plan and invent for it. [...] Deepest of despondency (as usual in commencing Nos.) (L5: 55).

The curtailed worksheet for Ws.8 (p.75), like that of Ws.7, shows that, if short of time and/or in adverse circumstances, Dickens may jettison chapter descriptions altogether, and fall back on chapter titling alone as the principal reminder of contents, supplemented of course by the relevant number plan entries.

Misfortune dogs him in the months following his dash to London to complete No.6: the serious illness of Charley, his eldest son, at school in London, which enforced the family's return in March during Ws.7; the difficult birth of Sidney, his seventh child, which so shocked Dickens that he is unable to work on Ws.8 for several days in April; then in May, a third mischance befalls him. A severe horse-bite leaves a nervous weakness in his writing arm (the right), delaying his start on Ws.9. His letters at the time confirm that, although he may plan and make a start on the opening ch.26 earlier in the month, he is physically unable to write at any length, until after he leaves for Brighton on 17 May to recover from the accident.

The number plan for No.9 is the shortest so far, Dickens perhaps hoping that it can be chapter-planned throughout, as in the penultimate and final worksheet for the first quarter. The weakness in his writing arm helps to explain number plan's brevity and the planning together of two final chapters.

The weakness may also account for the unusual large rounded hand of all three chapter titles, probably entered after the strain of writing the number. Hand and layout suggest that they are entered together, into the spaces left for them by the plans, a gapping tactic that he seems to have used for the first time in the 'Plan for ch.13' (see Ws.4 p.53).

Throughout Ws.9, he makes all entries in the worksheet in black, whereas he uses a bright blue ink to compose each chapter, except for the opening pages of ch.26. The commentary on Ws.9 shows how the two changes (moving from black to blue and back twice) enables Dickens to preserve his supply of the quick-drying bright blue for composition. In both number and chapter plan, he emphasises, by underlining, the significance of the preparatory ploy that connects Carker with Edith "before the wedding" (Ws.$9_{2,\ 13\ \&\ 14}$ p.79).

Still "bring[ing] on the marriage gradually" (Ws.9_2), in Ws.10 (p.83), Dickens abandons early an attempt in the light of his experience of No.7 at a two-chapter plan. He divides the marriage material in entries (4) and (6), so that he can end the second quarter with a wedding climax. Concerned as much with what follows the instalment as the instalment itself, the number plan prepares for the later development of Feenix, Miss Tox, Harriet, and the servant chorus. A detail concerning the marriage "coming off" (5) may be a left-hand side addition to the adjacent end plan for chapter thirty, made there because of the lack of space on the right-hand side. However, the contrast of hand between (5) and (18) and some similarity of entry (5) to entries (4) and (6) suggest that it is noted during number planning, because of its special significance as a crucial moment in the characterisation of Dombey.

Dickens's initial entry for ch.30 is a note of the text for the closing tableau, an end plan comparable to the endings of the chapter plans for Ws.4a and 5, and to the single entry end plan for ch.55. Planning is suggested by the deletion and re-ordering of "kneeling" and the insertion of "lying" (18). However, the note "Preparations for Cousin Feenix" (17), with its often-overlooked diagonal slash, is probably another memo to himself of the sort that records the location of a detail for future use. Referring to Feenix's association with the Brooke Street house, it also anticipates his later role as the senior family member at the wedding and beyond.

The two contrasting uses of the chapter description space are nicely illustrated in the entries for chs.29 and 31. As a summary, the notes for ch.29 are an orderly and stylish list, uniform in hand with title and carefully laid out, describing the content of the chapter in general terms. As a plan of a special sort, the notes for ch.31 delineate the structure of the day, giving a salient-point outline, which Dickens can elaborate from his easy recall of many imaginary rehearsals of the chapter. Apparently observing events as they happen, he lays down a tightly structured through plan to help him manage the narrative, and pace it to its measured end. The imperative "Begin" and the elided directive "back to dawn" confirm planning intent. Far from being occasional, as Butt and Tillotson imply in their summary (Butt and Tillotson, p.27), the detailed through plan will be matched by another quarterly climax at the end of No.15.

The worksheets of the second quarter as a whole reveal Dickens's determination to control the shape of the story, even if it means writing the occasional weaker chapter. He does so by extending the portrayal of the grieving Florence alone and without family support, sharing the narrative between Florence in Nos.6 and 8 and Dombey in Nos.7 and 9. He then plans to "bring [...] the marriage on gradually" in Ws.9, so that a climax can be reached in No.10. Despite the disruption caused by family illness, his wife's difficult labour and his own accident, he always manages to complete each worksheet, though obviously hindered by circumstances and by difficulties in the story itself. Nevertheless, from

Ws.6 to Ws.8, the number plans successively lose structure and extension. Compelled to "invent" rather than "plan" he very soon abandons chapter descriptions, whether plan or summary.

In Ws.9 and 10, Dickens recovers the development of the worksheet that he reached in Ws.5. Reviving an important device—begun in chs.13–15 (Ws.4 and 5)—in chs.26, 27 and 28, he leaves a space blank for chapter title and plans the chapter. Having composed and titled the chapter, and perhaps revised it during composition, he enters the title in the space left for it in the worksheet.[121] As before, Dickens identifies the lower left-hand space as an opportunity to memo ideas for future numbers (Ws.10_7). Once more in ch.30, he leaves recapitulations and lead-ins to invention and, by planning endings, anticipates the scope for narrative that precedes it (see ch.30). However, in the unusually long climactic chapter that closes the quarter, he through-plans the whole from dawn to dawn, ending as before with Carker on horseback. He finds the involvement of Carker, Dombey and Edith particularly absorbing, judging from the number of entries that concern them.

Third quarter: Marriage breakdown and Cuttle's life in the shop

Delaying the Dombey story in No.11, Dickens brings on the Mrs Brown subplot that will lead to the pursuit of Carker, to his death and ultimately to Dombey's ruin. Throughout the third quarter, he skilfully counterpoints the main plot with his many supporting intrigues, with the notable exception of No.14, where he once more interweaves narratives concerned with Dombey and Florence. The more numerous entries in each number plan reflect the growing complexity of the novel, as he introduces, advances or delays the various threads.

While the plots thicken in the third quarter, Dickens is also working quite deliberately on another sort connection between entries. The notes show how alert he is to pointedly draw out the various contrasting parallels of the third quarter: the "companion pictures" of the homes of the two brothers (Ws.11_1 p.87), the "contrast" of the two mothers and daughters (26); in Ws.12 (p.91), the "at home" of Dombey and that of the Toodles (14) and (22); and the "New Voices" in Mrs Skewton's death "in contrast to Paul's" (Ws.13_{34} p.95). Finally, before getting far into the composition of No.15, he makes his calculation of Florence's age (Ws.6a), and checks it against the timing of the second anniversary of Dombey's wedding, so that Edith can elope on the day of the second anniversary of "her wedding-Day" as part of her revenge (Ws.15_2 p.103).

There is an understandable tendency in accounts of the working notes to emphasise the separateness of the left-hand number plan from the right-hand chapter plan—a separation which is strengthened by the use of the word 'page' to describe either half. Chapter plans are expected to derive from number plans, as they usually do. In the first quarter, we have seen how some chapter plans, distinct from the more frequent right-hand chapter records, are entered on the left-hand half and used in a specific chapter during composition (Ws.3_{8-11} and Ws.4a). In the second quarter, one left-hand entry Ws.10_5 (p.83) is obviously intended for a specific chapter. In that instance, a chapter plan detail—Mr Dombey musing at table—displaced to the left-hand half later leaks back to the right-hand half during composition. Conversely, the chapter plan Ws.5a, and perhaps Ws.4a as well, are probably employed as separate sheets during the composition of individual chapters, before they are attached to the left-hand side.

In Ws.11–14, the relation between the left and right-hand side becomes more involved, largely because each number and chapter plan is longer and more detailed. Dickens sometimes goes between the two, treating them as interdependent rather than derivative. The plan for the opening ch.35 of Ws.12 p.91 is complementary to the corresponding entries in number plan; there is little overlap between the left-hand entries (2) and (3) and the right-hand entries (12)–(15). In Ws.13 (p.95), while the first item of entry (5) "Progress of domestic unhappiness" describes the general situation of the plan for ch.40, the second item "extravagance" is unmentioned but presumed in the chapter plan and written into the chapter during composition. In the same way, Bagstock's presence—noted in the number plan (4)—is woven into the final section of the chapter but not mentioned in its plan. In Ws.14 (p.99), the number plan for ch.42 makes it clear that Dombey's intention is "to reduce proud Edith" so that, in the chapter plan, Dombey's "instructions" need not be defined.

In Ws.11, however, the relation is more elaborate than any of the above. The number plan entries that relate to the opening chapter of the quarter ch.32 are unusually extended in entries (2)–(5). Dickens closely interweaves the left-hand entries (2)–(5) for ch.32 with the right-hand entries (12)–(16), so that in composition his entries become re-ordered as follows—(2), (4), (12), (13), (3), (15), (16)—while (14) is threaded into Toot's entry at (4) and his exit after (3). The "Glimpse of the chicken" entry (14) seems to reply to the otherwise unanswered entry (5) "Mr Toots and the chicken - qy". As readers, we can only assemble the two plans in the order suggested by their substance and appearance on the page. Dickens, on the other hand, can in his imagination separate and combine the materials of each entry, until he is satisfied with the narrative they generate. Although Dickens's summaries, like his plans, sometimes presume the substance of an entry in the number plan—compare for example Ws.4$_{1\ \&\ 10}$ (p.51)—none except ch.17 (later 18) have as intricate a relation to their number as the plan for ch.32. In this instance, the process being so intertwined confirms that the chapter description for ch.32 is a chapter plan.

With regard to ink changes in the quarter, a very limited supply of bright blue ink is reserved for the final ch.34 (cf. Nos.7 and 9). The commentary of Ws.12 again assumes that the use of blue—on this occasion a faint watery blue ink—is entirely consecutive, like the bright blue of Ws.7 (setting aside the unique entry Ws.7$_2$). The assumption again results in a more economical solution to the order-of-entry conundrum. Consecutiveness in the use of faint blue confirms that the title and description of ch.36 (later 37) follows its composition (and is a summary), and that the title and description of ch.37 (later 38) precedes its composition (and is a plan). Thus it also confirms that the accompanying indications used to identify the descriptions—similarity of title and description in ch.36 (later 37) and the directive and deletion in ch.37 (later 38)—are generally reliable.

The haphazard entries of Ws.13 (p.95) are similar to those of other midway worksheets, with the difference that almost all of its many entries find a place in the number in hand. Number planning is more tightly focused. The timing of related threads (Susan's dismissal and the installation of Pipchin) becomes more pressing as the crisis approaches. Nevertheless, as in the number plans of the other four worksheets of this quarter, some entries look to later instalments (see (13) and (14)).

Generally the chapter planning in the third quarter is more consistent in length, though still varying in the extent of its detail. The distinction between end-plans and through-plans is less evident. Most cover a series of salient points in each chapter, as though Dickens has now found the range of predictive allusion that is most useful to him. Having marked so emphatically the close of the first two quarters, he seems to have anticipated doing the same in the third. The notes show him planning to slow Carker's involvement in the marriage break-up (Ws.12_6). At first in Ws.15 (p.103), he plans to end with a climatic ch.48 (later 47), comparable to chs.16 and 31. He explains why he had to alter this initial plan; he re-adjusts their order, to leave the reader in a "pleasanter" frame of mind at the end of the number, dwelling on his reasoning as if—reluctant to lose a close parallel with the final chapters of Nos.5 and 10—he needed to reassure himself of the rightness of the decision (Ws.15_6 p.103).

In contrast to previous climactic ch.31 that closed the second quarter, ch.48 later 47 (p.103) has only one indication of planning intent, the substitution of "matter" for "reflection", implying that the substance of the digression should be more a matter of fact than opinion. The exposition concerning the development of Florence and the description of events that follows might be found in a summary, with the exception of the final sequence. Dickens attends to the close, anticipating that its outline will be a helpful aid to smoothing the transitions in a rapid and accelerating narrative. His concern for this basic but important aspect of the storyteller's craft—the management of the pace of different transitions—becomes explicit in the chapter plans of the double number (see Ws.19&20a_{33} p.123).

Although in the third quarter the scope of the worksheet entries enlarges with the entanglements of the story, there are no further developments in the sort of entry that Dickens makes there, other than those that show his interest in drawing out contrasting parallels between groups separated by social class and between events separated by time. As the worksheets accumulate, we can begin to see more clearly how he may use them retrospectively. He would certainly look back to pick out those entries that explicitly cue material for the next number (Ws.$8_{3\ \&\ 4}$ and Ws.$13_{2\ \&\ 14}$ pp.75 and 95) and those entries made "with an eye to the future" (Ws.11_8 p.87), particularly those to do with "the Machinery of the Tale" (e.g. Ws.7_{15} or Ws.15_{12} pp.71 and 103). He might watch the left-hand pages for those queries or underlined entries that, for a variety of reasons, might need further attention. Finally, when he needed to check the temporal consistency of the narrative, it seems very likely that he used both the left and right-hand of the accumulating worksheets, as a guide to accessing and tracking detail in his collection of the more distant back numbers. The small sheet Ws.6a undertaken at the start of No.15 shows how he uses worksheet and back number to calculate Florence's age and the timing of the elopement. No doubt he would do the same to check continuity of other details, particularly where the effect of retrospection intensifies pathos, for example, in the many departure scenes.

The later worksheets from Ws.9 to Ws.16 show that, in the creation of a chapter, from the imagined narrative to the finished text, there may be a continuing process of change. Beginning with an imagined narrative, Dickens has many opportunities to rehearse and change it. He may adjust the narrative to his number plan. He may eventually weave it into a putative chapter plan. He may revise the plan during its notation, hence the occasional query, deletion and revision. He may expand on what he has planned on the page, as he composes. He may also adjust its order, alter its emphasis, or insert new materials. Finally, even at proof stage, he has the opportunity to divide, transpose, add, correct or cut. The operation of such a varied cumulative method of working—apart from his powers of imagination—rests on an unusually retentive memory for detail and confident security of recall, as discussed in 'Memory, speech-making and planning', p.134.

Fourth quarter: Denouement

The last quarter of the novel falls into two sections, the first leading up to Carker's death and Florence's wedding (Nos.16–18), and the second to Dombey's ruin and Florence's reconciliation first to her father and then to Edith (Nos.19&20). Both sections are treated in a distinctively different way in their respective worksheets.

Number planning, already shrinking in Ws.15, diminishes as plotlines advance and the denouement becomes more predictable. In Ws.16 and 17, right-hand half entries are written in a fluent, even hand with a decisiveness that comes from Dickens's concentration on a closed set of problems. Forward-looking entries in the previous quarter suggest that he already has in mind how many of the intrigues are to be resolved and the few past mysteries explained, but in this quarter, he attends to when and in what order.

In Ws.16 (p.107), number planning is restricted to the romance plot, represented by the single entry "Return of Walter". In the number plan for Ws.17 (p.111), entry (1) sets up the chase, entry (2) prepares for the part Harriet will play later, through the connection to Morfin, and for her role in relation to Alice, and entry (3) announces the alteration to Dickens's intentions for Edith. Carker's death opens Ws.18. Dickens then devotes the rest of No.18 to the counter plot, restoring the community of the now crowded Shop and preparing for the marriage of the lovers (Ws.18$_{2-5}$ p.115).

In the three worksheets Ws.16–18, it is often difficult to detect with any certainty the function of the chapter descriptions, largely because so many entries are very brief. Nevertheless, whereas most chapter descriptions in the third quarter are chapter plans, in the last quarter before the double number, plans and summaries seem more evenly divided (see 'Appendix B' p.171). Dickens, with a clear idea of what remains to be done, has less need for chapter planning. For some chapters—those especially concerned with the "Machinery", for example the chapters of No.17—he borrows from the conventions of melodrama, preferring to control the detail of how to resolve the various plots in his imagination alone, as he did throughout previous novels (see the letter to Gaylord Clark, p.135). After the composition of each chapter, he keeps a brief, orderly record, presumably to provide a quickly accessible check on what he has covered.

Just because of the way these bare summaries pare down narrative, they often reveal Dickens's debt to theatre. They may give *dramatis personae* and setting, entrances and exits, forshadowings and climaxes, e.g. "Alice & Good Mrs Brown", "French men laying the supper", "To them Mr Dombey", "He [Morfin] shadows forth Mr Dombey's ruin" and "Scene between them [Edith and Carker]".

Nevertheless, many chapter descriptions in the final quarter can be identified as plans. The planning of ch.51, for example, a preparatory chapter that motivates the pursuit, shows planning intent by its deletions and revisions, by the re-ordering of its entries in composition and by making good an omission, the return of Mrs Chick to query the whereabouts of Florence. The description of ch.55, though brief, prepares for composition by a draft of the closing text (10), then, judging by the contrast of hand and layout, notes back in time to Carker's twofold "progress" towards Death (9)—referring to the emotional logic of the narrative, as well as his physical journey. The teasingly oblique title follows, its underlines positioned midway between title and the text below. The style of the title's entry in the manuscript confirms that Dickens devises it early; he may enter it there, as he begins to write the chapter. Dickens may also plan the middle ch.56. He appears to insert the title during composition; so in the worksheet, he leaves a generous gap, then plans by tilting the line, cramping his entries but keeping each group distinct and the order of incidents clear, and closing with the Chicken's final delivery.

Planning the double number

Dickens's worksheet for the double number is his plan for concluding the main plot (the failure of the Firm and the bankruptcy of Dombey), its inner plot (the relation of Dombey and daughter) and for winding-up the storylines of most named supporting characters.

In the number plan (Ws.19&20 p.119), he goes to the heart of the novel, preparing for the final stage in the relationship of father and daughter with entry (2) the birth of her child that moves Florence to relent and forgive, and entry (3) the repeated rhetorical device for ch.57 "Let him remember" prepared for in the left-hand side of Ws.6 (p.63). The power of memory to re-value the past and transform the present leads to Dombey's breakdown and to his rescue from suicide by Florence. With entry (4), Dickens is anticipating that the intensity of the reconciliation will need to be balanced by comedy. He details a broad comic inversion of male power in the main plot, and of romance in the counter plot, by winding up the MacStinger thread with the helpless Bunsby being processed like a slave towards marriage—to Cuttle's disbelief and discomfort.

The remaining left-hand entries are a unique rollcall of most named characters (excluding those mentioned in the number plan so far) in order to re-use or revive them in a way that completes their story. The proofs show the close attention Dickens gives to completing this curtain call of all the players (see commentary on Ws.19&20a p.125).

Turning to the right-hand half, with the same corroding black as that of the rollcall, Dickens plans ch.58. After its composition, he plans ch.59 in a denser black, then uses an unusual greeny blue ink to compose ch.59. When he returns to the worksheet and wafers Ws.19&20a into position—assuming his use of the ink is consecutive and unbroken, as seems likely—we can track his greeny blue entries from then on. He titles chs.58 and 59, titles and plans ch.60, enters a key idea for the next (as yet unnumbered) chapter, and lastly enters the number and title of the final chapter ch.62, all in greeny blue, after which he returns to black for the last time, to plan and compose ch.60. Without the ink change, the breaks within chapters and the movement between them would probably go undetected. This striking example of how an unbroken use of a coloured ink and quill affects entry order confirms comparable outcomes of the other isolated colour changes noted in Ws.7 and 12.

Many of the indications used to identify chapter planning in previous worksheets also appear in what is generally agreed to be self-evident chapter planning in the double number:

- the directives as in entries (17), (33) and (45)
- the preparation of text as in entries (22), (32) and (45)
- the inclusion of important detail in the manuscript that is omitted in planning, for example, the omission of Mrs Brown's back story in ch.58, or the omission of the apt part that Polly plays in ch.59, or of the role in ch.61 that Walter, as guide and protector, has in arranging Florence's meeting with Edith, and accompanying her to Brook Street
- the re-ordering of a plan in composition (see 'Composition and titling of ch.62' in Ws.19&20a p.125).

The re-ordering of earlier chapter plans in composition—in ch.26, for example, where the action follows Bagstock from the hotel to Mrs Skewton's and back—are minor adjustments, however, compared to those of ch.62. The difference arises from the greater compression of planning and composition in the double number. Dickens anticipated that managing such a variety of different problems in the double number would require a longer period of undisturbed concentration, which gave him the opportunity in the composition of ch.62 to reorder, recombine and add to what he had planned.

Two general planning procedures occur, also confirming the practice in previous worksheets, both associated with the use of greeny blue ink. They are the delay in titling chapters (chs.58–60) and the planning of two related chapters at the same time (chs.60 and 61). In the worksheets for single instalments, Dickens plans chs.33 and 34 together, and occasionally delays titling until a later chapter (see for example 'Appendix B', ch.26 p.169).

Dickens attends to planning rapid transitions in the double number, just as he did earlier worksheets. In ch.60, because of the number and variety of incidents, he points up how the narrative is to be carried from place to place by Cuttle (see entry (33) in Ws.19&20a p.123). For much the same reason, the management of transition becomes of special concern in planning the crises of climactic chapters in previous quarters (see 'Planning for transitions', p.140).

Mention has been made earlier how, from Ws.4 onwards, when Dickens plans chapters, he regularly defines their endings. In the more detailed chapter plans for Ws.5, he begins each chapter plan by identifying its end. When he returns to chapter planning in Ws.9, whether the chapter plan is an outline or more extended, he anticipates the detail of its ending. The procedure is especially evident in the closing chapter of each instalment.

However, in the double number, except for the final ch.62, planning each chapter's end is not a priority. In the absence of a lengthy number plan for the double instalment, chapter plans have to carry considerably more information than most of the plans for the single issues. Consequently, Dickens, while adding more matter as the opportunity arises in narration, also appears to rely on his memory to recall the retrospective allusions that end each chapter.

For example, the closing subject of the plan of the first chapter of the double number ch.58 "Alice's repentance and death" (18) is expanded in the text to include Alice's last wish that her mother reveal her blood relation to Edith, which is unmentioned in the chapter plan (though of course regularly hinted at earlier in the novel). The revelation leads to the long cadence to Alice's death, in which Dickens pleads for compassionate understanding of the harsh environment of "the mortal house on which the rain had beaten [...] in the wintry wind", an ending that recalls the ending of ch.33 entitled "Contrasts" in which Alice (unnamed) kisses Harriet when she leaves (465[511], cf. 786[871]).

Similarly, in the longest chapter of the number ch.59, Dickens ends not on the Florence's rescue of her father, the last note in its chapter plan (26), but on Miss Tox, who now perhaps for the last time coaxes the "bullet-headed" Robin into respectability, and on Polly. Unmentioned in the chapter plan, the latter is crucial to the chapter's end. He cues her presence by means of Mrs Pipchin's summons of a person she remembers as "Richards" to be her replacement—as she prepares to ride back to Brighton (rejoining Berinthia and Pankey) by Fly van in the comfort of Dombey's study chair, the "dead bargain of the sale" (793–94[879–80]). The chapter ends by repeating another contrast, the "shrill delight" awaiting Polly at her home in comparison with Dombey's deserted mansion "frowning like a dark mute on the street" (804[892]). The same extraordinary combination of innovation, reference and allusion characterises the end of all the other chapters; Dickens applies his energies and inventiveness to redoubling the reader's sense of a shared experience that is coming to a close.

While he revives and reuses recollection, he is also aware of the contours of each chapter, as he nears the boundary of the third printers sheet and the forty-eighth page of print. The critical chapter in that connection is ch.61. He accelerates Dombey's convalescence (37), so that he can devote the rest of the chapter to the longest unified passage of the double number, the final meeting of Florence and Edith (pp.613–20 in the part issue). Estimating forty-two MS pages for forty-eight of print and knowing that even a short final chapter requires a minimum of four MS pages, he cuts and pastes on the final page of ch.61 MS p.38, probably to shorten the last exchanges of Florence and Edith. However, having once saved space, he then cannot resist extending Feenix's gloriously comic pastiche of rhetoric and allusion by cramming in seven very closely written lines at the bottom of the page. He signs off his roll call (3)-(12) and its query of "Edith and Florence - certainly Edith and Cousin Feenix" (5), entering a heartfelt celebratory "Yes. All three", doubly underlining and marking the final entry of the worksheet (see Ws.19&20 p.119).

In executing his plan for the last chapter of the double number, true to his commitment to carry out "his care of him [Dombey] and his to the last", he radically changes the plan for ch.62, altering its emphasis and order. Instead of narrating the story of his protagonists' good fortune and success, he presents their future in three scenes introduced by a refrain concerned with "buried wine", derived from entry (44). The refrain, repeated twice, is written on the back of the manuscript, and coded for insertion, with his instruction to the compositor to leave a "white line", marking the passage of time between scenes, which makes possible, among other happy outcomes, the birth and growth of Florence's second child.

In the manuscript, the anticipated close "End with sea [...] and the invisible country far away" (Ws.19&20$_{45}$) is rewritten and lengthened. Dickens adds a paragraph on the significance of the voices in the waves to Dombey, speaking of his altered heart and Florence's "eternal and illimitable" love. Thus having given her love transcendent as well as moral significance, he addresses in a second paragraph what it might mean if her love were ultimately to be refused. The paragraph seems to imply that it is better to die young like Paul than to live on to become an aged Dombey, unaltered and redeemed by memory.[122] The tension between the two paragraphs may contribute to the cancellation of both.

Although Dickens did overwrite the number slightly, the deletion of the last two paragraphs could perhaps have been avoided, even with the late additions (see endnote 99). However, by their deletion he avoids contention, ending not on Dombey's "devotion to her little child – as if it were another Paul" or on the two children "as they go about together" but on his special attachment to little Florence, for reasons "known to no one but Florence". The paradox of the 'untold' story, implicit in Dombey's special relation to his granddaughter, is an oblique reminder—like the retrospective planning of the double number—of a story that has been told and in the final telling told again. Aware of the hazards of blank verse, he concludes with a sonorous heartfelt line "and smooths away the curls that shade her earnest eyes".[123]

Afterword

I began work for this ebook by photographing the original working notes in the National Art Library within the V&A, while at the same time studying the printed transcriptions of the worksheets wherever I could find them, including Horsman's edition of *Dombey and Son*. The original manuscript written with quill and ink on ordinary paper is still—a hundred and fifty years on—evocative of the occasion, which even facsimiles cannot fully convey. Horsman's printed version, however—and others like it—quite without individuality, can seem uninteresting and lifeless.

The transcriptions in this edition attempt to convey many of the features of the original in a way that, while assisting in the interpretation of the facsimiles, may also intrigue the reader. The layout and appearance of the handwritten word has been converted to a printed equivalent in Word 2010, with the addition of all accompanying conventional and idiosyncratic lines. If the reader studies a facsimile of a worksheet alongside its transcription, some of what Stone calls the 'immediacies' of the original should still be detectable in both (Stone, p.xxxi).

With regard to context of the working notes given in Horsman and Stone, I have added a more detailed account of how the novel was published in 'Section 1', and in the commentaries of 'Section 5' an outline of Dickens's other commitments and personal circumstances during the composition of each worksheet, gleaned from the labours of later researchers, particularly those responsible for the Pilgrim edition of the *Letters*. However, Dickens's order of work—of which the worksheets are only a part—had to be independently reconstructed. It involved scrutiny of the hand, quill and ink of the worksheet, manuscript and List of chapter headings, then ordering in time the various sorts of entries in the worksheets and the related tasks in manuscript, List, and proofs (as described in Horsman 1974 'Introduction', pp.xlv–vi).[124]

The reconstruction produces some unexpected results. For example, why does Dickens cover the left-hand side of Ws.5 with Ws.5a, instead of using the empty page beneath? And why is Ws.5a wafered into position after the composition of ch.14—as the right-hand edge of the added leaf suggests—when its entries clearly anticipate events described in that chapter? The likely solution is that Ws.5a has a special purpose. Dickens probably intended to use it as a separate sheet, keeping it alongside him as he composed ch.14. Then, adding a final entry (6) to the leaf, he may do the same again, as he composes ch.16.[125] Thus, Ws.5a helps him pursue the innovation in fictional method noted in Ws.5$_4$; Paul's experience of illness is to be "only expressed in the child's own feelings – Not otherwise described". The use of Ws.5a led me to look more closely at the point at which he added the other three attachments to their worksheets. Not that they might be used in the same way as Ws.5a (though Ws.4a may be), but that the timing of each attachment may be linked to a particular moment, which proves to be true of Ws.6a, and probably Ws.19&20a as well.

Another innovation occurs in the second quarter of the novel. Dickens experiments with a two-chapter number in No.10, making a note of the possibility at the start of Ws.10. The worksheet shows that he abandons the attempt early in the planning of the number, before he began composition. I detect

https://doi.org/10.11647/OBP.0092.09

a preparatory instance of that interest in No.7, which would have been a two-chapter number, had he not divided ch.20 at proof stage. He writes an unusually long chapter to open the number, and does the same in the closing chapter, after hastily planning an extension during its composition (and incidentally preserving unbroken the use of his bright blue ink).

Ordering entries and their associated tasks creates another significant recurrent dilemma. You cannot position on a timeline the 'chapter descriptions' (the entries immediately below the chapter title) without deciding whether those entries are made before composition and are plans, or are made after it and are summaries. Sorting out how to make that decision takes up most of 'Chapter descriptions as plans' in 'Section 6', p.137. One outcome is that, contrary to received opinion, there are many more chapter plans in the worksheets (for *Dombey and Son* at least) than chapter summaries. Establishing that many chapter descriptions are plans gives us fresh insight into Dickens's working methods, particularly his sensitivity to the approaching end of chapter and number.

When Dickens prepares for the final double number, he isolates himself from his London life for the best part of three weeks by moving to lodgings in Brighton. Tracing the course of his work, while he was living there, reveals the close attention he gives to the double number. The various indications of planning found there confirm the validity of the evidence used to distinguish plans from summaries in the single-number worksheets.

The timing of the change to the less satisfactory poorer blue inks—the watery blue and the greeny blue—also has a surprising outcome. Both of the changes to those blue inks coincide with a move by Dickens to a temporary residence, where he is soon obliged to use whatever ink is available. He has just returned temporarily to Devonshire Terrace (after his tenant vacated it) in No.12 and is in Brighton (in different lodgings from his previous visit) for the double number Nos.19&20. The concurrence of ink change with a temporary move strengthens the assumption that all uses of blue are—with two significant exceptions— consecutive and unbroken.

I summarise these investigations because they may be of interest to other researchers. They flow from the reconstruction of what is often a complicated sequence of events—the ordering in time of all aspects of Dickens's work in what he calls his "monthly harness" (L5:221) or "my month's dream" (L5:44). A full account of the order of entry, to do justice to the complexity of what he was attempting, requires a succinct way of identifying each entry. To meet that requirement, I add marginal numbers to all transcriptions, aware that they might slow reading, but hoping that they would ultimately make it easier to test evidence or follow an argument.

Dickens devises the worksheets to help him unify the novel by giving it shape, interweaving its many threads and drawing together its characters. The attempt brings with it "prodigious" and "infinite" pains. Approaching a climax, he complains "it takes so much time, and requires to be so carefully done" (L5:165). At the finish, he writes, "All through I have bestowed all the pains and time at my command upon it" (L5:271). Looking back, he believes "if any of my books are read years hence, Dombey will be remembered as among the best of them" (L5:611). The worksheets, with their ordered commentaries, give us the means whereby we can retrace some of his struggles.

I hope that the pursuit of the above outcomes will not deflect readers with an interest in how Dickens wrote *Dombey and Son*. The first four Sections, much of the commentaries, and of course all the facsimiles and transcriptions are intended for all readers, whether they are adapting the novel to other media, teachers and students in colleges and universities, members of reading groups, researchers in the field or Dickens enthusiasts. For the sake of readers, wherever they are, I have included references to easily accessible and inexpensive sources, as well as to the standard scholarly texts. Quotations from Dickens's letters to Forster are referred to using an online edition of Forster's *Life*, ebook 25851 in Project Gutenberg, downloaded to the free Kindle app, rather than the richly annotated Pilgrim *Letters*. Quotations from *Dombey and Son* are to both the hardback and paperback version of the Clarendon text; for more on 'References', see p.7. Most deletions made to the novel's text are restored in ebook 821 of Project Gutenberg. I have also included in the endnotes passages from all these sources.

Although Dickens's entries in the worksheet on Hablot Browne's illustrations are noted in the commentaries, there is unfortunately insufficient space in my chosen format to describe their detail, or to relate them to his changing responses to Browne's work.[126] The evidence for the contact between author and illustrator is considerable in the first half of the novel—for example in the letter to Browne quoted in connection with Dickens's vision of the first meeting of Dombey and Edith (see above p.136)—but, during the second half of the novel, there are few letters to Browne, and few entries in the worksheets concerning illustration. Their absence suggests perhaps either his resignation to Hablot Browne's shortcomings or some relaxation in his narrow conception of the role of the illustrator. A full account of the way the illustrations illuminate the text by visual allusion is given by Andrew Sanders in Appendix 2 of the Penguin Classics edition of *Dombey and Son* (London: Penguin Books, 2002), pp.950–57. There is also a substantial summary of 'Scholarship concerning illustration' in Leon Litvack's *Charles Dickens's "Dombey and Son": An Annotated Bibliography* (New York: AMS Press, 1999) pp.23–56.

To close this edition of the working notes, by way of a final comment on the relation of notes and text to illustration, it seems appropriate to end with an image of the novel's frontispiece, the last plate that Browne made for the novel. We know from Dickens's letter to his publishers that "Browne has come down here [Brighton] today [12 March 1848] with his frontispiece". The illustrator made a special journey from Croydon to show Dickens his sketch for the plate (L5:261). Presumably, it had the author's consent, and perhaps his approval. (There are signs in worksheets and letters that Dickens eventually stands back to allow his illustrator to form his own vision of the text (cf. endnote 53)).

In contrast to the cover design of the green wrapper, Browne's second rendering of the story is shaped, not by the fortunes of the Firm and the passage of time, but by an allegorical and symbolic re-interpretation of the text, focusing on Florence. With Paul, she forms a triangle, deeply cut in the foreground of the design. From there, the picture is divided into segments. In the upper right-hand segment are three episodes from the story of Florence, beginning with the death of her mother after the Paul's birth; followed below by a group—including an older Florence—delineated by their attitude towards the seated figure of an implacable unseeing Dombey; in the upper left-hand segment are four episodes from the story of little Paul, ending with his death; and between and above them, cut with the very lightest line, is a host of youthful angelic spirits, typified by their free-flowing robes, two of whom carry Paul upwards towards a mother figure, who welcomes him with open arms. On each side of the central triangle are emblematic images of Carker's violent death and of the death of the terrified Mrs Skewton, linked by the rise and fall of the steam train's smoke. Beneath the triangle, in a half-circle, is a fanciful depiction of figures in action: Walter struggling to survive the wreck of his ship, the lovers now reconciled, the radiant Cuttle celebrating the occasion, Florence preventing her father's suicide (imaged as a rescue from the sea, and encouraged by Paul), Old Sol mischievously carried on the waves by mermaids, and finally the figures of Rob and Miss Tox in a line from sextant and telescope to the sea, where Major Bagstock, helpless in the waters, is about to lose to his stick.

Browne, probably assisted by friend and co-worker Robert Young, among others, etches two copies of the sketch—after it had been reversed—on to the specially prepared steel. They organise the composition by using a full range of graded tones, a reflection of the eighteen days they had for the work, in contrast to the usual ten.[127] Browne manages to include a great deal of detail, which readers can recognise with the same pleasure they may have had in matching visual and textual detail in the earlier plates.[128]

However, even with its tonal variation, Browne's medium allows him only one reading of the novel. His design emphasises, in composition and detail, the role played by Florence (cf. Butt and Tillotson, p.95). Dickens, judging by his "immediate outline" might object to the omission of much of "the stock of the soup", especially the scenes that show the progress of the relation of Dombey and Florence (see endnote 42). He might also dislike Browne's repositioning of baby Paul and Florence to express their shared dependence on the mother—an example of an illustrator's interpretive freedom, which on occasion irritated Dickens considerably, if it clashed with his text or with his conception of the scene (see 2nd paragraph of 'Proofs' p.109).

Browne follows Carker's recollection of Florence as a little child "dark eyes and hair [and] a very good face" and his expectation that "I dare say she's pretty" (304[330]).[129] He depicts her with luxuriant hair let down, bonnet cast aside, shawl falling around her, long legs crossed, and a naked foot on the sand, while Paul lovingly rests a hand on her hair and shoulder. By such detail, Browne claims his own version of Florence. She is still the same loving young sister that we know from the text, who enjoys the needy affection of her little brother. She is also still the young girl, attending to her needlework, perhaps in the hope of pleasing her father. But for Browne, in his summary picture of her, at the heart of the novel, she is above all free from constraint and physically at ease with herself.

Frontispiece to *Dombey and Son* by Charles Dickens with illustrations by H. K. Browne (1848).

Appendices

A. Chapter number, title and length by part issue and date

No. of work-sheet	Date of Part	Chapter number	Chapter title (as published)	Chapter length
(1)	(2)	(3)	(4)	(5)
1	1846 Oct	1	Dombey and Son	7+¾
		2	In which Timely Provision is made in the best regulated Families	¼+7
		3	In which Mr. Dombey. as a Man and a Father ... the Home-Department	8
		4	In which some more First Appearances … the Stage of these Adventures	9
2	Nov	5	Paul's Progress and Christening	12+¾
		6	Paul's Second Deprivation	¼+15
		7	A Bird's-eye glimpse … also of the State of Miss Tox's Affections	4
3	Dec	8	Paul's further Progress, Growth and Character	14+½
		9	In which the Wooden Midshipman gets into Trouble	½+8+¾
		10	Containing the Sequel to the Midshipman's Disaster	¼+8
4	1847 Jan	11	Paul's Introduction to a new Scene	10+½
		12	Paul's Education	½+12+½
		13	Shipping Intelligence and Office Business	½+8
4a		Added leaf—a plan for the final episodes of ch.12, wafered to the bottom of the left-hand page of Ws.4		
5	Feb	14	Paul grows more and more Old-fashioned, and goes Home for the Holidays	17+¼
		15	Amazing Artfulness of Captain Cuttle, and a new pursuit for Walter Gay	¾+10
		16	What the Waves were always saying	4
5a		Added leaf—a plan for chs.14 and 16, wafered over the left-hand page of Ws.5		
6	Mar	17 (18)	Captain Cuttle … the young people — chs.17 and 18 are written as chs.18 and 17, and reversed at proof stage	8+½
		18 (17)	Father and Daughter	½+13+½
		19	Walter goes away	½+9
6a	Added leaf—entitled "Florence's age", pasted in error to Ws.6, probably written to prepare for ch.47 in No.15			
7	Apr	20	Mr. Dombey goes upon a Journey — Chs.20 and 21 are written as one chapter entitled "New Faces". It is divided in two at proof stage, and re-titled.	10+¼
		21	New Faces	¾+7+¼
		22	A Trifle of Management by Mr. Carker the Manager	¾+13
8	May	23	Florence Solitary, and the Midshipman Mysterious	16+¾
		24	The Study of a Loving Heart	¼+8+¼
		25	Strange News of Uncle Sol	¾+6
9	June	26	Shadows of the Past and Future	11
		27	Deeper Shadows	12+½
		28	Alterations	½+8
10	July	29	The Opening of the Eyes of Mrs. Chick	8+¾
		30	The Interval before the Marriage	¼+11
		31	The Wedding	12

https://doi.org/10.11647/OBP.0092.10

No. of worksheet	Date of Part	Chapter number	Chapter title (as published)	Chapter length
(1)	(2)	(3)	(4)	(5)
11	Aug	32	The Wooden Midshipman goes to Pieces	13+¼
		33	Contrasts	¾+8+¾
		34	Another Mother and Daughter	¼+9
12	Sept	35	The Happy Pair — Chs.35 and 36 are written as one chapter,	8+¾
		36	Housewarming — and divided at proof stage	¼+8+¼
		37	More Warnings than One	¾+7+¼
		38	Miss Tox improves an Old Acquaintance	¾+6
13	Oct	39	Further Adventures of Captain Edward Cuttle, Mariner	12+½
		40	Domestic Relations	½+11+½
		41	New Voices in the Waves	½+7
14	Nov	42	Confidential and Accidental	11+¾
		43	The Watches of the Night	¼+6+¼
		44	A Separation	¾+6+¾
		45	The Trusty Agent	¼+6
15	Dec	46	Recognizant and Reflective	9+½
		47	The Thunderbolt	½+13+¾
		48	The Flight of Florence	¼+8
16	1848 Jan	49	The Midshipman makes a Discovery	13
		50	Mr. Toots's Complaint	13
		51	Mr. Dombey and the World	6
17	Feb	52	Secret Intelligence	11+¾
		53	More Intelligence	¼+11+¾
		54	The Fugitives	¼+8
18	Mar	55	Rob the Grinder loses his Place	9
		56	Several People Delighted, and the Game Chicken Disgusted	17
		57	Another Wedding	6
19/20	Apr	58	After a Lapse	11+¼
		59	Retribution	¾+13
		60	Chiefly Matrimonial	9+¼
19/20a		61	Relenting	¾+8+½
		62	Final	½+4

Key to Appendix A

The numbered columns show the following:

(1) the worksheet number

As Dickens wrote one worksheet for each instalment, the number of each worksheet corresponds to that of the instalment. An additional leaf is attached to Ws.4, 5, 6 and 19&20 and numbered Ws.4a, 5a, 6a and 19&20a respectively. All are hyperlinked to their facsimile in 'Section 5'.

(2) the date of the instalment

Each number was published on the last day of the month, the 'magazine day' when monthly magazines generally went on offer to the public. It is usually described as belonging to the following month.

(3) the chapter number

The number of each chapter is hyperlinked to its start in the online version of ebook 821 in Project Gutenberg.

(4) the chapter title as published

(5) the length of each chapter as published in the instalment

The length of each chapter is measured by the number of full pages that it occupies, plus the proportion of the page (rounded to a quarter) which it may share with the chapter before and after. The opening page of the opening chapter and closing page of the closing chapter of the instalment are counted as full pages, even if they have blank lines before or after.

B. Chapter title history with purpose and features of chapter description

<table>
<tr><th>No. of work-sheet</th><th>No. of chapter</th><th>Title of chapter</th><th>History of chapter title entry</th><th colspan="2">Purpose of the chapter description</th><th colspan="2">Features of the chapter description</th></tr>
<tr><th>(1)</th><th>(2)</th><th>(3)</th><th>(4)</th><th colspan="2">(5)</th><th colspan="2">(6)</th></tr>
<tr><td rowspan="4">1</td><td>1</td><td>Dombey and Son</td><td>MS↔Ws / with the same revisions (3) in both</td><td>summary note</td><td rowspan="3">entered together after composition</td><td colspan="2">principal incident</td></tr>
<tr><td>2</td><td>In which Timely Provision… Families</td><td>revised (3) in Ws→MS</td><td>summary note</td><td colspan="2">defines chapter title</td></tr>
<tr><td>3</td><td>In which Mr. Dombey is… Department</td><td>revised (2) in MS→Ws</td><td>summary note</td><td colspan="2">the antagonists, Dombey and "Miss Nipper"</td></tr>
<tr><td>4</td><td>In which some… Adventures</td><td>MS↔Ws</td><td colspan="2">—</td><td colspan="2">—</td></tr>
<tr><td rowspan="3">2</td><td>5</td><td>Paul's Progress and Christening</td><td>revised in MS→Ws</td><td colspan="2">—</td><td>—</td><td rowspan="3">eight ideas for various numbers, entered before the Ws format was devised, and all written towards right-hand edge</td></tr>
<tr><td>6</td><td>Paul's Second Deprivation</td><td>MS→Ws</td><td>summary note</td><td rowspan="2">entered both together, with titles, after composition</td><td>defines chapter title</td></tr>
<tr><td>7</td><td>A Bird's-eye… Miss Tox's Affections</td><td>revised (2) in MS / revised in Ws, revised→Proofs, revised</td><td>summary note</td><td>Major and Miss Tox</td></tr>
<tr><td rowspan="3">3</td><td>8</td><td>Paul's further Character</td><td>revised (3) in Ws→MS, revised→Ws</td><td>summary note</td><td rowspan="3">entered together, after composition</td><td rowspan="3" colspan="2">an incident from each chapter, concerned with the power of money</td></tr>
<tr><td>9</td><td>In which the… Midshipman gets into Trouble</td><td>MS→Ws</td><td>summary note</td></tr>
<tr><td>10</td><td>Containing the Sequel to… Disaster</td><td>MS→Ws</td><td>summary note</td></tr>
<tr><td rowspan="3">4</td><td>11</td><td>Paul's Introduc-tion to a new Scene</td><td>revised in MS→Ws</td><td>summary</td><td rowspan="3">entered together, perhaps when ch.13 is being planned</td><td colspan="2">omits the long lead-in / gives setting, central episode and the repeated detail of the ticking clock</td></tr>
<tr><td>12</td><td>Paul's Education</td><td>MS↔Ws</td><td>summary</td><td colspan="2">situation and central scene / for "etc" see Ws.4a</td></tr>
<tr><td>13</td><td>Shipping Intelligence and Office Business</td><td>revised (3) in MS→Ws</td><td>plan</td><td colspan="2">gap for title / directive / omits Dombey / positions Walter's dispatch at end</td></tr>
<tr><td>4a</td><td colspan="7">Additional leaf—a list of ideas for second half of ch.12, which grows into a plan that is probably used in the composition of the chapter, and then wafered to bottom left-hand of Ws.4</td></tr>
<tr><td rowspan="3">5</td><td>14</td><td>Paul grows more… Holidays</td><td>revised in MS→Ws</td><td colspan="2">plan</td><td colspan="2">leaves gap for title / notes an ending then deletes it / principal incident / comment expressing intent / adds Ws.5a, plan from ailing Paul's POV</td></tr>
<tr><td>15</td><td>Amazing Artful-ness… Gay</td><td>MS↔Ws / with the same revision in both</td><td colspan="2">plan</td><td colspan="2">leaves narrow gap for title / dis-jointed layout / query / no mention of Walter's role / reply to query</td></tr>
<tr><td>16</td><td>What the Waves were always saying</td><td>MS↔Ws</td><td colspan="2">plan</td><td colspan="2">titled at start / gives opening and close / omits farewells / draft of closing texts / disjointed layout / re-uses Ws.5a after adding note on ever-flowing River</td></tr>
<tr><td>5a</td><td colspan="7">Additional leaf—a plan that is probably used to write chs.14 and 16, and afterwards wafered over left-hand of Ws.5</td></tr>
</table>

<table>
<tr><th>No. of work-sheet</th><th>No. of chapter</th><th>Title of chapter</th><th colspan="2">History of chapter title entry</th><th>Purpose of the chapter description</th><th>Features of the chapter description</th></tr>
<tr><th>(1)</th><th>(2)</th><th>(3)</th><th colspan="2">(4)</th><th>(5)</th><th>(6)</th></tr>
<tr><td rowspan="3">6</td><td>17
ch.18 in Ws & MS</td><td>Captain Cuttle does a little Business for the young people</td><td colspan="2">MS↔Ws</td><td>summary note</td><td>titled at start / restatement of title</td></tr>
<tr><td>18
ch.17 in Ws & MS and written first</td><td>Father and Daughter</td><td colspan="2">revised (2) in MS→Ws</td><td>summary</td><td>titled at start / title and summary evenly aligned and spaced / omits recapitulation and lead-in / four similar phrases, salient points in order / a fifth, inserted below title, avoiding underlines (cf. Ws.10_7) / smudges confirm all entries made together</td></tr>
<tr><td>19</td><td>Walter goes away</td><td colspan="2">inserted in MS→Ws</td><td>summary</td><td>titled at start / alludes to each section in MS order / taking tea, two awkward lovers-to-be / next day farewell to Sol and Cuttle / memo on Cuttle's watch</td></tr>
<tr><td>6a</td><td colspan="6">Added leaf on Florence's age, wafered in error to Ws.6 instead of being attached to Ws.15</td></tr>
<tr><td rowspan="3">7</td><td>20</td><td>Mr. Dombey goes on a Journey</td><td colspan="2" rowspan="2">written as one chapter in blue titled "New Faces" in MS→Ws / at proofing divided into two chapters and both titled / titles copied to Ws, and number heading added or adjusted</td><td>–</td><td>–</td></tr>
<tr><td>21</td><td>New Faces</td><td>–</td><td>–</td></tr>
<tr><td>22</td><td>A Trifle of Management …</td><td colspan="2">revised in MS→Ws</td><td>summary note, and a last minute plan</td><td>plot device: Rob a spy in the Shop / Toots episode added to extend ending</td></tr>
<tr><td rowspan="3">8</td><td>23</td><td>Florence Solitary, ... Midshipman Mysterious</td><td colspan="2">revised (3) in List→MS↔Ws</td><td>–</td><td>–</td></tr>
<tr><td>24</td><td>The Study of a Loving Heart</td><td colspan="2">MS↔Ws</td><td>–</td><td>–</td></tr>
<tr><td>25</td><td>Strange News of Uncle Sol</td><td colspan="2">MS↔Ws</td><td>–</td><td>–</td></tr>
<tr><td rowspan="3">9</td><td>26</td><td>Shadows of the Past and Future</td><td>entered in MS while writing chs.27 or 28 then→Ws</td><td rowspan="3">all titles copied to Ws at the same time, probably after writing ch.28</td><td>plan</td><td>gap for title / in MS, emphasises competition between Carker and Bagstock / the action follows the Major's exits and entrances</td></tr>
<tr><td>27</td><td>Deeper Shadows</td><td>revised in MS→Ws</td><td rowspan="2">planned together perhaps to delay writing at length</td><td>gap for title / opening items / various insertions / closing sequence</td></tr>
<tr><td>28</td><td>Alterations</td><td>MS↔Ws</td><td>gap for title / omits extemporised lead-in (discussion about Carker and Toots's visits, the farewells) / on arrival, surprise at changes / closure on Edith's feelings for Florence (underlined for future significance)</td></tr>
<tr><td rowspan="3">10</td><td>29</td><td>The Opening of the Eyes of Mrs. Chick</td><td colspan="2">revised (2) in MS→Ws</td><td>summary</td><td>titled at start / entries similar in structure, each opening with a name / sectioned as in MS / setting, situation, conflict, outcome</td></tr>
<tr><td>30</td><td>The Interval before the Marriage</td><td colspan="2">revised in MS→Ws</td><td>plan (plus memo entered during composition)</td><td>gap for title / description of the closing tableau / memo after title entry / Brook St satire prepares for Feenix's role at wedding</td></tr>
<tr><td>31</td><td>The Wedding</td><td colspan="2">MS↔Ws</td><td>plan</td><td>titled at start / detailed through–plan / change of speaker to develop Feenix and satire of aristocracy / directive at opening, and elision "Back to" at close, both implying intent</td></tr>
</table>

No. of work-sheet	No. of chapter	Title of chapter	History of chapter title entry	Purpose of the chapter description	Features of the chapter description
(1)	(2)	(3)	(4)	(5)	(6)
11	32	The Wooden Midshipman goes to Pieces	entered in Ws / not copied to MS at the start of composition / inserted later in MS	plan	title and plan uniform in hand and layout / combines LH and RH notes / together a full account of all episodes including the recapitulation (Mrs MacStinger and Rob) / re-orders "glimpse" / attention to closing text
	33	Contrasts	inserted in blue in MS while writing ch.34 in blue→Ws	chs.33 and 34 planned together	deletion to preserve a gap for title / Harriet entry omits the Morfin visit already noted in LH / ends with money gift to Alice
	34	Another Mother and Daughter	MS↔Ws		titled at start / opening / "Indication" re-ordered in MS / ending with "to return money" implying intention
12	35	The Happy Pair	MS↔Ws	planned, written and titled as one chapter, then divided and the new ch.36 numbered and titled at proof stage, but *not* copied to MS or Ws	titled at start / rethinks opening / combines LH and RH notes /assumes handkerchief scene that leads to Dombey's "discovery" / adds the dinner before the "at home" / inserts the first quarrel, Carker and Mrs Skewton present
	36	Housewarming	titled in proofs→ List[130]		
	37 36 in Ws	More Warnings than One	not titled at start in MS / title inserted later→Ws / (and MS re-numbered at a later point)	summary	numbered ch.36, in blue / title and summary uniform in hand and layout / outline of two warnings, Carker's to Edith (18) and Death's to Mrs S (19) / the effect of her stroke
	38 37 in Ws	Miss Tox improves an Old Acquaintance	Ws→List, revised / another title entered in MS during composition, then revised (see 'Appendix D')	plan	titled at start / opening directive / rethinks what Tox should wear / in MS, adds family reactions to Rob's deceitfulness, tying in subplot to theme of money misused
13	39	Further Adventures of Captain Edward Cuttle…	inserted in MS→Ws	plan	preserves gap for title / layout reveals how Dickens forms the chapter plan by assembling (and ordering) incident and character (see comment in Ws.13, p.96)
	40	Domestic Relations	MS→Ws	plan	titled at start / gives a selective two part entry for each of three sections /assumes LH Bagstock (see Ws.13₄) / "So to" warns of a transition (cf. chs.41 and 49).
	41	New Voices in the Waves	in MS titled, revised, deleted, restarted, and later retitled→Ws (see 'Appendix E')	plan	gap for title / notes subject, the death / queries the burial (34–35) / assembles the lead-in / in MS, adds Florence but omits a Pipchin scene (32) making room for (35) / 'so to' with directive, a warning of transition (33)
14	42	Confidential and Accidental	inserted in MS→Ws	plan	laid out to preserve gap for title / directive "open" / in MS Rob moved to recapitulation / omits Carker's 2nd meeting with Edith and Florence after Dombey is brought home
	43	The Watches of the Night	ch.43 titled in MS / revised, then initial title re-instated→Ws / while writing ch.43, divided in two / inserts number and title for ch.44→Ws	plan	gap for title / opening directive / deletion shows change of order (15) / closing text
	44	A Separation		summary note for ch.45 written first followed by summary for ch.44	for history of writing and summary of ch.44, see commentary of Ws.14, p.100
	45	The Trusty Agent	MS↔Ws		"Carker & Edith" suggests his growing mastery "by force" / last view before eloping
15	46	Recognizant and Reflective	ch.47 (initially ch.48) titled and entered as ch.48 in Ws→MS and written first / ch.46 titled and numbered in MS→Ws / ch.48 titled and numbered in MS→Ws under the chapter number heading for ch.47 /chapter number headings for chs.47 and 48 changed to 48 and 47	summary	title inserted / plot device, to link Rob and Mrs Brown without Carker knowing / two additions, Carker's and Edith's motives
	47	The Thunderbolt		plan	titled at start / hesitancy over how to describe digression / inclusive sequence of closing incidents / through-planned to end (cf. ch.31)
	48	The Flight of Florence		summary	deletion relates to transposition / title and summary uniform in hand and layout / last section begins the gathering of characters to Shop / mock suspense of Walter's arrival

No. of work-sheet	No. of chapter	Title of chapter	History of chapter title entry	Purpose of the chapter description	Features of the chapter description
(1)	(2)	(3)	(4)	(5)	(6)
16	49	The Midshipman makes a Discovery	MS started without titling, restarted, title inserted later→Ws (see 'Appendix E')	plan	leaves gap for title / entries (5)–(7) cover first three sections / entry (8) expresses Cuttle's agitation and builds up suspense / "So to" signals a narrative turning point needing preparation
	50	Mr.Toots's Complaint	titled in MS, revised→Ws and to List where, misremembering, CD makes an error and corrects it (see 'Appendix D')	plan	leaves gap for title / three entries for three sections, much added to and developed in MS / each distinct in hand and alignment / progressive loss of density with corrosion in (13), (14) and (15), with successive re-dipping or perhaps just a poor quill
	51	Mr. Dombey and the World	Ws→MS (see 'Appendix E')	plan	titles at start / deletion with revision / omission of Chick / order of reactions adjusted in MS
17	52	Secret Intelligence	inserted in MS→Ws	summary	each title uniform with description in layout and hand (though contrasting in size) / evenly corroded (6)-(11) but uneven where hand may be lighter or ink thinner (13)–(16) and progressively corroded (18 and 19) / brief orderly 'stage notes': characters and incidents with no signs of planning
	53	More Intelligence	titled in MS, revised→Ws	summary	
	54	The Fugitives	MS→Ws	summary	
18	55	Rob the Grinder loses his Place	Ws→MS	plan	layout & hand suggest end planning: draft of closing text, then changes in transport and in Carker, and last, the oblique title
	56	Several People Delighted, and … Disgusted	MS↔Ws	plan(?)	indications of planning: amount of detail, tilted and cramped entry, closing text / contra indica-tions: salient point(s) for each narrative section, and an orderly outline that resolves two plot-lines, the return of Sol and dismissal of Chicken (17)–(19), and prepares for the wedding
	57	Another Wedding	MS↔Ws	—	—
19/20	58	After a Lapse	MS started, titled, deleted, restarted, titled as before→Ws (see 'Appendix E')	plan	leaves gap for title / omits reactions to Firm's collapse / notes Morfin, the link to Harriet and Carker's intestacy / "Introduce" confirms planning intent / action follows Harriet to the penitent Alice on her deathbed / omits the mother's revelation of blood relationship
	59	Retribution	MS→Ws	plan	leaves gap for title / states subject / gives intermittent refrain marking order of departures / notes the loyal Miss Tox, and Dombey's crisis with (3), and Florence's rescue of her father (underlined with a flourish) / omits Polly's part in the drama and the quiet irony of the close
	60	Chiefly Matrimonial	Ws→MS	plan	enters title / identifies the marriages / gives Toots a new tag / instruction to open at the Blimber's / orders transition to Bunsby through Cuttle / then to Florence and Susan (in her servant dress) / in MS elaborates Toots' role
19/20a	61	Relenting	MS, inserted, turns leaf over, titles as before and restarts→Ws (see 'Appendix E')	plan	leaves gap for number and title / Edith to go to Italy with Feenix / Florence and Susan nurse the critically ill Dombey / a sequence: Feenix's request, Florence taken back to London and Brook Street, final meeting, Edith's revelation / in MS, opens with the nursing of Dombey, inserts presence of Walter, then follows plan
	62	Final	in MS probably leaves title gap, reinstates initial title of Ws / not copied to Ws	plan	enters and revises title in Ws / assembles plan with draft of ending (45) / in MS, all re-ordered, omitting "sketch", adding Toots the messenger, and rewording end (changed again at proofing)

Key to Appendix B

The numbered columns show the following:

(1) the worksheet number

As Dickens wrote one worksheet for each instalment, the number of the worksheet corresponds to the number of the instalment. Note an additional leaf is attached to Ws.4, 5, 6 and 19&20 and numbered Ws.4a, 5a, 6a and 19&20a respectively. All are hyperlinked to their facsimile in 'Section 5'.

(2) the chapter number

The number of each chapter is hyperlinked to its start in the online version of ebook 821 in Project Gutenberg.

(3) the chapter title as published

(4) a summary of the chapter title in worksheet, manuscript and elsewhere:

- '→' means 'transferred to', e.g. 'MS→Ws' means the title is first entered in manuscript, then transferred to worksheet,
- 'MS↔Ws' means that the appearance of the manuscript and worksheet does not reveal where the title is first entered, whether in manuscript or in worksheet,
- the number of revisions, if more than one, is shown in brackets.

(5) initial purpose of the chapter description, as shown by one of the following:

- 'summary note'—one or two entries written after composition,
- 'summary'—an outline usually of more than two entries, always written with the title after composition,
- 'plan'—always entered before composition, sometimes with the chapter title, but more often leaving a gap for the title to be inserted later,
- '(?)'—a query added in brackets means that the purpose cannot be described as plan or summary with any certainty, because of insufficient or conflicting evidence.

(6) features of description

The features noted are, for the most part, those mentioned in the commentary that suggest the purpose of the chapter description.

C. Transcription of the List of Chapter Headings

Purpose of the List

In light of how he has used the first five worksheets, Dickens decides that a list of chapter numbers and titles might be a useful adjunct, perhaps to remind him of the position of each chapter relative to other chapters, perhaps to get a view of the novel's overall progress. The List might also serve—if he had not yet received a copy of the previous number or its manuscript—as a note of the number of the opening chapter of the next number.

The List is not a preparation for the publication of a contents page. He would be aware that the printers assembled their contents pages from the eighteen published instalments and the proofs of the final double number. A contents page gives the opening page number of each chapter, which does not concern him. However, unlike a contents page that never gives the instalment divisions, the List usually implies the instalment boundary by its changes of hand.

Procedures in the List

Similarity of hand, quill and positioning of each chapter heading clearly shows that the headings for chs.1–16 are made on the same occasion, probably in the interval between the composition of Nos.5 and 6. From then on, with the exception of Nos.14 and 15, he completes one group of entries for each number.

From entry [6] to [12], it so happens that, when Dickens updates the List, he also changes ink colour with each group of entries. Entry [6] is in black, [6/7] in blue, [7/8] in black, [8/9] in blue, and so on, up to [12] in black. The changes in ink colour, together with the accompanying changes of alignment and hand, confirm that Dickens regularly updates his compilation during the writing of each number.

The timing of entries can also be traced in some detail. The listing for No.6 begins with the number entry for ch.17 (later 18), i.e. prior to the proofing of chs.17 and 18 when the first two chapters are reversed, and ends with the number error 'IX' for 19. The next entry [6/7] begins with the correction to the number heading of ch.19 and ends with the entry of the initial title given to ch.20, i.e. prior to the proofing of ch.20 when that chapter is divided and ch.20 retitled. When Dickens returns to enter [7/8], he begins by correcting the title of ch.20, includes the adjustments at proof stage and ends by titling ch.23, the first chapter of No.8. He revises that title in the List itself, copying the final version to the manuscript—an exceptional departure from his usual practice of revising in the manuscript, and a part of the general disruption to his usual procedures during the production of No.8 (see commentary on Ws.8, p.76). In [8/9], he completes the record for No.8 and most of No.9 except for the headings of ch.28, probably updating the record before he begins the final chapter of No.9. Then in [9/10], he copies in the headings of the four remaining chapters up to and including ch.31, thus completing the record for the first half of the novel.

For [11] and [12], Dickens continues the procedure, begun in No.10, of updating the List after finishing one number and before starting the next. Then for No.13, he reverts to his earlier practice of adding to the List before he has completed the number in hand. The handwriting of the chapter headings in Nos.14 and 15 is unusually varied, with several ink smudges that are untypical and a sure sign of rush. Despite dirty copy, we can be reasonably certain that Dickens makes at least two entries within the same number for the pivotal No.14 (see the conjectures in [13/14] and [14]). Similarly in the climactic No.15 he updates the List twice, entering [15a] after just one chapter the initial ch.48 ('The Thunderbolt'), followed later by [15b]. In the excitement of the moment and gripped by "the interest and passion of it", he overrides his established habit of making one entry for each number. For the remaining entries, he returns to his previous practice, making one entry each for Nos.16–18 and the two entries for the double number.[131]

There is also evidence of variation in the source that Dickens draws on when adding to the List. He may be copying (or recalling) what is entered in the manuscript, the worksheet or the corrected proofs. In entry [6], he enters the earlier order of chs.17 and 18 found in the worksheet and the manuscript, prior to their reversal in the proofs. In entry [8], on the other hand, he relies partly on the proofs and partly on the worksheet; the title of ch.36 appears only in proof, and the version of the title of ch.38 appears only in worksheet. On one unusual occasion, probably while writing ch.23, he revises a title in the List itself, and then copies the revision(s) into the manuscript (see entry [7/8] for ch.23).

Description of the transcription

Page size and layout (slightly reduced) is kept roughly proportionate to the original. A short unbroken black line from the left-hand edge is added to the transcript to show the boundaries that define each instalment. Below the black line is the number of the instalment in round brackets.

A short dotted red line from the right-hand edge shows the boundaries that define each group of headings that are entered together, with the exception of the boundary between the unique entries [15a] and [15b] that cannot be shown in this way (see commentary on [15a and b], p.178). Below the red line, a number in bold and in square brackets is given to the group of chapter headings that follows (the number also identifies the instalment(s), in part or whole, that each group covers). Its lower boundary gives a rough indication of the point at which the group is entered.

Each group of entries is accompanied, in the right-hand margin, by a brief description and comment on the group's main features. The broken double underlines of the chapter headings are typographical, while those of the chapter titles are 'drawn', in order to represent more clearly the broken underlines of the original. Changes in hand and ink in the original are imitated in the same way that they are shown in the transcriptions of the worksheets.

Aim of the transcription

The transcription corrects and adds to description of the List in the Clarendon edition of the novel ('Introduction', *Dombey and Son*, ed. Alan Horsman (Oxford: Clarendon Press, 1974 p.xliii). It aims to show visually most of the evidence in layout, hand and ink that enables us to conjecture how the order and content of its entries relate to those in the worksheets, the manuscript and proofs.

Transcription of the List of Chapter Headings

Dealings with the Firm of Dombey and Son - List of Chapter Headings

(No.1) Chapter I. [1–5]

Dombey and Son

Chapter II.

In which some timely provision is made for an emergency that will sometimes arise in the best regulated families.

Chapter III.

In which Mr Dombey, as a man and a father, is seen at the head of the home Department.

Chapter IV.

In which some more first appearances are made on the stage of these adventures .

(No.2) Chapter V.

Paul's Progress and Christening.

Chapter VI.

Paul's second deprivation.

Chapter VII.

A Bird's-eye glimpse of Miss Tox's dwelling-place; also of the state of Miss Tox's affections.

(No.3) Chapter VIII.

Paul's further progress, growth, and character

Chapter IX.

In which the wooden Midshipman gets into trouble.

Chapter X.

Containing the sequel of the Midshipman's disaster .

(No.4) Chapter XI.

Paul's introduction to a new scene

Entry [1–5] consists of the title heading and the headings for chs.1–16. They are distinguished by evenness of hand, a thin unvarying line, and regularity of alignment and spacing down and across the page.

Dickens writes without hesitation probably copying from the worksheet soon after he finished ch.16. The addition of 'some' to the title of ch.2 is assumed to be an error, the writer perhaps relying on memory and anticipating the title of ch.4.

Chapter XII .

Paul's Education .

Chapter XIII .

Shipping intelligence, and office business .

(No.5) Chapter XIV .

Paul grows more and more old-fashioned, and goes home for the holidays

Chapter XV .

Amazing artfulness of Captain Cuttle, and a new pursuit for Walter Gay .

Chapter XVI .

What the waves were always saying .

(No.6) Chapter XVII . [6]

Father and Daughter .

Chapter XVIII .

Captain Cuttle does a little business for the young people.

Chapter XIX .

Walter goes away . [6/7]

(No.7)

Chapter XX .

<New faces> Mr Dombey goes upon a journey. [7/8]

Chapter XXI .

New faces

Chapter XXII .

A trifle of management by Mr Carker the Manager.

(No.8) Chapter XXIII .

Florence solitary, and

Domestic and <~~Fxxxigxxxx~~(?) Foreign.> T'he Midshipman Mysterious

Chapter XX~~III~~ IV. [8/9]

The Study of a loving heart .

Entry [6] consists of the headings for chs.17 and 18 together with the chapter number heading for ch.19, mistakenly entered as ch.9. Dickens copies in these entries probably before he finishes and titles ch.19 (the last chapter of No.6) and certainly before he transposes chs.17 and 18 at proof stage.

Entry [6/7] consists of the correction to the numbering of ch.19 and its title, the number heading and the initial title of ch.20. The entries coincide with the bright blue ink used for all of No.7. Dickens copies them in before writing ch.22 (the last chapter of No.7) and before dividing ch.20 at proof stage.

Entry [7/8] consists of the deletion of the initial title for ch.20, the entry of the revised title and the headings for chs.21–23. Dickens probably copies in these entries while he is writing ch.23 in black. When he comes to devising a title for ch.23, he enters it first in the List, then revises it there (twice), and lastly copies the final version into the gap in the manuscript and later into worksheet (see 'Appendix D', ch.23, p.185).

Entry [8/9] consists of all the headings for chs.24–27. The amendment to the number heading for ch.24 is a running correction. His use of blue ink here coincides with its use in No.9 from MS p.6 of the first chapter (ch.26) to the end of the last chapter (ch.28). Dickens enters the headings, before he begins to write ch.28.

Chapter XXV.

Strange news of Uncle Sol.

(No.9) Chapter XXVI.

Shadows of the past and future.

Chapter XXVII.

Deeper Shadows.

Chapter XXVIII. [9/10]

Alterations

~~The opening of the eyes of M[rs] Chick~~

(No.10) Chapter XXIX.

The opening of the eyes of M[rs] Chick

Chapter XXX.

The interval before the Marriage.

Chapter XXXI.

The Wedding.

(No.11) Chapter XXXII. [11]

The Wooden Midshipman goes to pieces.

Chapter XXXIII.

Contrasts.

Chapter XXIV. (X inserted: XXXIV)

Another mother and daughter.

(No.12) Chapter XXV. (X inserted: XXXV) [12]

The Happy Pair.

Chapter XXXVI.

House warming

Entry [9/10] consists of the headings for chs.28–31. Dickens begins by giving the title of ch.29 to ch.28, forgetting that he had not yet entered the title of the final chapter in the previous number. He corrects the error and completes the headings up to and including ch.31, copying in these entries when he has finished ch.31, thus completing the entries for the first half of the novel.

Entry [11] consists of the headings for chs.32–34. Dickens writes with the same blue he has just used for ch.34, the final chapter of No.11, misnumbering ch.34 as ch.24.

Entry [12] consists of the headings for ch.35–38. Dickens copies in these entries but, continuing from the previous entry, misnumbers the first chapter as ch.25. He corrects the number headings of both chs.34 and 35, and completes the headings up to and including ch.38 (the last chapter of No.12). He is perhaps copying from the worksheet, but correcting as he goes from his memory of the changes made to second proofs of ch.35. He gives the earlier unrevised title for ch.38 only found in Ws 12.

The listings of both this and the previous two numbers are added after he completes each number, reflecting his confidence in the progress of the narrative.

Chapter XXXVII .

More warnings than one .

Chapter XXXVIII .

Miss Tox cultivates an old acquaintance .

(No.13) Chapter XXXIX . **[13]**

Further adventures of Captain Edward Cuttle, Mariner.

Chapter XL.

Domestic Relations.

Chapter XLI .

New Voices in the waves. **[13/14]**

(No.14) Chapter XLII .

Confidential and Accidental.

Chapter XLIII

The Watches of the Night. **[14]**

Chapter XLIV .

A separation

Chapter XLV .

The trusty Agent.

(No.15) Chapter XLVI. **[15a]**

Recognizant and reflective. & **[15b]**

Chapter XLVII .

The Thunderbolt .

Chapter XLVIII .

~~The Thunderbolt~~ . The Flight of Florence.

Entry [13] consists of the headings for chs.39 and 40 and the number heading for ch.41. Dickens copies in these entries before he has titled ch.41 (the last chapter of No.13).

Entry [13/14] consists of the title for ch.41, the headings for ch.42, and the number heading of ch.43. Dickens probably copies in these entries before he has completed or titled ch.43, for the first time interrupting composition during or as he begins the second chapter of a number.

Entry [14] consists of the title of ch.43 and the headings for chs.44 and 45. Dickens probably copies in these entries as soon as he has finished ch.45 (the last chapter of No.14). Ink flow in the titles of chs.44 and 45 is unusually erratic. Dickens seems to overwrite "Agent".

Entries for No.15, like those for No.14, are made in two stages. In the first stage, covered by [15a], Dickens enters the just the number headings for chs.46–48 followed by the title of the chapter he had just finished "The Thunderbolt" (initially intended as the last chapter). In the second stage, after writing the other two chapters and re-thinking the chapter order, he makes entry [15b], in which he deletes the initial title of ch.48, re-titling it "The Flight of Florence", and transfers the titles of chs.46 and 47. The separation of the two entries is clear from the marked contrast of hand. (The second double underline beneath ch.48 seems inadvertently to have been repeated, perhaps made by mistake or—more likely—being accidentally caught on paper that Dickens may have used as blotting paper or as a hand-rest).

For the first and only time, in keeping the record for Nos.14 and 15, Dickens makes two entries in each number, interrupting composition in the middle of both. There is an unusual number of smudged entries. He seems energised by the approaching crisis, taken up with the reactions of each of the four protagonists in turn. His hurried engagement with this task is in keeping with his involvement in the narrative; in his excitement, he goes between manuscript and worksheet more often than usual.

Entry [15a] confirms the order of entry given in the commentary for Ws.15 (p.104) and the interpretation of Dickens's 'Comment' (p.105). See also endnote 89 and 92.

(No.16) Chapter XLIX. **[16]**

The Midshipman makes a discovery.

Chapter L .

Mr Toots's ~~sore~~(?) complaint.

Chapter LI.

Mr Dombey and the World . **[16/17/18]**

(No.17) Chapter LII.

Secret Intelligence

Chapter LIII.

More Intelligence.

Chapter LIV.

The Fugitives.

(No.18) Chapter LV.

Rob the Grinder loses his place. **[18]**

Chapter LVI.

Several people ~~pleased,~~ delighted and the Game chicken disgusted.

Chapter LVII.

Another wedding.

(Nos.19/20) Chapter LVIII . **[19&20]**

After a lapse

Chapter LIX.

Retribution.

Chapter LX .

Chiefly Matrimonial.

Entry [16] consists of headings for chs.49–50 and the number heading of ch.51, entered before beginning work on ch.51, the last chapter of No.16. Titling ch.50, Dickens appears to misremember, and then correct the title (see ch.50 'Appendix D').

Entry [16/17/18] consists of the title of ch.50, all the headings for chs.52–54 and the number heading for ch.55. Dickens copies in these entries probably when he has completed ch.54, the last chapter of No.17. It is the only entry when he completes the record for two numbers and prepares for a third.

Entry [18] consists of the title of ch.55 and the headings for ch.56 and 57. Perhaps entering the title of ch.56 from memory, Dickens miswords the title, and at once corrects the error. The underlines are applied to only one version, confirming that the change is a running correction, not a revision. He completes the record, without going on to number the first chapter of the double number, perhaps anticipating that he will begin his preparation for Nos.19&20 without the usual break.

Entry [19&20] consists of headings for chs.58–60, made during or after the completion of ch.60.

[19&20a]

Chapter LXI.
= = =

Relenting
= = =

Chapter XLII.
= = –

Final.
= =

Entry [19&20a] consists of the headings for chs.61 and 62 entered overleaf on the last page of the List when he has completed ch.62.

D. Revisions to chapter titles in manuscript, worksheet and List

In his introduction to the Clarendon edition, Horsman makes a general comment on manuscript revisions that 'deletions are not recorded because, with very few exceptions, they cannot be read' (Horsman 1974 Introduction, p.xliv). While this appears to be the case for the body of the text, it is fortunately not true of most revisions to chapter titles in manuscript, worksheet and List.

Partially visible words can be identified with near certainty. It is also sometimes possible to make a reasonable guess at groups of words that are in part indecipherable, while single words that are entirely obscured can sometimes be conjectured from their length and context. Only a few revisions are completely unreadable (see chs.7, 8, 29 and 38). However, even in these instances it is helpful to know that revisions are present.[132]

In the manuscript, after the early chapters, Dickens invariably underlines the chapter title as he enters it, doing the same for title revisions. The broken double underlines that are given to chapter titles probably began as his routine signal to compositors to use uppercase type.[133] They are used throughout, with the result that, because he tends to vary the size and spacing of the underlines with each revision, they are important in distinguishing one revision from another.

From the transcriptions below, it seems that, for the first few chapters, Dickens often revises in the worksheet but that after ch.8 he finds it more useful to revise in manuscript during or soon after composition. On one occasion (ch. 23) he appears to enter the chapter title first in his "List of Chapter Headings", and takes the opportunity to revise there. On several other occasions, e.g. for chs.38 and 62, he reverts to his earlier practice of entering the chapter title first in worksheet, presumably because he is confident in his choice of title. As with so many of his practices in the working notes at this stage of his career, he is quick to adapt to changing circumstances.

Each title and each revised title are shown separately, with their location, and in the order in which they are made. No attempt is made to give the evidence for this summary of outcomes, as the underlines and layout that reveal order are often too closely written to be transcribed without magnification. However where there is doubt about the order, location or substance of a revision, conjectures are followed by a query in brackets.

Chapter one

(1) Dombey and Son (Ws)

(2) Dombey and Son (MS)

(3) In which Dombey and Son are presented to the reader. (Ws)

(4) In which Dombey and Son are presented to the reader. (MS)

(5) Dombey and Son. (MS and Ws)

The original title, the revised title and the reinstated title appear in both worksheet and manuscript. In the manuscript, each version is underlined; in the worksheet, only the final title is underlined. A probable explanation is that Dickens entered the title in the worksheet (1) and then manuscript (2), then revised it by adding "In which" and "are presented to the reader" in the worksheet (3), copied the same additions to the manuscript (4), but finally re-instated the initial title in both the worksheet and manuscript (4).

Chapter two

(1) In which timely provision is made for a[n] ~~Family~~ emergency that will sometimes arise in the best regulated families. (Ws)

(2) In which timely provision is made for an emergency that will sometimes arise in the best regulated families. (MS)

The correction in (1) suggests that (1) precedes (2), i.e. the title is entered first in the worksheet, revised there, then copied to the manuscript.

Chapter three

(1) In which Mr Dombey is beheld in the bosom of his family. (Ws)

(2) In which Mr Dombey is seen in the bosom of his family. (Ws)

(3) In which Mr Dombey, as a man and a Father, is seen at the head of the home Department. (Ws)

(4) In which Mr Dombey, as a man and a father, is seen at the head of the home-department. (MS)

Dickens rewords and revises in the worksheet, delaying transfer to the manuscript until he has a final version. He underlines only the final version in the worksheet and in the manuscript.

Chapter five

(1) Paul's Progress (MS)

(2) Paul's Progress and christening. (MS)

(3) Paul's Progress and christening (Ws)

Dickens titles and revises in the manuscript, and then transfers the final version to the worksheet.

Chapter seven

(1) CHAPTER IV In which a xxxxxxxxxxxxxxxxxxxxxxxxxxxxxxxx glimpse is afforded of Princess's Place. (MS)

(2) CHAPTER IV In which a bird's-eye glimpse is afforded of Princess's Place. (MS)

(3) CHAPTER VII A Bird's eye glimpse of Miss Tox's dwelling place. Also of the state of Miss Tox's affections (Ws)

(4) CHAPTER ~~IV~~ VII ~~IN WHICH~~ A BIRD'S-EYE GLIMPSE ~~IS AFFORDED~~ OF ~~PRINCESS'S PLACE.~~ Miss Tox's dwelling place; ~~and~~ also of the state of Miss Tox's affections. (Corrected proof of (2))

Dickens titles and revises in the manuscript (1) and (2). When transferring the revised version to the worksheet, he makes further changes (3). Using the proofs of (2), he brings the title into line with (3), at the same time substituting a semicolon for the stop and using a lower case 'a' in "Also" (4).

Chapter eight

(1) Paul's further ~~progress~~ progress, and character. (Ws)

(2) Paul's further progress, growth and character. With some account of Mrs Wrychin's establishment. (Ws)

(3) Paul's further progress, growth and character. With some account of Mrs Pipchin's establishment. (Ws)

(4) Paul's further progress growth, and character. With some account of Mrs Pipchin's xxxxxx xxxxxxxxxxx establishment(?) (MS)

(5) Paul's further progress growth, and character. With some account of Mrs Pipchin's establishment (MS)

(6) Paul's further progress, growth, and character. (MS)

(7) Paul's further progress, growth, and character. (Ws)

Dickens begins by revising in the worksheet alone. To (1) he adds "growth" and "With Wrychin's establishment" (2), following the second change of name in the left-hand entry Ws.3_2. He then alters "Wrychin" to "Pipchin" (3) after the fourth and final change of name in Ws.3_2. When he transfers (3) to the manuscript, he extends the description of Mrs Pipchin's establishment (4) and revises that version at least once (5). The presence of versions (4) and (5) is confirmed by two distinct sets of underlines. Finally in (6), he deletes all mention of Mrs Pipchin and returns to an early version of Paul's progress (2). He then copies (6) to (7), underlining it in Ws.3 for the first time.

Chapter eleven

(1) Paul's education (MS)

(2) Paul's Introduction to a new Scene. (MS)

(3) Paul's Introduction to a new Scene. (Ws)

Dickens titles and revises in the manuscript, and then transfers the final version to the worksheet.

Chapter thirteen

(1) Sailing Orders. (MS)

(2) Shipping Business. (MS)

(3) Sailing Orders, and Office Business. (MS)

(4) Shipping Intelligence and Office Business. (MS)

(5) Shipping Intelligence and Office Business (Ws)

Dickens titles and revises in the manuscript, and then transfers the final version to the worksheet.

Chapter fourteen

(1) Paul goes home for the holidays. (MS)

(2) Paul grows more old-fashioned and goes home for the holidays. (MS)

(3) Paul grows more and more old-fashioned and goes home for the holidays. (MS)

(4) Paul grows more and more old-fashioned and goes home for the holidays.(Ws)

Dickens titles and revises in the manuscript, and then transfers the final version to the worksheet.

Chapter fifteen

(1) Artfulness of Captain Cuttle, and a new pursuit for Walter Gay. (MS)

(2) Artfulness of Captain Cuttle, and a new pursuit for Walter Gay. (Ws)

(3) Amazing Artfulness of Captain Cuttle, and a new pursuit for Walter Gay. (MS and Ws)

Dickens titles in the manuscript and transfers the title to the worksheet. "Amazing" appears to be an afterthought, added to both the manuscript and the worksheet at the same time.

Chapter seventeen (later chapter eighteen)

(1) Relatives and Friends (MS)

(2) Relatives and Friends of Florence. (MS)

(3) Father and Daughter. (MS)

(4) Father and Daughter. (Ws)

Dickens titles and revises twice in the manuscript, and then transfers the final version to the worksheet. Unlike title revisions in previous chapters that are all cumulative, building on earlier versions, revision (3) is an emphatic change of focus.

Chapter twenty

(1) New Faces (MS and Ws)

(2) Mr Dombey goes upon a journey (Corrected proof of (1))

(3) Mr Dombey goes upon a journey (Ws)

Dickens enters the title (1) in the manuscript and in the worksheet (in blue). At the proof stage, he divides ch.20 into two, re-titling ch.20 "Mr Dombey goes upon a journey" and titling the new ch.21 "New Faces". In worksheet, he deletes (1), copies in "Mr Dombey goes upon a journey" for ch.20. (He also enters a new chapter number heading for ch.21, titles it "New Faces", and adjusts the initial ch.21 to 22).

Chapter twenty-two

(1) ~~Xxxxx~~(?) Management of Mr Carker the Manager. (MS)

(2) A trifle of Management by Mr Carker the Manager. (MS)

(3) A trifle of Management by Mr Carker the Manager. (Ws)

Dickens, writing all of the manuscript of the seventh instalment in blue, also revises there in blue—the deletion may be "Alert/Astute/Adroit" or some such word with similar risers—and later transfers the final version in black to the worksheet.

Chapter twenty-three

(1) Domestic and Fxxxgxxxx(?) (List)

(2) Domestic and Foreign . The Midshipman Mysterious (List)

(3) Florence solitary, and the Midshipman Mysterious. (List)

(4) Florence solitary, and the Midshipman Mysterious. (MS and Ws)

Having left a gap for the title in manuscript during the composition of chapter twenty-three, Dickens titles in the List, revises there two or three times, then transfers the final version to the manuscript and the worksheet.

Chapter twenty-seven

(1) Darker and deeper Shadows. (MS)

(2) Deeper Shadows. (MS)

(3) Deeper Shadows. (Ws)

Dickens titles and revises in blue in manuscript, but transfers the final version to worksheet in black, probably after he composed ch.28 in blue in manuscript, and returned to black to complete the record (see 'Titles of chs.26, 27 & 28', p.81).

Chapter twenty-nine

(1) The eyes of Mrs Chick are opened all at once (?). (MS)

(2) The eyes of Mrs Chick are opened. (MS)

(3) The eyes of Mrs Chick are opened. (Ws)

(4) The opening of the eyes of Mrs Chick. (MS)

(5) The opening of the eyes of Mrs Chick. (List)

Dickens enters the title (1) in the manuscript as he begins the chapter. Later, he lessens the irony, revising the title to (2), which is copied to the worksheet (3). When he decides soon afterwards to use the wording of the title as the basis for the lettering of the first illustration in No.10 "The eyes of Mrs Chick are opened to Lucretia Tox", perhaps to avoid repetition he restyles the title in the manuscript to its final version (4). This is also the version he copies into the "List of Chapter Headings" (5). However, he may leave the title that he had already copied to the worksheet unchanged, because the version there serves as a record well enough.

Chapter thirty

(1) Before the Wedding (MS)

(2) Before the Marriage (MS)

(3) The Interval Before the Marriage (MS)

(4) The Interval before the Marriage (Ws)

Dickens titles and revises in the manuscript, and then transfers the final version to the worksheet.

Chapter thirty-eight

(1) Miss Tox cultivates an old acquaintance. (Ws after 'ch.37')

(2) Miss Tox renews acquaintance (?) with Rob the Grinder. (MS)

(3) Miss Tox improves an old acquaintance. (MS)

(4) Miss Tox cultivates an old acquaintance. (List)

Dickens may first title the chapter in worksheet, where the chapter is numbered ch.37. In manuscript, where the chapter is numbered ch.38, he revises the wording as he enters it, then, bringing it closer to the version in the worksheet, revises it again (the published version). When he transfers the title to the List, where the chapter is numbered ch.38, perhaps overlooking the revision in manuscript, he re-enters the initial title only found in worksheet.

Chapter forty-one

(1) The great(?) sea shore. (MS)

(2) The sea shore. (MS)

(3) New Voices in the Waves. (MS)

(4) New Voices in the Waves. (Ws)

Dickens titles and revises twice in the manuscript, and then transfers the final version to the worksheet. The second revision, like that of ch.18, brings a change of subject, in this case making a comparison more explicit.

Chapter forty-three

(1) The Watches of the Night (MS)

(2) The Vigils of a Night (MS)

(3) The Watches of the Night. (MS)

(4) The Watches of the Night. (Ws)

During or perhaps after composition, Dickens titles, revises, then reinstates the initial title in the manuscript, transferring the final version to the worksheet.

Chapter fifty

(1) Mr Toots's love(?) and friendship (MS)

(2) Mr Toots's complaint. (MS)

(3) Mr Toots's complaint. (Ws)

(4) Mr Toots' ~~sore~~(?) complaint (List)

Dickens titles and revises in manuscript transferring the final title to worksheet. When he enters the title in the List, he appears to mistake the title, then to correct it. The conjecture "sore" is suggested on the following grounds (1) it is the right length (2) like the deleted word it has no letters with risers or tails (3) Dickens has already given Toots the word "sore" to describe his love (ch.32, 448^{492}) (4) the collocation is a common one in biblical and Shakespearian language.

Chapter fifty-three

(1) Further Intelligence. (MS)

(2/3) More Intelligence. (MS)

(3/2) More Intelligence. (Ws)

Dickens titles, revises in the manuscript, and transfers the final version to the worksheet (or vice-versa).

Chapter fifty-eight

(1) After a lapse (MS)

(2) ~~After a lapse~~ (MS)

(3) After a lapse. (MS)

(4) After a lapse. (Ws)

In the manuscript, Dickens enters the title, which he deletes along with the opening paragraph. He replaces them with a slip where he rewrites the paragraph, and reinstates the deleted title. He then transfers the title to the worksheet.

Chapter sixty-two

(1) Final (Ws)

(2) The last bottle of the old Madeira (Ws)

(3) Final (MS)

Dickens enters a title in greeny blue ink and later revises it. During composition, after using the "old Madeira" as a recurring motif in the text, he reinstates the initial title in the manuscript.

E. False starts in the manuscript at chapter openings

Dickens occasionally begins a chapter, falters, turns the leaf over and starts again. Sometimes, instead of turning over the leaf, he writes a fair copy on a slip of paper, perhaps with more revisions, which he sticks over his first attempt. The five false starts listed below—often interesting for what they reveal of Dickens's stylistic sensitivities—show how his entry of chapter titles varies:

- he may title as he writes and revises the text, then start again, repeat the title and continue to revise the text as he writes (chs.51 and 58)
- he may title as he writes, revise the title and the text, then start again, leave a blank line, continue to revise the text and insert a different title later (ch.41)
- he may leave a narrow gap, write on (creating a broken sentence) and soon after sqeeze in a title. He then deletes the whole, enters the same title, full-sized and well spaced, and revises the text (ch.61)
- he may leave a gap, write on, revise the text, then start again, leave a gap, continue to revise the text and insert a title later (ch.49).

These false starts show that Dickens sometimes leaves a blank line for the title, that he usually begins again because of dissatisfaction with the text, and that he may often, having left a blank line, insert (and revise) a title soon afterwards. We also know from colour changes that he may delay entering a title until well into the chapter, or even until he begins the next chapter.

Chapter forty-one

Chapter XLI.
The ~~great~~(?) sea shore.
All /^is going on as it was wont! The waves

Chapter XLI.
New voices in the waves.
All is going on as it was wont.~~to~~(?) The waves are hoarse with repetition xxxx xxxx
xxx of their mystery the dust lies piled upon the xxxx shore …

Dickens titles, revises, then after a line abandons what he has written. Turning over the leaf he begins again, leaving a blank line for a different title that is entered later.[134]

Chapter forty-nine

(Dealings in the Firm of Dombey and Son —————————— N°. XVI

Chapter XLIX.

It was long before Florence awoke. The day was in its prime, the day was in its wane, and still she slept on, unconscious of her strange bed, of the noise and turmoil of the street, of the
~~xxxxxxxxxxxxxxxxxxxxxxxxxx~~ light that shone ~~xxxxxxxxxxxxxxxxxxxxxxxxxx~~ Weary exhaustion
xxxxxxxxxxxxxxxx outside the shaded window. Txxxxxxxxxxxxxxxxxxxxxxxxxxxxxxxxxxxxxx
xxxxxxxxxxxxxxxxxxxxxxxxxxxxxx both in mind and body, she slumbered …

(Dealings in the Firm of Dombey and Son —————————— N°. XVI

Chapter XLIX.
The Midshipman makes a discovery.

It was long before Florence awoke. The day was in its prime, the day was in its wane, and still, weary in mind and body, xxxxxxxxx she slept on; unconscious of her strange bed, of
Perfect ~~xx~~
the noise and turmoil in the street and of the light that shone outside the shaded window. ^Unconsciousness of what had happened …

Dickens enters the part and chapter number heading, leaves a narrow blank line for the title, composes the first two sentences but revises the third so extensively that he decides to abandon the page. He strikes out the whole of what he has written, turns the leaf over and begins again, entering the part and chapter number heading and leaving a gap as before, into which he later inserts a title in smallhand.

Chapter fifty-one

Chapter LI
Mr. Dombey and the World.

Where is the proud man <all the ~~while~~(?)time>while the days go by? Is he sitting by his
daunted
blackened fire, like the ~~frightened~~ traveller on the Prairie waiting until the

Chapter LI
Mr. Dombey and the World.

doing Does he ever think
What is the proud man ^all the xxxxxtime while the days go by? ^~~Has he any thought~~ of his
[daughter xxor
wonder
xxx ^where she is gone?

Dickens transfers the title from the worksheet, then writes on. However, when he begins to extend the simile, he turns the leaf over and begins again. He enters the title and writes on as before, omitting the comparison. The false start with the identical repeat of the title confirms that the title is entered before he begins to compose.

Chapter fifty-eight

Chapter LVIII .

After a Lapse .

Dickens enters the title and writes the first paragraph, making many revisions. Then he takes a blank slip of paper, makes a fair copy (with the title), cuts it to size and attaches it over his first attempt. It is possible to read the same title beneath, but little of the corrected text.

Chapter sixty-one

Chapter LXI .
Relenting
Florence had need of help, the father's need of help, it made Susan's aid invaluable.

Chapter LXI .

Relenting
was sore, and
Florence had need of help. The father's need of it ^ made the aid of her old friend, invaluable

Dickens leaves a narrow gap for the title, writes the first line, and then squeezes the title into the spaces (the risers of "Rel" lie between the broken underlines) and finally strikes through the whole. He turns the page over and starts again, this time confidently titling as he writes.

F. Use of blue inks in worksheet, manuscript, List and proofs

The table below shows when Dickens uses a blue quill and ink. It lists the number he is working on, the sort of blue he is using, the point at which he begins to use it in each number, the entries that are made in blue—with a note on function—and when and how its use is interrupted by a change to black:

• in No.7	in bright blue	LH (2) the backstory of Edith and her mother;
	in black	RH (7), (8), (11) & (13) preliminaries,
		LH (1), (3) & (4) initial plan;
	in bright blue	MS and RH (9) title and composition of ch.20 (later 20 & 21), List [6/7],
		MS composition and title of ch.21 (later 22),
		Proofs (ch.20 divided into 20 & 21),
		LH (6) additional plan for ch.22,
		MS composition of extension to ch.22;
	in black	RH (10) & (12) titles for chs.20 & 21, etc.
• in No.9	in bright blue	MS composition of second half of ch.26 and its title;
	in black	RH (13)–(17) plans for ch.27 and (20) for ch.28;
	in bright blue	MS composition and title of ch.27, List [8/9], MS composition and title of ch.28;
	in black	RH (6), (12) & (19) titles of chs.26, 27 & 28.
• in No.11	in bright blue	MS composition and title of ch.34, title of ch.33, List [11];
	in black	RH (18) & (34) titles of chs.33 & (34), etc.
• in No.12	in watery blue	RH (17)–(19) title and summary of ch.36(later 37), Proofs (ch.35 divided into chs.35 and 36),
		LH (6) comment and RH (15) underlines,
		MS composition of ch.38,
		LH (8) comment;
	in black	MS change of 'ch.36' to 'ch.37', List [12].
• in Nos.19&20	in greeny blue	MS composition of ch.59,
		RH (15) title for ch.58 and (20) for ch.59, (28) title and (30) & (31) plan for first part of ch.60, (36) plan for first section of ch.61, (40) number heading and (41) title of ch.62;
	in black	RH (32) & (33) plan for second part of ch.60, etc..

The table above is derived from Dickens's order of work, as reconstructed in the commentaries to the worksheets in 'Section 5'. It reveals the extent to which it has been possible to preserve consecutiveness in his use of blue ink—given the other constraints: the function of chapter descriptions, the history of titling, the layout of entries, and their other qualities of hand, quill and ink.

It shows that in No.7 he begins by making a single isolated entry (2) in bright blue, and that all his other bright blue entries in No.7, other than (2), are consecutive, i.e. uninterrupted by the use of black. Likewise, the bright blue entries in No.11, the watery blue entries in No.12 and the greeny blue entries of Nos.19&20 are all uninterrupted by entries in black. It also shows that, although Dickens writes most of No.9—the second half of ch.26 and all of chs.27 and 28—in bright blue, he interrupts its use on one occasion only to plan for chs.27 and 28 in black.

For explanations and conjecture on Dickens's use of blue inks, see 'Ink colour' in 'Section 2', p.21 and the relevant commentaries in the worksheets of 'Section 5'.

Abbreviations used in the table are the same as elsewhere. They are:

- 'LH' means the left-hand half of a worksheet
- 'List' refers to "List of Chapter Headings"
- 'MS' means the manuscript of the novel
- 'RH' means the right-hand half of a worksheet
- numbers in round bracket refer to the marginal numbers given to entries in the transcription of each worksheet
- numbers in square brackets refer to the numbered entries in 'Appendix C'.

Bibliography

Ackroyd, Peter, *Dickens: A Memoir of Middle Age* (London: Vintage Books, 2012).

— *Dickens* (London: Sinclair–Stevenson Ltd., 1990).

Butt, John and Tillotson, Kathleen, *Dickens at Work*, 2nd ed. (Oxford: Methuen, 1968).

Churchill, R. C., *A Bibliography of Dickensian Criticism* (London Macmillan Press, 1975)

Clark, Lewis Gaylord, 'Charles Dickens', *Harpers New Monthly Magazine*, vol.25 (1862), 376–80.

Collins, Philip (ed.), *Charles Dickens The Public Readings* (Oxford: Clarendon Press, 1975), https://doi.org/10.1093/actrade/9780198125013.book.1

— *Dickens Interviews and Recollections*, 2 vols. (London: Macmillan, 1991).

Deane, Bradley, *The Making of the Victorian Novelist: Anxieties of Authorship in the Mass Market* (London: Routledge, 2003).

Dickens, Charles, *Bleak House*, eds. George Ford and Sylvère Monod (New York: Norton, 1977).

— *Dickens Journals Online* (University of Buckingham), http://www.djo.org.uk/household-words.html

— *Dombey and Son* (London: Bradbury & Evans, 1848).

— *Dombey and Son*, ed. Alan Horsman, Clarendon Dickens series (Oxford: Clarendon Press, 1974), https://doi.org/10.1093/actrade/9780198124917.book.1

— *Dombey and Son*, ed. Alan Horsman, Oxford World's Classics series (Oxford: Oxford University Press, 2008).

— *Dombey and Son*, ed. Andrew Sanders (London: Penguin Classics, 2002).

— *Dombey and Son*, ebook 821, Project Gutenberg, http://www.gutenberg.org/ebooks/821 (released 1 February 1997)

— *Letters of Charles Dickens*, Pilgrim edition, eds. Graham Storey, Kathleen Tillotson and Madeline House, et al., 12 vols. (Oxford: Clarendon Press, 1982–2002).

— *Little Dorrit*, eds. Stephen Wall and Helen Small, rev. ed. (London: Penguin Classics, 2003).

— *Our Mutual Friend*, Oxford Illustrated Dickens series (Oxford: Oxford University Press, 1974).

— *Pickwick Papers*, ed. James Kinsley (Oxford: Clarendon Press, 1986), https://doi.org/10.1093/oseo/instance.00121338

Dolby, George, *Charles Dickens as I Knew Him* (London: Everett & Co., 1912).

Forster, John, *Life of Charles Dickens*, ed. J. W. T. Ley (London: Cecil Palmer, 1926).

— *Life of Charles Dickens*, 3 vols. in 2 (Boston: James R. Osgood & Co., 1875), ebook 25851, Project Gutenberg, http://www.gutenberg.org/ebooks/25851 (released 20 June 2008)

Gager, Valerie L., *Shakespeare and Dickens: The Dynamics of Influence* (Cambridge: Cambridge University Press, 1996).

Hammerton, J. A. (ed.), *The Dickens Companion,* Charles Dickens Library, vol.18 (London: Educational Book Co. Ltd., 1910).

Hardy, Barbara, *Dickens and Creativity* (London: Continuum, 2008), https://doi.org/10.5040/9781474211321

Hartley, Jenny, *Charles Dickens and the House of Fallen Women* (London: Methuen, 2008).

Herring, Paul D., 'Number Plans for *Dombey and Son*', *Modern Philology* 64 (1966), 151–87.

James, Henry, 'Preface to *The Tragic Muse*', http://www.gutenberg.org/files/20085/20085-h/20085-h.htm#PREFACE

Johnson, Edgar D. H., *Charles Dickens: An Introduction to his Novels* (Princeton: Princeton University Press, 1968).

Litvack, Leon, *Charles Dickens's 'Dombey and Son': An Annotated Bibliography* (New York: AMS Press, 1999).

Low, Annette, 'The Conservation of Charles Dickens' Manuscripts', *V&A Conservation Journal*, no.9 (October 1993), http://www.vam.ac.uk/content/journals/conservation-journal/issue-09/

Monod, Sylvère, *Dickens the Novelist* (Norman: University of Oklahoma Press, 1968).

O'Gorman, Francis (ed.), *A Concise Companion to the Victorian Novel* (Oxford: Blackwell, 2005).

Patten, Robert L., *Dickens and His Publishers* (Oxford University Press, 1978; reprinted by The Dickens Project, University of California, Santa Cruz, 1991).

Philpotts, Trey, *The Companion to Dombey and Son* (Great Britain: Liverpool University Press, 2014).

Purton, Valerie, *Dickens and the Sentimental Tradition* (London: Anthem Press, 2012), https://doi.org/10.7135/UPO9780857289070

Schlicke, Paul (ed.), *The Oxford Reader's Companion to Dickens* (Oxford: Oxford University Press, 1999), https://doi.org/10.1093/acref/9780196662532.001.0001

Slater, Michael, *Dickens and Women* (London: J. M. Dent & Son, 1983).

— *Charles Dickens: A Life Defined by Writing* (New Haven and London: Yale University Press, 2009).

— *The Great Charles Dickens Scandal* (New Haven and London: Yale University Press, 2012).

Smith, Grahame, *Charles Dickens A Literary Life* (London: Macmillan Press, 1996), https://doi.org/10.1007/978-1-349-24489-8

Stone, Harry, *Dickens and the Invisible World* (London: Macmillan Press, 1979), https://doi.org/10.1007/978-1-349-05072-7

— (ed.), *Dickens' Working Notes for His Novels* (University of Chicago Press, 1987).

Sucksmith, H. P., 'Dickens at Work on *Bleak House*', *Renaissance and Modern Studies* 9 (1965), 47–85.

Tomalin, Claire, *The Invisible Woman* (London: Viking Penguin, 1990).

Turner, Mark W., '"Telling of My Weekly Doings": The Material Culture of the Victorian Novel', in: *A Concise Companion to the Victorian Novel,* ed. Francis O'Gorman (Oxford: Blackwell, 2005), pp.113–33, https://doi.org/10.1111/b.9781405103206.2004.x

Wall, Stephen (ed.), *Charles Dickens A Critical Anthology* (London: Penguin Books, 1970).

Endnotes

1 Rotation of text to any angle within a text box was the crucial development in Word 2010 at the time.

2 Double quotation marks are used for Dickens's own words and singles for all others.

3 This quote is from the fifth paragraph of the Preface to *The Tragic Muse* by Henry James (http://www.gutenberg.org/files/20085/20085-h/20085-h.htm#PREFACE). He is not thinking specifically of *Dombey and Son* but of the nineteenth-century realist novel in general.

4 Turner's article is in *A Concise Companion to the Victorian Novel*, ed. Francis O'Gorman (Oxford: Blackwell, 2005), pp.113–33 (p.119).

5 Quoted from Paul Schlicke's article '*Dombey and Son*' in *The Oxford Reader's Companion to Dickens*, ed. Paul Schlicke (Oxford: Oxford University Press, 1999), pp.183–86.

6 'Manuscript' (with the abbreviation 'MS') in this study refers to the manuscript of the novel. To avoid ambiguity, it excludes the working notes, i.e. the monthly worksheets and other notes, although these have become bound into Volume 1 of the manuscript of the novel.

7 The origin of what became a monthly standard is documented in chapter three of *Dickens and His Publishers* by Robert Patten (Oxford: Oxford University Press, 1978; reprinted by The Dickens Project, University of California, Santa Cruz, 1991), pp.45–74.

8 The cover design of the green wrapper is reproduced to scale and in colour at the front of this book. It is used as the frontispiece, in black and white, in both the Clarendon hardback and the Oxford World's Classics paperback (where it is also much reduced).

9 Readers would most likely look at the two illustrations, question their significance, and have each one in mind as they began reading, whereas the reader of the volume publication came across the illustrations as they read the text, the printer having inserted each plate near to the page carrying the relevant narrative.

10 In the old currency of pounds, shillings and pence (or £sd), 12d (pence) = 1/- (shilling) and 20/- = £1. John Dickens's income from the Naval Pay Office began at a little under £200 p.a. when he married in 1809, rose to over £400 in the 1820s, and then fell back (Slater, p.8 and p.12). With the income and status of a member of the aspiring middle class, he owned a standard set of literary volumes of the previous century, which his eldest son—'a terrible boy to read'—devoured (Peter Ackroyd, *Dickens* (London: Sinclair–Stevenson Ltd., 1990) p.44). However, in a more frugal lower-middle-class home,

https://doi.org/10.11647/OBP.0092.11

buying a novel would probably be a rare event, though its members might pay a shilling for a monthly instalment. When the father was imprisoned for debt in 1824, his son was earning 7/6 per week as a child worker. Later Dickens began earning as an office boy in 1828 at a starting wage of 10/6 per week. Scrooge's pay to his only clerk Bob Cratchit at 15/- a week for a man with six children was a starvation wage. For information on 'money values' and 'readership', see Shlicke, pp.381–83 and pp.487–89; for economic data, see measuringworth.com.

11 Unlike the individual parts, many of these 'first issue' first editions, bound up by owner or publisher from the parts, are at the time of writing (2015) in general circulation and occasionally offered for sale.

12 The place of the mode of production in cultural history is outlined in the introduction to *The Making of Victorian Novelists* by Bradley Deane (London: Routledge, 2003), pp.ix-xvi, and in the article by Mark Turner, '"Telling of My Weekly Doings": The Material Culture of the Victorian Novel', in: *A Concise Companion to the Victorian Novel*, ed. Francis O'Gorman (Oxford: Blackwell, 2005), pp.113–33. An account of some of the issues is also given in chapter two of *Charles Dickens: A Literary Life* by Grahame Smith (London: Macmillan Press, 1996).

13 For an overview of the novel, see Schlicke's article, '*Dombey and Son*'. For a longer account of Dickens's life at the time of the novel's composition, see chapter eleven in *Charles Dickens: A Life Defined by Writing* by Michael Slater (New Haven and London: Yale University Press, 2009). Leon Litvack gives a brief summary of Robert Patten's account (see endnote 7) of the effect of novel's success on Dickens's financial arrangements in his annotated bibliography *Charles Dickens's 'Dombey and Son': An Annotated Bibliography* (New York: AMS Press, 1999), entry no.21, pp.19–20.

14 Butt and Tillotson describe the narrative content of the design in detail in *Dickens at Work*, 2nd ed. (Oxford: Methuen, 1968), pp.92–94.

15 His difficulties, as he saw them, are recounted in a letter to Forster in August 1846:

> "You can hardly imagine [...] what infinite pains I take, or what extraordinary difficulty I find in getting on FAST. Invention, thank God, seems the easiest thing in the world; and I seem to have such a preposterous sense of the ridiculous, after this long rest" (it was now over two years since the close of Chuzzlewit), "as to be constantly requiring to restrain myself from launching into extravagances in the height of my enjoyment. But the difficulty of going at what I call a rapid pace, is prodigious; it is almost an impossibility. I suppose this is partly the effect of two years' ease, and partly of the absence of streets and numbers of figures. I can't express how much I want these. It seems as if they supplied something to my brain, which it cannot bear, when busy, to lose. For a week or a fortnight I can write prodigiously in a retired place (as at Broadstairs), and a day in London sets me up again and starts me. But the toil and labour of writing, day after day, without that magic lantern, is IMMENSE!! I don't say this at all in low spirits, for we are perfectly comfortable here, and I like the place very much indeed, and the people are even more friendly and fond of me than they were in Genoa. I only mention it as a curious fact, which I have never had an opportunity of finding out before. My figures seem disposed to stagnate without crowds about them (*Life* 423[K:8591]; for the reference conventions, see overleaf, endnote 18).

16 The term 'worksheet' (abbreviated to 'Ws') is used for the number plan and chapter plan together, in order to avoid the confusion that often arises from using 'number plan' for the worksheet as a whole and for those parts of the left-hand page that are plans for the number. The difference is

variously made by other writers using a finer distinction, e.g. 'Number/number', 'number-plan/number plan', which seems less memorable and more difficult to sustain.

17 A wafer was a small disk of paste which became moist when you wetted it. Dickens uses the disks in the working notes to join leaves together. Quick-drying, the disks and leaves appear without exception to have stayed exactly where Dickens placed them.

18 References are to two versions of John Forster's *Life of Charles Dickens*: the first, edited by J. W. T. Ley (London: Cecil Palmer, 1926), by page number, and the second, ebook 25851 in Project Gutenberg, downloaded to Kindle, by 'location' number. The editor's reasons for using Kindle, rather than direct reference to ebook 25851, are given in 'References', p.7.

19 Dickens himself valued his working notes sufficiently to want them preserved along with the manuscripts of his novels. The manuscript of *Dombey and Son* is just one of many complete manuscripts of Dickens's novels in the V&A's Forster Collection, all of which have working notes of some sort.

20 After writing this section, the editor discovered Valerie Purton's work on 'sentimentalism'. She suggests that the warm friendliness of Dickens's mature prose style develops from his experience of the drama and fiction of sentiment from Henry Fielding to Charles Lamb, a legacy that is prominent in *Dombey and Son*, 'his greatest triumph in the sentimentalist tradition'. See Valerie Purton, *Dickens and the Sentimental Tradition* (London: Anthem Press, 2012), pp.123–39.

21 John Butt in his article 'Dickens at Work', *Durham University Journal* (June 1948) cited in R. C. Churchill, *A Bibliography of Dickensian Criticism* (London Macmillan Press, 1975), p.29 and Sylvère Monod in *Dickens, romancier. Étude sur la création littéraire dans les romans de Charles Dickens* (Paris, 1953) translated by the author as *Dickens the Novelist* (Norman: University of Oklahoma Press, 1968). They may have been encouraged by the publication of Eric Bolls' article, 'The Plotting of *Our Mutual Friend*', in *Modern Philology* 42 (1944) cited in Churchill p.115, on the working notes for *Our Mutual Friend* that are held in the New York Public Library.

22 For more on the details of the conservation of the manuscript, see Annette Low, 'The Conservation of Charles Dickens' Manuscripts', *V&A Conservation Journal*, no.9 (October 1993), http://www.vam.ac.uk/content/journals/conservation-journal/issue-09. The position of the worksheets in the manuscript of the novels varies. In *Little Dorrit*, for example, each worksheet is placed at the start of the relevant instalment.

23 There are some minor differences between the description of the notes here and that of the Clarendon edition of *Dombey and Son* (Horsman 1974, 'Introduction', pp.xliii-xlvi), and a few disparities, e.g. the description of the left-hand page of Ws.5 and the description of the "List of Chapter Headings". The treatment of transcription is of course quite different.

24 Horsman seems to confuse leaves and pages in his description of the "List of Chapter Headings" (Horsman, p.xliii). There are six pages in all. Dickens uses both sides of three leaves (one is still joined to another to form the only uncut foolscap sheet in the entire manuscript of working notes and text).

25 The three wafered additions were probably attached to their worksheets by Dickens himself some time during his work on the relevant number, whereas the leaves on "Florence's age" (Ws.6a) were always separate pages, until pasted on to the back of Ws.6 after his death, when all the working notes were bound up with the manuscript of the novel. For an account of 'wafering', see above endnote 17.

26 Dickens was waiting in June 1846 for the delivery of "the big box" containing his writing materials (L.4:373).

27 Cutting and mending a pen was clearly a skill that every clerk or teacher would be expected to have, and one that every properly-schooled early-nineteenth-century boy would be expected to learn. An office boy working for *Household Words* later recalls that he was not allowed to cut Dickens's quills, implying that Dickens took special care over it and/or was used to doing the job himself (see Philip Collins (ed.), *Dickens Interviews and Recollections*, 2 vols. (London: Macmillan, 1991), 2:196. The process of cutting a quill to a thin, medium or broad tip and splitting the end to help the flow required skill and practice (which accounts for the search for an acceptable steel substitute between 1830 and 1860). The 'pen-knife' evidently had a sharper blade than the ordinary present-day pen-knife; it could be honed to a razor-sharp edge. Dickens may have more often avoided the delay of re-cutting by simply taking up a fresh pen; he writes in a letter of 1842, "As my pen is getting past its work I have taken a new one" (L.3:160). Perhaps not regularly re-cutting his own quills, he did not keep a pen-knife handy, like Mr Merdle who, needing a sharp blade to bleed himself to death, has to borrow a pen-knife from his daughter-in-law (*Little Dorrit*, eds. Stephen Wall and Helen Small (London: Penguin classic, 2003) pp.680–83.

28 Where the space is limited, reference to left-hand and right-hand half of the worksheet is sometimes abbreviated to 'LH' and 'RH' respectively.

29 Readers of the digital version of this book, who interrupt the text to follow hyperlinks, may be able to return to the text either by 'alt + left arrow' or by a 'Go back' facility, depending on their software and/or system. Similarly, the command to rotate (between portrait and landscape mode) varies with different software (in Adobe, it is 'ctrl' + 'shift' '+' or '-').

30 One of the few mistakes in underlining chapter titles is in ch.62, where Dickens, underlining the first revision of the title in the worksheet, gives a pair of underlines to the first syllable of "Final" (a 'run-on' error); see Ws.19&20$_{42}$ p.123 and cf. 'Appendix C', entry [15b], p.178 (a 'transfer' error).

31 Word 2010 allows the use of drawn straight lines ('shapes') to distinguish various degrees of thickness, four of which are used in transcription (a half, three-quarter, one and one-and-a quarter points). The program provides as many degrees ('gradients') of blackness as there are percentage points.

32 All transcribers comment on individual instances of corrosion and sometimes use it to detect concurrent entries, but none give a wider account of it, perhaps because of its unreliability. The perception of corrosion is affected by the quality of the light source and by the colour of the surroundings. It is also possible that environmental pollution has created some corrosion since Butt began his work in the 1940s.

33 The diagonal slash first appears in the earliest surviving pages of notes: for No.41 of *The Old Curiosity Shop*, then in the two pages of notes for Nos.4 and 6 of *Martin Chuzzlewit* (a general precursor of the format of the working notes); see Stone, pp.8–9 and pp.42–45.

34 In this respect, Dickens seems to take more care in the manuscript (his copy text) than in the notes. It is likely that he used blotting paper of some sort to accelerate drying; some of the random marks resemble the transfer typical of the blotting paper of a hundred years later. Cf. the many references to blotting and blotting paper in *Household Words* and *All the Year Round* at http://www.djo.org.uk/household-words.html.

35 Among the errors is Paul Herring's misreading of 'awful' for 'artful' ; see 'Number Plans for *Dombey and Son*', *Modern Philology* 64 (1966), 151–87, p.171.

36 Many of the critical comments on Stone's transcriptions also apply to those of Trey Philpotts's transcriptions in his "Companion to Dombey and Son" (Great Britain: Liverpool University Press, 2014). His transcriptions are reduced photographic copies of Stone's, but with the two halves of each worksheet placed on opposite pages and without the facsimiles that were intended to accompany them.

37 At the age of seventeen, Dickens learnt the Gurney system of shorthand, after only a six-month struggle—it usually took two years. He went on to become an outstanding practitioner by all accounts, including his own tongue-in-cheek boast to Wilkie Collins many years later: "I dare say I am at this present writing [6 June 1856], the Best Hand Writer in the World" (L.8:130). He still had the facility when he tried to teach it, forty years on, to one of his sons, Henry Fielding (about nineteen at the time), who gives a memorable account of his lessons. His father's sample speeches were the source of so much laughter for both of them that Henry made little progress (Collins (1991) 1:164).

38 Herring, Paul D., 'Number Plans for *Dombey and Son*', *Modern Philology* 64 (1966), 151–87.

39 Overlooking how entries are grouped is relatively common. Even Sylvère Monod, usually a careful commentator on the notes, seems to misread significant groupings in Ws.2 (Monod, 1968, p.259).

40 This apt phrase 'the marriage storm' is adapted from Butt and Tillotson, where they describe the 'real storm-centre of the novel' (see *Dickens at Work*, p.103).

41 As each original manuscript leaf is mounted on a white sheet, any entries on the verso side are revealed by cutting a window in the mounting sheet. A photograph of the window and what it reveals can then be taken without removing the manuscript leaf from its mount. The only verso entry in the worksheets (apart from that of the exceptional Ws.6a) is Ws.1 verso, which because of its smaller size is displayed in portrait mode.

42 Dickens's outline to Forster is as follows [the paragraphing is the editor's]:

> I will now go on to give you an outline of my immediate intentions in reference to Dombey. I design to show Mr. D. with that one idea of the Son taking firmer and firmer possession of him, and swelling and bloating his pride to a prodigious extent. As the boy begins to grow up, I shall show him quite impatient for his getting on, and urging his masters to set him great tasks, and the like. But the natural affection of the

> boy will turn towards the despised sister; and I purpose showing her learning all sorts of things, of her own application and determination, to assist him in his lessons; and helping him always. When the boy is about ten years old (in the fourth number), he will be taken ill, and will die; and when he is ill, and when he is dying, I mean to make him turn always for refuge to the sister still, and keep the stern affection of the father at a distance. So Mr. Dombey—for all his greatness, and for all his devotion to the child—will find himself at arms' length from him even then; and will see that his love and confidence are all bestowed upon his sister, whom Mr. Dombey has used—and so has the boy himself too, for that matter—as a mere convenience and handle to him. The death of the boy is a deathblow, of course, to all the father's schemes and cherished hopes; and 'Dombey and Son,' as Miss Tox will say at the end of the number, 'is a Daughter after all.'....
>
> From that time, I purpose changing his feeling of indifference and uneasiness towards his daughter into a positive hatred. For he will always remember how the boy had his arm round her neck when he was dying, and whispered to her, and would take things only from her hand, and never thought of him. ... At the same time I shall change her feeling towards him for one of a greater desire to love him, and to be loved by him; engendered in her compassion for his loss, and her love for the dead boy whom, in his way, he loved so well too.
>
> So I mean to carry the story on, through all the branches and offshoots and meanderings that come up; and through the decay and downfall of the house, and the bankruptcy of Dombey, and all the rest of it; when his only staff and treasure, and his unknown Good Genius always, will be this rejected daughter, who will come out better than any son at last, and whose love for him, when discovered and understood, will be his bitterest reproach. For the struggle with himself which goes on in all such obstinate natures, will have ended then; and the sense of his injustice, which you may be sure has never quitted him, will have at last a gentler office than that of only making him more harshly unjust....
>
> I rely very much on Susan Nipper grown up, and acting partly as Florence's maid, and partly as a kind of companion to her, for a strong character throughout the book. I also rely on the Toodles, and on Polly, who, like everybody else, will be found by Mr. Dombey to have gone over to his daughter and become attached to her. This is what cooks call 'the stock of the soup.' All kinds of things will be added to it, of course (*Life* 472–73[K:9244–65]; for the full reference, see endnote 18).

43 On the back of Ws.1, Dickens enters the number heading for a fourth chapter (ch.22) in the same hand as the other three number headings, showing that they were very probably entered altogether. For the later transfer of number heading and title to the front of the worksheet, see the last entries in the commentary on Ws.1 (recto), p.41.

44 Like the number heading for ch.4 (see above), its title is entered on the under (verso) side of Ws.1, sometime after the entry of the number heading.

45 This chapter's function as a short, alternative ch.4 accounts for its unusual brevity; it is only four printed pages and, with ch.16, one of the shortest (see chs.7, 16 and 62 in 'Appendix A'). It became ch.7.

46 Georgina recorded that an average day's work for him was two to two-and-half sides of manuscript, and a very, very hard day's work was four of them (Collins, 1991, 1:119). However, Dickens's written output cannot be used as a measure of creativity. Charley, his eldest son, records that his father used to say that it was his business to sit at his desk during just those particular hours of the day [ten o'clock to lunchtime]: 'I have known a day to have been barren of copy, but to have been a very good day, notwithstanding. [...] I learnt to know well, that he had been, almost unconsciously, diligently thinking all round his subject' (*ibid.*, 1:120).

47 Readers without access to the critical Clarendon text, or who in any case wish to read the longer cuts in their context, may prefer to download ebook 821, the free edition of the novel in Project Gutenberg, where most—but not all—of the longer cuts have been silently restored (see http://www.gutenberg.org/ebooks/821).

48 Forster considered that, of all the letters he received from Dickens, the following passage written towards the end of August 1846 threw more 'illuminative light' onto his life as a writer than any other:

> But the difficulty of going at what I call a rapid pace, is prodigious; it is almost an impossibility. I suppose this is partly the effect of two years' ease, and partly of the absence of streets and numbers of figures. I can't express how much I want these. It seems as if they supplied something to my brain, which it cannot bear, when busy, to lose. For a week or a fortnight I can write prodigiously in a retired place (as at Broadstairs), and a day in London sets me up again and starts me. But the toil and labour of writing, day after day, without that magic lantern, is immense!! I don't say this at all in low spirits, for we are perfectly comfortable here, and I like the place very much indeed, and the people are even more friendly and fond of me than they were in Genoa. I only mention it as a curious fact, which I have never had an opportunity of finding out before. My figures seem disposed to stagnate without crowds about them (*Life* 423[K:8595]; for the full reference, see endnote 18).

49 In the paragraph beginning "After another cold interval" at the word "font", Forster cuts "a rigid marble basin which seemed to have been playing a churchyard game at cup-and-ball with its matter-of-fact-pedestal, and to have been just that moment caught on top of it" (Horsman 1974 p.59 n.2; in ebook 821, K:1103, Project Gutenberg, http://www.gutenberg.org/ebooks/821 downloaded to Kindle). For the use of ebook 821, see 'References' p.7.

50 A second proof of ch.7 has the following added to the ending (deleted by Forster and adapted by Dickens to form the first paragraph of the opening of No.3):

> Beneath the watching and attentive eyes of Time—so far another Major—his slumbers slowly changed. More and more light broke in upon them; distincter and distincter dreams disturbed them; an accumulating crowd of objects and impressions swarmed about his rest; until he woke—a Schoolboy!

51 One number followed by another superscripted (and both bracketed together) is a combined page reference to the Clarendon text in hardback and paperback (see 'References', p.7).

52 Dickens may have coalesced his memories of Mrs Roylance and memories of another landlady (see Michael Slater, *Dickens and Women* (London: J. M. Dent & Son, 1983), p.389 n.41).

53 Dickens was aware of the difficulty that his visual imagination and retentive memory posed for his illustrators. In connection with John Leech's illustration for the Christmas book for 1846, *The Battle of Life*, he writes ruefully "You know how I build up temples in my mind that are not made with hands (or expressed with pen and ink, I am afraid), and how liable I am to be disappointed in these things" (*Life* 440[K:8945]).

54 The third paragraph of Dickens's second preface to *Pickwick Papers*, written in September 1847, begins:

> It was observed in the Preface to the original Edition, that they [the parts] were designed for the introduction of diverting characters and incidents; that no ingenuity of plot was attempted, or even at that time considered

> very feasible by the author in connexion with the desultory mode of publication adopted [...] on one of these points, experience and study have since taught me something, and I could perhaps wish now that these chapters were strung together on a stronger thread of general interest. (*Charles Dickens: A Critical Anthology*, ed. Stephen Wall (Harmondsworth: Penguin Books, 1970), pp.80–84), p.81.

The worksheets for *Dombey* show Dickens striving for a "stronger thread of general interest" with considerable "ingenuity of plot" and much else besides that contribute to the unity of the novel.

55 One of the reasons Dickens preferred monthly over weekly publication was that the former gave him more "elbow room" and "open places in perspective" in comparison with the compressed "teaspoonful" instalments of the latter (see below, endnote 103).

56 At issue here is whether the descriptions are plans made before composition or summary records made after it. Butt and Tillotson's pioneering *Dickens at Work* seems to have had an unfortunate effect in this respect. When they give close attention to the evidence (particularly of colour) supporting the view that a few notes are written after composition, they give the impression that many, or even most, descriptions are retrospective summaries. Generalisations along these lines find their way into Paul's Herring's article and into many introductory accounts of the working notes.

57 In Dickens's letter to Forster on 5 July 1846 he mentions "a great surprise for people at the end of the fourth number, [the death of Paul, later moved to the fifth number] and I think there is a new and peculiar sort of interest, involving the necessity of a little bit of delicate treatment whereof I will expound my idea to you by and by" (*Life* 404[K:8229]; for full reference, see endnote 18).

58 See *Dombey and Son*, ed. Alan Horsman (Oxford: Clarendon Press, 1974)—hereafter 'Horsman 1974' and followed, for example, by 'Introduction', p.xxix n.1; see 'References (2)', p.7.

59 Horsman 1974, 'Appendix D', pp.865 and xlviii.

60 The unpublished passages in the manuscript of No.5 are only available in the hardback critical Clarendon edition. Containing some characteristic examples of Dickens's inventive exuberance and his "preposterous sense of the ridiculous", comic matter is often the first to be sacrificed when he is correcting an over-run (see Horsman 1974, p.183 n.1 and p.185 n.2, both from ch.14, extensions of Paul's conversation with Toots and Miss Blimber respectively, and p.207 n.1, p.214 n.1 and p.217 n.4, all three cut from ch.15). No cuts were made to ch.16. Unfortunately, none of the cuts are restored in Project Gutenberg's ebook 821.

61 The final "too" is not in the published text. The editor supplies it from Horsman's account of the reading versions in 'Appendix D' of the hardback Clarendon edition (pp.862–65). According to Horsman, when Dickens began public readings for his own benefit in 1858, the story of "Little Dombey" was the first to be taken from a full-length novel. The version with the "too" added to the last word of the reading is in the Berg copy held by the New York Public Library (Horsman 1974, 'Appendix D', p.865). The detail is not mentioned in Philip Collins's edition of *Charles Dickens: The Public Readings* (Oxford: Clarendon Press, 1974). The added word helps convey the authenticity of the aging Dickens's management of pathos.

62 The quotations are from the last letters that Dickens sent to Forster while writing the novel and living abroad. The passage in the *Life* is best read as a whole [paragraphing is the editor's but the ellipses are Forster's]:

> I left him on the 2nd of February with his writing-table in readiness for number six; but on the 4th, enclosing the subjects for illustration, he told me he was "not under weigh yet. Can't begin." Then, on the 7th, his birthday, he wrote to warn me he should be late. "Could not begin before Thursday last, and find it very difficult indeed to fall into the new vein of the story. I see no hope of finishing before the 16th at the earliest, in which case the steam will have to be put on for this short month. But it can't be helped. Perhaps I shall get a rush of inspiration …
>
> I will send the chapters as I write them, and you must not wait, of course, for me to read the end in type. To transfer to Florence, instantly, all the previous interest, is what I am aiming at. For that, all sorts of other points must be thrown aside in this number.[…] I hope when I write next I shall report myself in better cue …
>
> I have had a tremendous outpouring from Jeffrey about the last part, which he thinks the best thing past, present, or to come."[140] Three more days and I had the MS of the completed chapter, nearly half the number (in which as printed it stands second, the small middle chapter having been transposed to its place). "I have taken the most prodigious pains with it; the difficulty, immediately after Paul's death, being very great. May you like it! My head aches over it now (I write at one o'clock in the morning), and I am strange to it. …
>
> I think I shall manage Dombey's second wife (introduced by the Major), and the beginning of that business in his present state of mind, very naturally and well. … Paul's death has amazed Paris. All sorts of people are open-mouthed with admiration. … When I have done, I'll write you such a letter! Don't cut me short in your letters just now, because I'm working hard. … I'll make up. … Snow—snow—snow—a foot thick." The day after this, came the brief chapter which was printed as the first; and then, on the 16th, which he had fixed as his limit for completion, the close reached me; but I had meanwhile sent him out so much of the proof as convinced him that he had underwritten his number by at least two pages, and determined him to come to London. The incident has been told which soon after closed his residence abroad, and what remained of his story was written in England (*Life* 481–82[K:9444–62]; for the full reference, see endnote 18).

63 Dickens was also surely aware—though he does not make it explicit in the worksheets until Ws.15$_{28 \& 29}$—that he often uses the house stairs as a setting for moments of dramatic intensity.

64 The change in function of John Carker follows from the alteration in "Walter Gay's Destiny". Dickens adds to his outline to Forster (see above) his initial intention for Walter:

> "About the boy, who appears in the last chapter of the first number, I think it would be a good thing to disappoint all the expectations that chapter seems to raise of his happy connection with the story and the heroine, and to show him gradually and naturally trailing away, from that love of adventure and boyish light-heartedness, into negligence, idleness, dissipation, dishonesty, and ruin. To show, in short, that common, every-day, miserable declension of which we know so much in our ordinary life; to exhibit something of the philosophy of it, in great temptations and an easy nature; and to show how the good turns into bad, by degrees.
>
> If I kept some little notion of Florence always at the bottom of it, I think it might be made very powerful and very useful. What do you think? Do you think it may be done, without making people angry? I could bring out Solomon Gills and Captain Cuttle well, through such a history; and I descry, anyway, an opportunity for good scenes between Captain Cuttle and Miss Tox. This question of the boy is very important. … Let me hear all you think about it. Hear! I wish I could."… (*Life* 473[K:9268–75]; see above).

Although Dickens "ultimately acquiesced" to Forster's advice to "reserve [Gay] for a happier future", he seems to lose his earlier imaginative involvement in the character.

65 The manuscript and the first proof read "she had only reckoned up thirteen".

66 The numbering of pages is consecutive across instalments, and the same as the single-volume first edition (1848).

67 The relevant moments marking time passing are: 344–46[375–76], the stipulation of the packet; 507–08[558], the death of Mrs Skewton; 528[582], the opening of the packet after one year; and 569[627], the mention of Mrs Skewton's death at Carker's breakfast with Dombey.

68 This account of the change to a bright blue ink for Ws.7_2 confirms that of Horsman. He asserts that the long entry on Edith must be made 'before what follows in brown' (Horsman 1974, 'Introduction', p.xxx). Although conjecture, the account seems a likely explanation of other crucial details, which Horsman does not explore.

69 It just possible that the entry of the number heading for ch.21 is inserted and that the numbering of ch.22 was initially ch.21. However, Dickens' changes to Roman numerals are generally more obvious than the proposed changes would be. The last broken underline of chapter twenty-two, positioned under the "II" is probably entered at the same time as the "XX".

70 From letters and surviving proofs, it is clear that Dickens often sent the first chapter of a number to the printers as soon as he had written it. See Horsman 1974, 'Introduction', p.xlv, and L5:23.

71 For the first illustration, Dickens wrote Browne a long letter on 10 March 1848 giving him a full account of the characters involved, sometime before he had written the second half of ch.20 (see 3rd paragraph onwards p.136). He received the preliminary sketch he had asked for on the 15th, and in reply asked for a few changes but also told Browne that there was no need for a second sketch "It is so late" (L5:33 and 35). Dickens's note for a second illustration is just that, with no lettering. Browne would probably be concerned to keep the illustration less visually crowded to speed up production, which regularly involved making a sketch, a copy, and two identical engravings in reverse on a steel plate for each illustration.

72 Understandably, Browne gives the scene an indoor setting, with much less detail, for the second illustration. He would have had early notice of the more elaborate scene for the first plate. However, though still hard pressed, he and his engravers were quite able to complete the second plate within the nine or so days that remained. He was probably given shorter notice for the second illustration of No.8, another closing scene involving Carker on horseback, on that occasion addressing Florence (see ch.24).

73 Dickens keeps a record of cuts that he values. Typically, he garners one of Mrs Skewton's effusive half-remembered quotations. See paragraph beginning "Really,' cried Mrs Skewton": "one might almost be induced to cross [...] is his prophet". It re-appears 372[406 & n.].

74 The use of bright blue differs in No.9 from its use in No.7. In Ws.9, Dickens makes all entries specific to the worksheet in black (as well as the first five or six manuscript pages of ch.26). In Ws.7, he uses the bright blue for all manuscript pages and for three groups of entries in the worksheet. For a description of the differences see 'Appendix F'; for a fuller account, see the commentary on the bright blue entries and the biographical introduction in each worksheet.

75 The following detail is worth noting, as part of the unusual history of the relation of Ws.9 to the manuscript (cf. Horsman 1974, 'Introduction', p.xxxii.). One difference, between the published text and the manuscript, relates to the visit to Kenilworth in ch.26. When Dickens writes ch.27, he adds to the Kenilworth excursion an initial morning visit to Warwick Castle, partly to satirise, through Cleopatra, the current vogue for the Middle Ages. In the published text of ch.26, "Warwick … to" (360[393]) and "Warwick and" (361[394]) is added to "Kenilworth". The failure to bring ch.26 into line with ch.27 in the manuscript confirms that ch.26 was unavailable (probably being at the printers) when he composed ch.27.

76 The editors of ebook 25851 in the Gutenberg Project have 'to himself' before 'both', which is not present in Ley's text of Forster's *Life*, though it may be present in the text they are editing, *Life of Charles Dickens*, 3 vols. in 2 (Boston: James R. Osgood & Co., 1875).

77 The character of Feenix opens out, not inconsistently, with the progress of the narrative, one of the many "branches and offshoots and meanderings that come up" (see the fourth paragraph of the "outline" in endnote 42).

78 Paul Schlicke (ed.), *Oxford Reader's Companion to Dickens* (Oxford: Oxford University Press, 1999), pp.185–87.

79 At the moment of the Staplehurst railway disaster, Dickens had apparently taken the manuscript of the next number of *Our Mutual Friend* out of his pocket (L11:56–57).

80 Consecutiveness in the use of the blue cannot be assumed (cf. Ws.7 and Ws.9). Two assumptions are made here: that Dickens's tenant used and left behind a supply of watery blue ink, and that Dickens used what was clearly a poor ink because no other was available to him. There may have been similar local circumstances to account for his use of the unusual greeny blue, in the later stages of his work on the double number, while in lodgings in Brighton.

81 Dickens may have planned for Dombey to welcome Pipchin in some way. Or perhaps the plans for both chs.40 and 41 preceded the composition of either, and this detail of the plan for ch.41 was made redundant by Dombey's reference in ch.40 to the re-employment of Pipchin—possibly through the good offices of Carker (542[598]). There are other instances of the pairing of chapter plans, notably chs.33 and 34 (see Ws.11). However, the contrast of hand, as well as that of tone and substance, makes the pairing of chs.40 and 41 less likely.

82 The collocation "room enough" is derived from Prince Hal's speech over the dead Hotspur. It occurs once in connection with burial in Shakespeare's plays (Act V, scene 4, line 94 in *Henry IV Part One*. See, for example, http://www.shakespeare-online.com/plays/1kh4_5_4.html). Dickens has an actor's memory for the plays, quoting extemporaneously whenever needed.

83 The grounds for placing entries for ch.45 before those for ch.44 are (a) the late addition of the number heading for ch.45; (b) the positioning of the title of ch.44, well to the left, to create space for the summary of ch.44; (c) the layout of the summary for the ch.44 entry (22), shaped around the number heading for ch.45; and (d) the double underline flourish beneath "M[r] Toots", signalling the end of the entries for Ws.14. Another consideration is ink flow, which appears unreliable throughout the

right-hand page. Dickens may be finding it difficult to control the ink, possibly re-dipping more often, but more likely simply responding to a reluctant quill. As the ink thins, it appears less dense, e.g. (15) to (19), (21) to (22), (26) and (5). Nevertheless, the progressive nature of the fading ink confirms the order of entry suggested by the layout, that the summaries of both chs.45 and 44 (in that order) follow the composition and titling of ch.45.

84 Dickens habitually registers his pleasure in the characterization of Toots by enlarging his name. Other instances occur in Ws.11_5 p.87, Ws.13_8 p.95, Ws.16_{12} p.107, and Ws.18_3 p.115.

85 The last three manuscript paragraphs of ch.45 are as follows:

> Edith saw no on that night, but locked her door, and kept herself alone. She did not weep; she showed no greater agitation, outwardly, than when she was riding home. She laid as proud a head upon her pillow as she had borne in her carriage; and her prayer ran thus:
>
> "May this man be a liar! For if he has spoken truth, she is lost to me, and I have no hope left!"
>
> "This man", meanwhile, went home musing to bed, thinking, with a dainty pleasure, how imperious her passion was, how she had sat before him in her beauty, with the dark eyes that had never turned away but once; how the white down had fluttered; how the bird's feathers had been strewn upon the ground" http://www.gutenberg.org/files/821/821-h/821-h.htm#link2HCH0045).

As usual, the editors of ebook 821 silently restore these three paragraphs, adding small changes of their own to paragraphing and punctuation (which in this copy the editor has corrected). The last paragraph pointedly refers back to moments earlier in the chapter (see 600 and 602[662 & 665]).

86 *Dombey and Son*, ebook 821, Project Gutenberg, http://www.gutenberg.org/ebooks/821

87 Although Dickens seems to have given Forster general authority to make whatever amendments were needed, it seems unlikely that he had particular approval for the cut at the end of ch.45. The cut shows the intensity of Edith's (and Carker's) feelings, which helps to motivate Dickens's plan for their adultery and Edith's suicide. He was certainly aware that the loss of three paragraphs was damaging. Apparently advised by Forster to clarify Edith's motives—see *Life* 483[K:9478]—he tries to make up for loss at the end of ch.46 (616–18[681–82]).

88 The 'Home'—a refuge and reformatory for about a dozen or so young women who were destitute, abused, petty criminals and/or 'fallen'—demanded his time and energy, particularly before and after its opening in mid-November 1847. He is the chief organiser and fund holder for the project on behalf of the philanthropist Angela Burdett-Coutts. For its influence on his presentation of women in the novel, see Jenny Hartley, *Charles Dickens and the House of Fallen Women* (London: Methuen, 2008), pp.131–41.; Michael Slater, *Dickens and Women* (London: J. M. Dent & Son, 1983), pp.341–44; and Claire Tomalin, *The Invisible Woman* (Viking Penguin, 1990), pp.86–88.

89 The List confirms the order of work thus far. It differs from that of Graham Storey and K. J. Fielding in L5:197 n.7. Similarity of hand suggest that the chapter number headings, the title "The Thunderbolt" and the chapter description for ch.47 share the same quill (as they do in the "List of Chapter Headings"), in contrast to the distinctive hand and quill of the titles and descriptions of chs.46 and 48 and entry [6]. Horsman seems to agree with this reading (Horsman 1974, 'Introduction', p.xxxiv-v). See also endnote 92 below, for the evidence on the order of entry.

90 If Dickens were writing for a present-day audience, he would perhaps have kept to his original intention for Edith. However, he re-imagines an outcome for Edith without distorting his earlier conception of her. Indeed the rapidity with which he seems to have taken up Jeffrey's objection to her adultery (mentioned later in the same paragraph of *Life* 484[K:9485]) suggests he was uneasy about attempting to include it. Similarly his initial intention for Walter, who was at first meant to slowly follow "that common, every-day declension of which we know so much in our ordinary life" (see endnote 62 above). However, Dickens has little imaginative commitment to the man who returns as Walter. He does not mention him in his plan for Florence's journey to Brook Street in ch.61 (see Ws.19&20a$_{38}$ p.123); perhaps, for a moment, he overlooks Walter, who, as Florence's caring protector, ought to be included (cf. the omission and later insertion of Mr Toodles' consent to his wife's return to the Dombey mansion (Horsman 1974, 'Footnote', p.753 n.2).

91 Dickens estimates accurately the length of the instalment. The proofs for No.15 have only one deletion of any length, a cut of a single line from one of Carker's self-revealing speeches (not restored in ebook 831); after "Bah" (617[681]) he deletes "I never respected man yet, and should know men, pretty well". The tone and substance of the deletion is reminiscent of Iago's exchanges with Roderigo in *Othello*. Similarly, the "moving accidents" in Walter's tales to the young Florence in ch.6 (80[84]) may be a verbal echo of Othello's story of his wooing of Desdemona (I_3). Dickens's debt to Shakespeare is less in pointed longer quotation and more in spontaneous borrowings of rhythms, words and phrases.

92 The order of entry in the commentary contradicts n.7 in L5:197, where the editors of the *Letters* read Ws.15$_6$ to mean that Dickens wrote ch.46 first and then "The Thunderbolt" as the last chapter. Ws.15$_6$ can be read to mean the reverse, that Dickens wrote "The Thunderbolt" first, i.e. before ch.46 and the unwritten middle chapter that was "meant to have led up". This order is in keeping with the pencilled page numbering of the compositor in the manuscript, the initial entries in the "List of Chapter Headings", and the changes in hand and quill noted in the worksheet's commentary. In both readings, however, there is the unwritten middle chapter that is clearly referred to in the *Life* 483[K:4979] (and see endnote 118). Herring in his article on the number plans confirms the order of entry that is chosen in the commentary (Herring 177–78).

93 The cut amounts to three lines at the end of the paragraph beginning "As to Perch" near the end of ch.51:

> Mrs Perch frets a good deal, for she fears his confidence in woman is shaken now, and that he half expects on coming home at night to find her gone off with some Viscount, 'which', as she observes to an intimate female friend, 'is what these wretches in the form of woman have to answer for, Mrs P. It ain't the harm they do themselves so much as what they reflect upon us, Ma'am; and I see it in Perch's eye' (Horsman 1974, p.689 n.5, or http://www.gutenberg.org/files/821/821-h/821-h.htm#link2HCH0051).

94 Dickens's busy lifestyle creates hazards for even his most well informed biographers. In the passage in the *Life* referred to here, Forster writes No.14 meaning 15, and 15 meaning 16 (*Life* 483–84[K:9482–85]). Modern biographers have the benefit of the work of many other researchers, which can create other sorts of pitfalls. Slater, relying on Horsman, no doubt because of his meticulous work on the text of *Dombey*, accepts his extraordinary statement that the number plans for Nos.9–15 show Dickens

'moving forward with very few queries or second thoughts', whereas there are more queries in that section of the notes than any other (see Horsman 1974, 'Introduction', p.xxxii and Slater 2009, p.267). Horsman's comments on the working notes are occasionally unreliable; he does not give them the same close attention that he bestows on the text of the novel.

95 Harriet, like Toots and Cuttle, has a crucial role in the denouement. They move the action from one group of characters to another, enabling Dickens to dramatize their interrelation, unwind his intrigues and enlarge his themes.

96 The revelation accounts for the resemblance to Edith of the painting, commented on by Carker and presumably modelled by Alice (455^{500}). Dickens's increases the effect of a typically melodramatic moment of discovery by preparing for it with hints earlier (see for example 554^{610}).

97 The colour of the greeny blue ink has been brightened in transcription for the sake of clarity. Its incidence can clearly be seen in the original. Unfortunately even in full colour facsimile, the greeny blue is sometimes difficult to distinguish from black ink. It is closely described in Stone (pp.51–52).

98 For a paragraph on Mr Toodles, see ch.59 (793^{880}); for the Skettles, see the second sentence of ch.60 (805^{892}); for Miss Tox, see 829^{920} in the paragraph beginning "Ambitious projects", from "Miss Tox" to "in the least"; and for a phrase on Diogenes, see—after the "white line"—the last passage in the novel ($833^{924–25}$) .

99 Dennis Walder's note to the paperback Clarendon text that Dickens 'had overwritten the concluding number by seven lines' (Horsman, 2008, p.967) probably following the editors of the *Letters* (L5:263 n.5). According to Horsman, the proofs went beyond the forty-eight pages allowed for in the number, 'though not by much'. He gives the overwriting and the additions made to proofs as the reason for the deletion of the two final paragraphs (Horsman 1974, 'Introduction', p.xxxvi). However, the first issue of the first edition of the novel, which included all additions and has the same pagination as the part issues, has eighteen blank lines in its last page of print. Moreover, if the additional line that is given to most of the last two chapters (pp.613–24) was added to all, the cancelled paragraphs might be comfortably restored. It seems the decision to delete may have been made for other reasons. The two cancelled paragraphs are restored in ebook 821 Project Gutenberg, http://www.gutenberg.org/files/821/821-h/821-h.htm#link2HCH0062, as follows:

> The voices in the waves speak low to him of Florence, day and night—plainest when he, his blooming daughter, and her husband, beside them in the evening, or sit at an open window, listening to their roar. They speak to him of Florence and his altered heart; of Florence and their ceaseless murmuring to her of the love, eternal and illimitable, extending still, beyond the sea, beyond the sky, to the invisible country far away.
>
> Never from the mighty sea may voices rise too late, to come between us and the unseen region on the other shore! Better, far better, that they whispered of that region in our childish ears, and the swift river hurried us away!

100 The experience of reading Dickens in parts is largely lost in reading a single volume edition, even if the part divisions are shown. The Clarendon text gives the part number at the top of the verso page and the chapter number on the page opposite, and registers the number division with an 'END OF NO' as a footnote or as a line of text. However, to approach the experience of handling a part issue,

the modern reader needs the division to be registered much more forcibly, perhaps by *turning* a leaf to the recto page containing the part heading (part number, long title, date) or, better still, to one that contains the front image of the next number's green cover (which has the design, number, date, price, long title, etc.).

101 Of course, backward reference is not possible in the opening number. Dickens disguises this problem by beginning 'in the middle of things', which naturally opens the way to supplying the past.

102 The count of pages is based on the pagination and layout of the first edition, which is the same as that of the part issues (as in 'Appendix A').

103 Comparing the composition of weekly to that of monthly instalments, Dickens writes:

> The difficulty of the space [in *Hard Times* (1854)] is CRUSHING. Nobody can have an idea of it who has not had an experience of patient fiction-writing with some elbow-room always, and open places in perspective. In this form [the weekly serial], with any kind of regard to the current number, there is absolutely no such thing (*Life* 565[K:11849]).

104 Dickens numbers the manuscript pages of each instalment as he writes them, excepting for the opening page of the number, which he leaves unnumbered. Each instalment is numbered continuously across chapters but separately from other instalments. Consequently, when he writes ch.48 (later 47) before the other two chapters, he leaves its pages unnumbered; they are numbered in pencil by the compositor. The numbering of the printed parts, on the other hand, is one sequence from pp.1–624.

105 Although Dickens does not number or title the new chapter in the manuscript, he does appear to insert a short paragraph to mark the ending of the first day, "So passes the night … home", which suggests that he may anticipate the possibility of splitting the chapter earlier than Horsman implies (Horsman 1974, 'Introduction', p.xlv). He also adds "Many" to the opening phrase of the next paragraph, emphasising the passage of time between the two halves of ch.35. Marking the passage of time by a chapter break was probably another reason for dividing the chapter. Its effect qualifies somewhat Dombey's rush into marriage.

106 To preserve the introduction of the counter plot of ch.4, Dickens postpones a chapter on Miss Tox and the Major (a short four-page chapter, written as an alternative to the longer ch.4) then "with great pangs" makes deep cuts in chs.1–3 (see Ws.1, p.40).

107 Horsman notices that the cut is made in Forster's hand (Horsman 1974, 'Introduction', p.xxxiv) probably with Dickens's general consent. The cut reveals the depth of feeling that binds Edith and Carker together; the deletion may be reticence on Forster's part. He had become, by this stage, Dickens's touchstone to the moral (and religious) sensitivities of his readership. Dickens anticipates the role by his own callow undertaking in the preface to *Pickwick Papers* not to "call a blush to the most delicate cheek"—the very constraint that he later came to satirise in *Our Mutual Friend* in the character of Podsnap, apparently in some respects modelled on the aging Forster.

108 Dickens exploits the same convenient conversion elsewhere in the manuscript (adding 'I' to ch.21 and ch.37) and in worksheet (adding 'I' to ch.47 and perhaps to ch.21, and deleting 'I' in ch.48).

109 The importance of the back numbers—and of the relation the worksheet has with them—is sometimes overlooked. Dickens would have been sent his copy of the current number as soon as it was issued. Before that, his manuscript would also presumably have been returned with the proofs. For his use of the worksheets in Ws.6a, see the 'Outcome' paragraph in p.69.

110 See Valerie Gager, *Shakespeare and Dickens: The Dynamics of Influence* (Cambridge: Cambridge University Press, 1996), pp.47–55. She goes on to demonstrate the range and detail of Dickens's command of quotation from Shakespeare.

111 *Harpers New Monthly Magazine*, vol.25, 1862, p.379. See also Butt and Tillotson (p.28), quoting from the article in *Harpers New Monthly Magazine.* They are misled by its author, Lewis Gaylord Clark, who writes that it was 'written about this period [Oct.1849]'. Clark, the editor of the *Knickerbocker Magazine* from 1833 to 1860, was using a number of letters, written to him by Dickens, and confused dates. The editors of the *Letters* pursue the quote to the *Knickerbocker Magazine* and give a date for the letter as June or July 1839 (see L1:558). It occurs verbatim in the magazine (August 1839, 14, p.196). The earlier date of 1839 makes it clear that Dickens is referring to the composition of the three earlier novels, not, as Butt and Tillotson assume, to account for the presumed lack of a master plan for *Dombey and Son* and the later novels. Tillotson does not use the publication of a second edition (1968) to correct the error, believing 'None of our conclusions is seriously affected' (Preface to the second edition, *Dickens at Work* (Oxford: Methuen, 1968) p.11).

112 Browne's original sketch has not survived. The published illustration shows the alterations that Dickens asked for.

113 Though he refers to his "monthly work", Dickens avoids the term 'worksheet', describing the left-hand as "number plan" and the worksheet as a whole as "mems", i. e. literally 'things to be remembered' implying rather more than 'records'.

114 Cf. Dickens's comment on the novel's title: "I think it an odd one, and therefore a good one" (L.1:615).

115 The only clear instance of a planning entry (not a query or a postponement) being set aside without comment is Ws.13_{32}, perhaps referring to a cancelled meeting of Mr Dombey and Mrs Pipchin.

116 H. P. Sucksmith's article on Dickens's working notes for *Bleak House*, although more wide ranging and interpretive, reaches by a different route a comparable position to this conclusion (see *Renaissance and Modern Studies* 9 (1965), 47–56).

117 This sentence presumes that Dickens began ch.48 (later 47) for No.15 before the other two (for the weight of evidence, see endnote 87).

118 After receiving advice from Forster that he should clarify Edith's motives before the elopement, Dickens replies:

> I have not elaborated that, now, because (as I was explaining to Browne the other day) I have relied on it very much for the effect of her death. I have no question that what you suggest will be an improvement. The strongest place to put it in, would be immediately before this last one ["The Thunderbolt" at this stage ch.48]. I want to make the first two chapters as light as I can, but I will try to do it, solemnly, in that place." (L5.197)

The "place" he refers to is the end of a middle chapter, which he seems to have abandoned. Instead he places "Carker's state of mind" and "Dark indication of Edith's state of mind" at the end of ch.46. The evidence for ch.46 being written after "The Thunderbolt" rather than before, as noted in L5.197 n.7, is summarised in endnote 87. The editors of volume five of the *Letters* suggest that the "middle" chapter might have had more on Carker and Edith, a conjecture that appears to sets aside the last entry in Ws.14_{20} "the last view of them before the elopement".

119 Dickens writes to Forster probably in connection with Pecksniff, about the way characters can "open out": "given what one knows, what one does not know springs up" (L3:441).

120 Dickens probably anticipated the innovation in fictional method (evident in Ws.5 and 5a) from the moment he decided that Paul should die. He hints at it in a letter to Forster on 5 July 1846:

> I shall certainly have a great surprise for people at the end of the fourth number [the death of Paul, initially planned to end No.4]; and I think there is a new and peculiar sort of interest, involving the necessity of a little bit of delicate treatment whereof I will expound my idea to you by and by (*Life* 404[K:8229]).

121 This crucial gapping tactic is apparently overlooked by Butt and Tillotson in their comment on the worksheet facsimile of Ws.7 for *David Copperfield* and the discussion of chapter plan and summary that follows in *Dickens at Work*, pp.25–27.

122 For the deleted paragraphs, see (833 n.6 [967 n.925]) and to read the revised passage in context, see the end of ch.62 in http://www.gutenberg.org/files/821/821-h/821-h.htm#link2HCH0062. For a close reading in the light of the 'sentimentalist tradition', see Purton pp.135–39.

123 The last three lines of the novel as published, before the two canceled paragraphs, falls comfortably into blank verse (or perhaps in this instance into hexameters). Dickens defends his use of blank verse, in a letter of 25 April 1844 to Hon. Charles Watson:

> I am perfectly aware that there are several passages in my books which, with very little alteration—sometimes with none at all—will fall into blank verse, if divided into lines. It is not affectation in me, nor have I the least desire to write them in that metre; but I run into it, voluntarily and unconsciously, when I am very much in earnest. I even do so in speaking.
>
> I am not prepared to say that this may not be a defect in prose composition; but I attach less importance to it than I do to earnestness. And considering that it is a very agreeable march of words, usually; and may be perfectly plain and free; I cannot agree with you that it is likely to be considered by discreet readers as turgid or bombastic, unless the sentiments expressed in it, be of that character. Then indeed it matters very little how they are attired, as they cannot fail to be disagreeable in any garb.(L 4.112–13)

124 The conservator Annette Low, who worked on the recent remounting of all Dickens's manuscripts, notices that the 'different quills and nibs and change in ink supplies [...] give valuable evidence of his process of planning, writing and correcting' (Annette Low, 'The Conservation of Dickens' Manuscripts', *V&A Conservation Journal*, 9 (1993), http://www.vam.ac.uk/content/journals/conservation-journal/issue-09

125 Horsman makes a similar conjecture in connection with the cover design, though without any supporting evidence (Horsman 1974, 'Introduction', p.xviii). He suggests Dickens had Browne's cover design before him, with its picture of the waves of a moonlit sea at night and contrast to the

sunlit day (the lower right- and left-hand), when he described the horror Mrs Skewton's death. The relevant passages are the opening paragraph of ch.41, and its repetitions (559–61$^{617–19}$).

126 All references to illustration will be found on the left-hand side of the worksheets, showing that Dickens mentions them as a requirement of the number, though they mostly concern moments in individual chapters. They are as follows: Ws.1_8 Ws.4_6 Ws.6_5 Ws.7_6 Ws.10_8 and Ws.$12_{5\,\&\,7}$.

127 Browne's own estimate of the time needed to etch two sketches for a single number is in Collins's *Dickens Interviews and Recollections* (1:128–29).

128 In the serialised publication, the illustrations were separated from the text, located between advertisements and the opening of the story, rather like two frontispieces. Given a clue by the lettering, readers would have to actively seek out the relation of text and illustration.

129 Cf. Lady Skettles's comment "What eyes! What hair! What a lovely face!" (197^{211}).

130 In manuscript and worksheet, ch.35 is not divided. The title of the new ch.36 is given at proof stage. It also appears in the "List of Chapter Headings" (see 'Appendix C').

131 The quotation is from a general comment by Forster on Dickens's work on *Dombey and Son* during his "residence abroad" from June 1846 to March 1847 (see *Life* 482$^{K:9462}$).

132 The editor's experience of reading the underside of the opening of ch.51 with the aid of a strong light source suggests that, although laborious, it may well be possible to read these few titles in the same way. Presumably all deletions might be read with infrared photography as used by John D. Gordon in 1943 and Ada Nesbit in 1952 to uncover Georgina's censorship of Dickens's papers (Slater, 2012, pp.112 and 116).

133 George Ford and Sylvère Monod confirm this point in the Norton edition of *Bleak House* (New York: Norton, 1977), p.773.

134 In the manuscript, Dickens instructs the printer to leave "a white line" in the early part of ch.62, after "marriage bells". He may think of the gap he leaves for titles in the worksheet and manuscript as an imitation of composing practice.

This book need not end here...

At Open Book Publishers, we are changing the nature of the traditional academic book. The title you have just read will not be left on a library shelf, but will be accessed online by hundreds of readers each month across the globe. OBP publishes only the best academic work: each title passes through a rigorous peer-review process. We make all our books free to read online so that students, researchers and members of the public who can't afford a printed edition will have access to the same ideas.

This book and additional content is available at:
https://www.openbookpublishers.com/product/469

Customize

Personalise your copy of this book or design new books using OBP and third-party material. Take chapters or whole books from our published list and make a special edition, a new anthology or an illuminating coursepack. Each customized edition will be produced as a paperback and a downloadable PDF. Find out more at:
https://www.openbookpublishers.com/section/59/1

Donate

If you enjoyed this book, and feel that research like this should be available to all readers, regardless of their income, please think about donating to us. We do not operate for profit and all donations, as with all other revenue we generate, will be used to finance new Open Access publications.
https://www.openbookpublishers.com/section/13/1/support-us

CPSIA information can be obtained
at www.ICGtesting.com
Printed in the USA
BVOW07*1918140917
494824BV00003B/3/P

9 781783 742240